Researching Teaching

Researching Teaching:
Methodologies and Practices for Understanding Pedagogy

Edited by

John Loughran

UK   Falmer Press, 1 Gunpowder Square, London, EC4A 3DF
USA   Falmer Press, 325 Chestnut Street, 8th Floor, Philadelphia, PA 19106

First published in 1999

A catalogue record for this book is available from the British Library

ISBN 0 7507 0948 0 cased
ISBN 0 7507 0947 2 paper

Library of Congress Cataloging-in-Publication Data are available on request

Jacket design by Caroline Archer

Typeset in 10/12pt Times by
Graphicraft Limited, Hong Kong

Printed in Great Britain by Biddles Ltd., Guildford and King's Lynn on paper which has a specified pH value on final paper manufacture of not less than 7.5 and is therefore 'acid free'.

Contents

Contents

List of Tables and Figures

1   Researching Teaching for Understanding

John Loughran

Introduction

As a high school science teacher I was often concerned about thinking of interesting ways of teaching my students. However, the rush and bustle of school life quickly taught me that most things were urgent and immediate. It was important to be ready to move when the bell rang at the end of a lesson, there was a constant need to respond quickly to events, and time was always a resource that was in short supply. Therefore, attempting to genuinely engage students in their learning was more an idealistic goal than a common achievement. To realize the goal meant attempting to balance the constant (non-direct teaching) demands of school while attempting to know more about how students learnt and how particular teaching strategies genuinely impacted on students' learning outcomes. This tension between the nature of teachers' work and the time, energy and expertise necessary to inform practice through research, I believe, is a constant dilemma for teachers.

Much of my knowledge about teaching and learning was tacit and therefore implicit in my actions as I was rarely required (or encouraged) to make it explicit through articulation — to myself or to others. In retrospect I sometimes wonder what I thought researching teaching might have meant or what it might have involved. However, I do not think I would be exaggerating to say that I thought researching teaching was something which was the domain of others (academics) far removed from the actual classroom, sadly reinforcing the stereotype so well described by Schön (1983) of the swampy lowlands of practice and the elevated highlands of theory. I also think that my view then was perhaps not all that different from many of my colleagues and was probably a part of the ongoing tension inherent in teachers' work.

The idea that researching teaching required some form of study at a distance from real classrooms was perhaps superficially influenced by an understanding of research as a form of knowledge and an approach to practice which was far removed from the work of teachers. Such a view would see schools as simply being a data source which, following data collection and analysis, could lead to conclusions which might be reported — but not necessarily in a form that would be particularly accessible or helpful to teachers in their everyday classroom practice.

I was reminded of this view of researching teaching when a colleague (Jeff Northfield) invited me to collaborate with him when he was himself struggling to 'make sense' of his experiences during (and following) his return to high school teaching. In *Opening the Classroom Door* (Loughran and Northfield, 1996), Jeff, as an experienced teacher educator and educational researcher noted that:

> For many years I have pondered the way in which teacher knowledge and experi-
> ence has been regarded by teachers and other educationalists. I have repeatedly
> heard comments such as, 'I am only a teacher' when teachers introduce themselves
> at the start of a new course; 'It is only about me and my teaching' when sharing
> their experiences, and; 'It is only in my classroom in my school', which indicates
> that teachers feel their knowledge and experience does not extend beyond their
> own situation. I find myself thinking the same way about the story of my experi-
> ences in the secondary classroom . . . many teachers have learned to rely on educa-
> tional ideas coming from outside the profession. Policy and curriculum ideas have
> generally been produced by others, with teachers the first targets of the change
> process. Teacher ability to adapt ideas to suit particular contexts have been part of
> the rhetoric but it has been rare to have the introduction of new ideas associated
> with the time and support needed for teachers to implement new approaches with
> understanding. Teacher personal opinions have had little place in the introduction
> of most educational change. Teacher knowledge and experience is rarely regarded
> as a sound basis for shaping educational change. Teacher knowledge has been
> regarded as idiosyncratic and difficult to analyse and be understood in any gener-
> alizable way.
>
> While teachers may acknowledge external knowledge as having higher status
> than their own knowledge, they are quick to point out that educational theories
> and ideas are often irrelevant in assisting them to address day-to-day teaching
> concerns. After returning to school teaching I can identify closely with the teacher
> feelings about the educational knowledge that matters. From the perspective of an
> educational researcher I had to come to terms with the teacher knowledge I was
> gaining. It was extremely powerful but closely linked to a particular class of
> students in particular contexts. It was difficult to analyse and communicate to
> others. My day-to-day concerns did not seem to fit with the diverse range of ideas and
> theories I had in my background. Teaching made me feel that my growing know-
> ledge was limited, like the teachers who made the comments at the start of this
> section . . . For me, the return to teaching was often a confusing and unsettling
> experience . . . The dailiness of teaching and its unpredictability appeared to domin-
> ate my reflections . . . My attempt to analyse and communicate my understanding
> of teaching and learning at the end of the year was only partly successful . . . Very
> vivid and significant teaching episodes should have been a basis for understanding
> but it was difficult to separate my own responses and the missed opportunities
> from any coherent description of progress . . . On reflection, my frustration during
> the year was in trying to analyse the day-to-day teaching experiences in a way that
> might lead to consistent improvement in classroom interactions. I was also strug-
> gling to find ways of communicating my 'teacher knowledge'. I was experiencing
> the earlier observations made about teachers and their knowledge, yet feeling that I
> should have been able to better understand and use my experience. I would argue
> [now] that teacher knowledge has different characteristics in the way it is developed
> and used. (Loughran and Northfield, 1996, pp. 134–5)

Jeff's reflections on his experiences reminded me of the importance of researching teaching in ways that are both accessible to teachers and useful in their work and this is difficult if research is something done to teachers rather than with them — or by them. In essence, if teachers' knowledge is to be better understood, to be helpful, informative and valuable to the profession and the educational community at large, then researching teaching needs to be similarly understandable, useful and valuable to teachers. However, this is difficult to achieve if research is not an important part of teaching and teachers' work. In fact, it is this notion of research being separate from the work of teachers that led Northfield (1997) to develop a compelling argument about the status of teacher-research in his paper 'It is interesting . . . but is it research?' in which he (in a similar way to the extract above) begins to unravel the thinking which underpins the 'typical' understanding of research in comparison to the type of research that teachers may find helpful and choose to be engaged in.

In many ways I would now argue that an important way of conceptualizing research is by considering it to be seeking answers to questions and, in regard to researching teaching, that the questions are those which are important in the teaching and learning environment. Therefore, the approach (method) to the research depends on the questions and the type of evidence (no matter the form: quantitative, qualitative or both) one might consider appropriate and helpful in answering those important questions.

Researching teaching, then, is something which may be conducted in a variety of ways and the diversity of approaches needs to be recognized, acknowledged and understood; particularly by teachers as they are (hopefully) the end users — if not always the producers — of the knowledge. However, understanding teachers' perceptions of, and approaches to, research is important and it has been through involvement in the PEEL (Project for the Enhancement of Effective Learning) (Baird and Mitchell, 1993; Baird and Northfield, 1992) and PAVOT Projects (Perspective and Voice of the Teacher) (Northfield, Mitchell and Loughran, 1997) that much of my understanding and appreciation of researching teaching has developed.

The PEEL project (which is more fully examined by Mitchell in Chapter 4 in this volume) highlights the importance of researching teaching for teachers but, importantly, does so with a direct link between the research and teachers' practice. For the past 15 or so years, PEEL teachers have been involved in examining their teaching and its impact on students' learning as they have worked towards answering the question, 'How can we help our students become active (rather than remain as passive) learners?' This research question has spawned numerous projects and has been one of the most remarkable stories of ongoing research and the development of understanding of classroom teaching and learning that I have encountered. What may (by some) be regarded as a simple question has led to the development of a knowledge base and of teaching procedures and strategies which both resonate with, and are accessible to, teachers as they strive to enhance their students' metacognition (Flavell, 1976; White, 1988).

As a result of the PEEL project, teacher-research projects have been encouraged and developed through PAVOT. Again, understanding what research means and how it is interpreted and used by teachers is important but it is clear that there are a number of important features which have become identifiable through these projects. These features are comprehensively outlined by Loughran and Northfield (1997) but, for now, some of these features include:

- The need to recognize that teachers begin with comprehensive 'big picture' aspirations as they begin to study their classrooms. Most frequently, their studies centre on classroom concerns which represent persistent tensions, dilemmas and difficulties. They are reluctant to focus on more narrowly defined areas as they remain aware of the complexity and uniqueness of their classrooms and the way many factors interact in these settings.
- Teachers focus on their classroom issues and are conscious that this limits generalizability to other situations (e.g. 'It is only my classroom' and 'No-one else will be interested' are common teacher responses).
- The complexity and perceived uniqueness of teacher concerns makes communication to others difficult and teachers tend to feel isolated with their concerns.
- The primary role of the teacher means that new findings and teaching become interwoven. Teachers feel they need to act immediately on new possibilities and adjust their teaching. The research focus therefore alters, as adjustments are made, and new insights and possibilities emerge. Hence the intertwining of teaching and researching is such that as one alters so does the other so the traditional notion of research of 'holding the problem in place while it is researched' is not really possible as the problem develops, shifts and changes as it is responsive to the continual shifts in the teaching.
- Teachers have shown little interest in merely studying a problem to clarify it, or prove its existence. As just stated, they want to do something about it. This means that their research almost always includes designing and implementing new approaches — classroom interventions that are intended to achieve change. However, teachers (unlike traditional researchers) have to deal with the consequences of their interventions as part of their daily routine with the class. Negative consequences can affect a class for the remainder of a year. This means that research can be a high-risk activity for teachers and significantly affect their primary role as a teacher.
- For most teachers, the primary purpose in studying their teaching is to teach more effectively in their own classroom settings. This is a very personal purpose and is one that is usually not part of the research agenda for an academic researcher who is researching other people's classrooms and wider contexts.

Therefore, in researching teaching there are a number of important issues to be considered and to be communicated to the educational community. In many ways, the work of PEEL and PAVOT is similar to the development of self-study in education faculties, which continues to grow and gain acceptance in the research community.

The S-STEP (Self-study in Teacher Education Practice) SIG (Special Interest Group) of AERA (American Education Research Association) has become a major source of research into the teaching practice of teacher educators with the main intent that such research will inform practice. A most important touchstone for this work is the book by MaryLynn Hamilton (*Reconceptualizing Teaching Practice: Self-study in Teacher Education*, 1998) which illustrates a variety of approaches to researching teacher education practice. The wave of self-study research has highlighted interesting parallels with some of the tensions and dilemmas of researching teaching whereby attempts to better align the learning through research and the actions of practice become problematic as the two become more closely intertwined and personal.

It is this need to continue to forge stronger links between research and practice that was the genesis of this book. At the first S-STEP Conference at Herstmonceux (UK) in 1996 I was amazed by a presentation of a longitudinal research project being conducted by a group of teachers in Alaska. Not only was their research approach very well organized, and their data collection clear and appropriate, but their presentation took a form that caused me to question some of my 'taken for granted' assumptions about researching teaching. This group of teachers presented their research findings as a play (Austin et al., Chapter 7) and it demonstrated such a clear understanding of their work that it caused many conference participants to reconsider not only their own research positions, but also the manner in which they offered their knowledge to the educational community.

The participants in this book have continued this challenge by being willing contributors in a project to demonstrate a diverse range of approaches to the researching of teaching. It is an attempt to highlight the need for all in education to 'reframe' our understanding of our taken-for-granted notions of researching teaching. The book is organized in sections that are designed to illustrate particular themes so that the overall project offers a coherent pathway along a continuum of approaches to methodologies and practices in researching teaching.

Researching Teaching Through Pedagogy

The first section is *Researching Teaching Through Pedagogy*. This section of the book opens with Max van Manen's chapter in which his exploration of our understanding of pedagogy illustrates a number of important issues both about pedagogy and how research approaches impact on it. Max's work with anecdotes illustrates the value of exploring new ways of looking into pedagogy through students' eyes and offers a powerful way for teachers to reconsider their classroom practice and their students' learning.

Chapter 2 is by David Treagust and Allan Harrison. They illustrate how an expert pedagogue's approach to, and practice of, teaching can be 'unpacked' and 'defined' in ways that are particularly apt in helping us to understand the complex nature of teaching and learning and the value of being able to describe and analyse teaching. Their analysis sheds new light on teachers' skills in a way that goes far beyond a technical-rationalist approach.

The third chapter in this section is by Ian Mitchell, the co-founder of the PEEL project. In this chapter, Ian gives a full account of the PEEL project and how it has developed interesting ways of researching teaching that are 'teacher-friendly' and 'academically valuable'. Ian puts a compelling case for working with teachers in ways that help to develop a rich understanding of teaching and learning so that it might highlight the difficulties associated with articulating and documenting teachers' professional knowledge-in-action.

Researching Teaching Through Collaboration

The second section of the book is *Researching Teaching Through Collaboration*. The first chapter in this section is by John Smyth and documents his approach to genuinely working with teachers in researching their practice whilst maintaining a real desire for the research to be an integral part of the change process in schools — a change process (hopefully) driven by teachers. John's approach to research clearly demonstrates how working in partnership with schools opens up the possibilities for teachers to use initiatives and opportunities in ways that can be more advantageous and beneficial to the local school community than could realistically be possible by simply implementing bureaucratically mandated 'reform'.

Peter Grimmett and Maureen Dockendorf's chapter follows Smyth's and their work illustrates the tensions, difficulties and dilemmas faced by an 'external expert researcher' working in collaboration with a 'teacher-researcher' in an attempt to support teacher-research groups. Their chapter illustrates both interesting research and an interesting approach to conveying that to others. Their chapter represents two experiences but as one story: 'Maureen was engaged in practice with other practitioners; Peter's practice was engaged with her practice as one of the facilitators. It was not meta-facilitation; just another form of facilitation. Facilitation, we both soon learned, was like stepping into a labyrinth. There were times when we didn't know which way to turn to make sense of what we were experiencing. We were frequently stymied. It was like fighting a monster in the triton-chamber. We felt like Theseus and wanted to call Ariadne to our aid. But there was no Ariadne in our story — only ourselves. If the monster was to be slain, then we had to find a way to do it. Because the monster was of our making, not a wicked king's! The monster was us!'

Following on from Peter and Maureen is the work of Terri Austin and her Alaskan Teacher Research Network (ATRN). This chapter highlights how important it is to research teaching in ways that are appropriate for the end users of the knowledge and how valuable it can be to document and disseminate that knowledge in creative and engaging ways. Their play is a fine example of how research and practice can be closely linked, and although reading the play is clearly different to experiencing the performance, it more than adequately illustrates their approach to, and understanding of, researching teaching.

The final chapter in this section is by Tom Russell and Shawn Bullock. In this chapter, Tom — the teacher educator — and Shawn — one of his student-teachers — document their learning together about teaching and learning about teaching. This chapter also highlights the importance of being able to understand and articulate the specialist knowledge of teaching and how important and valuable this can be for a beginning teacher — and a teacher educator. Again, Tom and Shawn illustrate their findings in a way that challenges the stereotype for disseminating research knowledge. As they state, 'When we began this research, we put our faith in a process with little sense of the possible outcomes. The risk of unknown outcomes is inherent in all research, just as it is inherent in teaching. While many of the details of our teaching may be unique to our personal classrooms, we are pleased to have discussed both the science classroom and the science teacher education classroom in one piece of research. We will be pleased if others interested in experience-first teaching approaches that value personal learning from experience find meaning for their own science or teacher education classrooms.'

Researching Teaching Through Context

The third and final section of the book is *Researching Teaching Through Context*. In this case, the contexts are the content of technology studies, physics student-teacher education, assessment and reflective practice. Chapter 9 by Alister Jones explores issues associated with teaching particular content (technology) and the difficulties that can be inherent in implementing curriculum change; particularly if the change is outside one's specialist content field. Alister's examination of teachers teaching technology brings to the surface the importance of helping teachers recognize the difference between their teaching intents and their teaching actions, hence researching teaching has important and immediate lessons for teaching.

Chapter 10 by Helmut Fischler outlines a comprehensive study into the development of student-teachers learning about physics teaching. In this chapter, Helmut applies a research method that uses repertory grids 'as a tool for gaining information about the developmental process that leads to the identification of conceptions'. Through this research project, Helmut demonstrates how student-teachers' conceptions of physics and their conceptions of teaching itself may actually be at odds in their practice. Through this project, the importance of researching teaching in teacher education programs is raised in a way that highlights the importance of synthesizing our existing research knowledge in ways that genuinely inform teacher education practice.

Beverley Bell and Bronwen Cowie worked together to research formative assessment. Assessment is one of those areas of teaching that is so important to teachers (in particular) as it has such an influence on what teachers and students 'see' as directing actions in a teaching and learning environment. Beverley and Bronwen note that, 'as researchers, [we] valued both the research and development strands to enable us to document teachers' tacit knowledge and practice. Although we have both secondary and tertiary teaching experiences ourselves, we enjoyed being surprised and amazed at the unanticipated data and the complexity of the formative assessment process as it emerged in the data analysis. Hence, both the teachers and the researchers gained from having one aspect of teachers' knowledge and professional practice articulated, described and theorized.'

The final chapter is by Christopher Day and examines reflective practice and its importance in the development of teachers' professional knowledge. Chris outlines the nature of reflective practice and the value and purpose of researching this field of teaching knowledge so that teachers' career development and professional knowledge development might be better articulated and linked. As Chris so thoughtfully argues, 'a necessary condition of effectiveness as a teacher is regular reflection upon the three elements that make up teaching practice: the emotional and intellectual selves of the teacher and students; the conditions which affect classrooms, schools and students' learning and achievements; the experience of teaching and learning.' Chris' examination of reflection is an appropriate way of reconsidering some of our goals and aspirations for researching teaching.

Richard White closes the book with a personal view of how he has seen researching teaching develop in his time as a professor of education. He reflects on his involvement in researching teaching and how methodologies and practices have shifted over the years and the importance of this shift for the development of our understanding of the complex nature of teaching and learning.

This book has been organized to specifically offer a diverse range of approaches to researching teaching in the hope that it will help to highlight the importance of knowing about the intricacies of teaching in ways that might not be so evident through more traditional forms of research. I have also specifically chosen forms of documentation that might similarly challenge our taken for granted ideas about dissemination and presentation of research findings. I trust reading this book will be as interesting for you as it has been for all of us involved in this project.

References

BAIRD, J.R. and MITCHELL, I.J. (1993) *Improving the Quality of Teaching and Learning: An Australian Case Study — The PEEL Project*, 2nd Edition, Melbourne: Monash University Printery.

BAIRD, J.R. and NORTHFIELD, J.R. (1992) *Learning from the Peel Experience*, Melbourne: Monash University Printery.

FLAVELL, J.H. (1976) 'Metacognitive aspects of problem solving', in RESNICK, L.B. (ed.) *The Nature of Intelligence*, Hillside, NJ: Erlbaum.

HAMILTON, M.L. with LABOSKEY, V., LOUGHRAN, J.J., PINEGAR, S. and RUSSELL, T. (1998) *Reconceptualizing Teaching Practice: Self-Study in Teacher Education*, London: Falmer Press.

LOUGHRAN, J.J. and NORTHFIELD, J.R. (1996) *Opening the Classroom Door: Teacher, Researcher, Learner*, London: Falmer Press.

LOUGHRAN, J.J. and NORTHFIELD, J.R. (1997) *Developing Quality Criteria for Teacher Research: a Beginning Point for Considering What Counts*. A paper presented at the Conference of the International Study Association on Teacher Thinking, Kiel, Germany.

NORTHFIELD, J.R. (1997) 'It is interesting . . . but is it research?' Paper presented at the 28th Conference of the Australasian Science Education Research Association, Adelaide, Australia.

NORTHFIELD, J.R., MITCHELL, I.J. and LOUGHRAN, J.J. (1997) 'Understanding the impact of context in promoting quality learning', ARC (Australian Research Council) proposal to the Department of Employment, Education, Training and Youth Affairs, Melbourne, Monash University Faculty of Education.

SCHÖN, D.A. (1983) *The Reflective Practitioner: How Professionals Think in Action*, New York: Basic Books.

WHITE, R.T. (1988) *Learning Science*, Oxford: Blackwell.

Section One

Researching Teaching through Pedagogy

2   The Language of Pedagogy and the Primacy of Student Experience

Max van Manen

Introduction

I have often wondered why it is that some cultures seem to have a language or words for things that another society lacks. Of course, it is commonplace to point out environmental determinants: how the Inuit living in the Northern Arctic have a highly differentiated vocabulary for snow and ice where in most societies one only has a few general terms. The physical environment of human beings provides for experiences that people in different geographical locations may not encounter. And therefore, the language forms associated with these experiences may not be trans-latable into languages where the ecological conditions are very different. But how does this sit with terms that describe human relationships? More particularly, does the absence of an equivalent for the word pedagogy in some languages reflect a different preoccupation with children, a different approach to children or even culturally different ways of perceiving and thinking about children?

Why No Pedagogy?

The example of Britain is suggestive of such a question. In a paper entitled 'Why no pedagogy in England?' Brian Simon (1981) states that 'the concept of "pedagogy" has actually been shunned in England'. Why, when in the nearest continental coun-tries such as Holland, Belgium, Germany, and in Scandinavian countries, the concept of pedagogy has such a very extensive and widely discussed tradition? According to Simon this occurred partly because the members of the most prestigious edu-cational institutions, such as the ancient universities of Oxford and Cambridge, have 'contemptuously rejected' the idea that a professional knowledge base is required for the job of teaching. Simon (1981) argues that the class system in England led to an emphasis on socialization. Even though the teacher had certain pastoral care responsibilities in terms of upbringing, in the situation of upper middle class culture there was an emphasis on traditional rules and values in the operation of the public school systems. The suffering of excessive pestering, bullying, cruel practices, sexual abuse, and rigid routines took their toll amongst the children but problems such as these did not allow for systematic pedagogical questioning of how to be attentive to children's experiences and how to deal with them appropriately.

Another reason that pedagogy did not fare well amongst the scholarly elite in England seems to be the power of cultural assumptions about inborn talent. The concept of pedagogy is rooted in the recognition of the human capacity for learning and in the general human condition of this capacity. A more class-oriented view sees education as a selective instrument. Simon (1981) feels that certain assumptions of innate intelligence amongst the educational elite did not seriously allow for the idea that whatever a teacher could do would make a real difference in a child's cognitive and emotional development.

As a footnote to Simon's reflections on the question 'Why no pedagogy in England?' it should be pointed out, as well, that he interprets the concept of pedagogy primarily in a scientific-technical manner. He seems especially interested in the reason for the absence of inquiry into the methods and effective techniques of teaching. He understands his own question as asking, 'Why no science of pedagogy in England?' (Simon, 1981). But hereby he already gives a very different twist to the notion of pedagogy, different from the way it has been part of the educational tradition just across the Channel separating England from the rest of the continent. There the notion of pedagogy has a long and complex history. As a practice, pedagogy describes the relational values, the personal engagement, the pedagogical climate, the total life-worlds and especially the normativity of life with children at school, at home, and in the community. And as an academic discipline, pedagogy problematizes the conditions of appropriateness of educational practices and aims to provide a knowledge base for professionals who must deal with childhood difficulties, traumas and problems of childrearing. Central to the idea of pedagogy is the normativity of distinguishing between what is appropriate and and what is less appropriate for children and what are appropriate ways of teaching and giving assistance to children and young people.

The Erosion of Pedagogy

The situation in North America, Canada, and Australia seems somewhat different. Unlike England, the term pedagogy is no longer avoided in English-speaking communities. On the contrary, pedagogy has turned into a genuine fashion word. The term now appears frequently across a great variety of educational and other theoretical discourses. And yet, if we look somewhat closer at these usages then it appears that this language of pedagogy very often covers things that have little, if anything, to do with understanding the lifeworlds of children.

If we look at the larger context then it would appear that there are three main developments with reference to the notion of pedagogy in the English-speaking world (outside of England). One recent trend is towards an increased substitution of the term pedagogy for the vocabulary of teaching, instructional programs, curriculum, etc. A second trend is the appropriation of the term pedagogy by post-structuralists and new theorists. The third trend is interesting because it seems to move towards a kind of thinking that appears pedagogical and it seems to be searching for a new language to express and address pedagogical preoccupations. In looking at the larger picture, there seems to emerge the strange situation that the populariza-tion of the term pedagogy is actually aiding the process towards an erosion of the sensibility of pedagogy (as the normative practice of dealing with children), while at the same time there actually is a movement towards a normative pedagogical sensibility in education but under a different nomenclature: the language of moral education and moral discourse about teaching and life in classrooms.

With respect to the first trend, there is obviously an increasingly widespread usage of the term pedagogy. If we do word searches of publications and articles with pedagogy in the title, then we see a curious phenomenon. Up to the early 1970s the term pedagogy was scarcely used. Between 1975 and 1985 books and articles with pedagogy in the title became increasingly noticeable, especially, of course, in the literature of critical pedagogy (Freire, 1970; Apple, 1990; Giroux, 1981) etc. And after the mid-1980s there seems to have been an explosive usage of the term pedagogy.

But as suggested above, in the general domain of education the new coinage of the term pedagogy may strangely be responsible for a certain erosion of pedago-gical sensitivities. It appears that the term pedagogy is often simply used as a buzz-word that has replaced the terms teaching, instruction, or curriculum. So instead of speaking of the 'teaching of mathematics' or 'whole language curriculum' one now tends to speak of the 'pedagogy of math' and 'whole language pedagogy'. And yet, like most fashion words, there is a certain extra something that is expressed in the usage of the term.

I have asked teachers what they feel is the sense of meaning of the term pedagogy — for example: 'What do you feel is the difference between the expres-sion "language pedagogy" and "language teaching"?' Teachers say things such as: 'The word "pedagogy" seems to add a philosophic element, it seems to hint at what is at work behind the phenomena.' And, invariably, they immediately ask: 'Well, what does pedagogy *really* mean?' This response is not surprising. Often fashion words are fuzzier and less clearly delineated than the terminology that has more established currency. The word may not yet be completely functional in the relev-ant language games that belong to people's life-worlds. In education, fashion words often get formally sanctioned by certain major figures in the educational power hierarchy after the term has already functioned in the progressive, creative, but still marginal labours of less influential, less well-connected scholars. This is the reality of the 'sociology of research' that is rarely acknowledged in critical studies. Just as in the designer fashion industry, ideas from street culture sometimes get picked up and formally introduced to the fashion world, so the term pedagogy has become appropriated by the research leadership — but ironically, sometimes for non-pedagogical ends. By this I mean that the term pedagogy was initially made popular through influential inquiries and theories that were highly rationalistic, completely ignoring the original normative (moral, relational, ethical) core meanings (for a discussion of this trend see van Manen, 1997).

The second trend describes how pedagogy has become a key term in post-structuralist thought and in what is sometimes called 'new order theory'.[1] In the domain of post-structuralist critical theory there also occurs a kind of erosion of pedagogy, especially in the 'new' discourse of pedagogy. This erosion is a function of new theories, needing a language for radicalizing consciousness but having no use for the reference to *paides* or child. Some commentators speak of a new order where the old notion of pedagogy as dealing with children is deconstructed and a new pedagogical project is produced that involves approaches such as psychoanalytic readings of contemporary culture, media studies, cultural studies, literary criticism, gender politics, management studies, and so on. Therefore, McWilliam (McWilliam and Taylor, 1996) can say in her introduction to the edited volume *Pedagogy, Technology, and the Body*, 'Despite its etymology, much of the current writing about pedagogy does not refer specifically to the science of educating children' (p. 1). Instead a whole array of new topics is unfolded.

Some of this literature does, however, examine the relations that teachers and other professionals maintain with children. These titles cover an exotic range of topics: 'Beyond the missionary position: Teacher desire and radical pedagogy' by Erica McWilliams; 'Eros, eroticism and the pedagogical process' by bell hooks; 'Visualizing safe sex: When pedagogy and pornography collide' by Cindy Patton; 'Queer theory, homosexual teaching bodies, and infecting pedagogy' by Peter G. Taylor; 'Is there a queer pedagogy?' by Debra Britzman. These works include 'the interrogation' of the meaning of professional relations between professional pedagogues and the children or adults they serve. In the words of McWilliam and Jones (1996): 'Medics, ministers, priests and pedagogues — all stand unfrocked in the new order. And this sensitivity is due in no small measure to the work of feminists who have challenged the cult of personality in the classroom' (p. 127).

Why use the word 'defrocked'? Perhaps the intent is to deconstruct the supposed higher values of the practice of pedagogy by hinting at its shady sides. For example, Jane Gallop (1988) explodes the meaning of pedagogy in a manner of suspicion that is shockingly accusative. She winkingly points to the Greek link between pedagogy and pederasty (child molesting). In the words of Gallop: 'Pederasty is undoubtedly a useful paradigm for classic European pedagogy. A greater man penetrates a lesser man with his knowledge. The student is empty, a receptacle for the phallus; the teacher is the phallic fullness of knowledge' (1988, p. 43).

New order theorists describe teaching as erotic seduction of the innocent student (coded as female) by the desirous teacher (coded as male). The teacher intro(se)duces the student into a lifelong scholastic love affair with a 'body of knowledge' — but in this process the teacher's own body may become the literal body which the student comes to crave and desire and vice versa.

In educational contexts it seems that the public constantly hears of cases where teachers, priests, police, physicians, and other professions responsible in various ways for the welfare of children have betrayed their sacred trust. Sexual abuse and harassment seems rampant. But, this literature goes much further than merely scrutinizing predatory practices. It sees the forces of erotic needs, wants, demands, and desires embedded deeply in our cultural psyche and hidden in our discursive practices, in such a way that only psychoanalytic, or critical, inquiries are able to retrieve things like the sexual politics of the pedagogical relationship.

So, the new theorists help us to become aware of how complex, ambiguous, implicative, and fragile, human relationships are, and how nothing is sacred in our new postmodern world. Even those who are critical of the sometimes excessive nature of the new order theories may be willing to admit that our knowledge forms and practices are often built on naive assumptions concerning the intentionality of human motivations, inclinations, predicaments, and propensities. And yet, the so-called 'new pedagogies' are subject to their own vulnerabilities. New theorists, themselves, run the risk of becoming enchanted with the accusatory or titillating products of their own obsessions, polemics, and fascinations. The image of the teacher as rapist of children may have 'positive' shock-value, but it can also function as the expression of a hidden craving of the theorizer whose provocative metaphors and discourses about the pedagogy of desire mask voyeuristic and ambiguous desires, equally insidious to the welfare of children. In other words, just as biographic and critical investigations into Sigmund Freud's theorizing have unmasked some shady sides of the great psychiatrist, so the post-Lacanians and other post-structuralists could benefit from critical 'interrogations' to unmask their own hidden obsessions, perversions, narcissisms, and manias.

But quite apart from the above issues, the main argument in this text is that the term pedagogy is being depredated from our children under the well-intentioned guise of their liberation from systemic cultural oppression and abuse. This appropriation away from a child-oriented discourse of the term pedagogy by post-structuralists, cultural theorists, and psychoanalytically oriented educationists is unsettling insofar as it contributes to an erosion of the fragile spirit of pedagogy: the caring commitment to remain interested in the question of how to live responsibly and appropriately with children, not for our benefit but for theirs.

Against these drifts in the erosion of pedagogy, there is a more hopeful trend emerging. Partly as a reaction, it seems, against the influence of increasingly rationalistic, technocratic, and corporatist movements in education we see a renewed interest in the question of the ethos of pedagogical practices. First there are educators who seek to recover something that has been long absent from North American educational thought: an ethics-sensitive language of teaching and an epistemology of practice that is guided by an interest in the child's experience and in the relational sphere between teachers and their students. Alan Tom (1984), John Goodlad (Goodlad, Soder and Sirotnik, 1991), Philip Jackson (Jackson, Boostrom and Hansen, 1993), Hugh Sockett (1993), Nel Noddings (1992), David Hansen (1995) and others have begun to argue that the most unfortunate fact about contemporary discourses and practices of education is that they have tended to become overly rationalistic, behavioristic, scientistic, and managerial. And yet, the latest push in education is towards even more pronounced rationalized practices. We see this in developments such as charter schools set up on the market place model, outcomes-based evaluation of teachers, privatization of government responsibilities (such as monitoring and testing of achievement levels by for profit companies), corporate funding of educational institutions in exchange for advertising visibility. What we are witnessing is a new form of enterpreneurship in education — based on the thought that teaching is simply a skill with commodity value in the market place. Privatization of educational, healthcare, and social welfare programs have the effect that professional associations and educational unions are losing control over their professional body. Private charter schools are allowed to hire teachers at a lower pay scale than offered by the public system. In the Edmonton Journal of 24 June 1998, the salary of a beginning teacher at a local charter school was cited as $15,000 (Canadian) as compared to $35,000 for a beginning teacher with the public system. The hiring policies and practices of school systems are driven by the corporatist values of business models; teachers are simply treated as replaceable workers.

So, in spite of these developments, it is significant that there is a strong counter-current noticeable in this conversion to free market ideology and technical solution-based approaches. Educators who worry about this trend argue that we need to ask the question of what it would mean if teachers were treated as moral agents with a practical professional language. A professionally acknowledged moral language would allow teachers to think of their daily practices as essentially pedagogical interactions. Sockett argues that the invention of a moral language enables teachers to talk about their everyday activities in a manner that many of them experience as freeing (Sockett, 1993). Finally there is an accepted vocabulary for making conversationally available the kinds of topics, concerns and problems that are at the heart of teaching and of dealing daily with children. For example, educators now can make sense of teaching and learning events as processes of encouragement or discouragement, which are moral versions of concepts such as punishment, praise, blame and so on.

The Reflexive Nature of Pedagogy

It is now a well-known principle of inquiry that the object of our study is always contaminated by the frame of our observational stance. In the literature of research on teaching this is easily demonstrated. If your outlook as a researcher is outcomes- or results-based then everything the teacher does seems to have consequences for the effectiveness of the classroom. If you regard teachers as rational actors then all you may see is teachers making decisions from one moment to the next. If you are preoccupied with the issue of reflective teaching then you will primarily see teachers operating at various levels of reflectivity in their classrooms. If you look for the presence of moral values in teaching then everything the teacher does seems to have moral significance. Our interpretive frame seems to account for our perceptiveness as well as for our blindness. Thus, when Shulman observes an outstanding teacher (as in his description of Nancy) he sees a highly rationalistic practice (Shulman, 1987). But when Sockett would observe Nancy he sees a thoroughly moral practice (Sockett, 1987).

Since we have to accept that what we see is a function of our stance, this poses a self-reflective or hermeneutic constraint on our understanding. As the philosopher Grondin points out, the contemporary situation is such that we not only know that all knowledge and understanding is interpretive but also that we are reflexively aware of this condition (Grondin, 1994, p. 14). So it is not just our task to interpret what we see, we are also challenged to provide interpretive acknowledgment that our understandings are indeed interpretive. Therefore, it is not good enough to simply admit that the accounts we provide are interpretations. The condition of reflexivity adds a level of self-consciousness to our interpretive act: they become exemplary of the forms of life that engenders these particular interpretations.

In other words, the practice of teaching can be regarded as a living recommendation for showing what teaching is (or should be). Whether we like it or not, in all our actions we set examples for what we think teaching is. And this is where the principle of reflexivity is important: we know that everything — literally every little thing we do or do not do — in our interactions with children has significance. Why? Because as teachers we stand in relations of influence to our students. And we are reflexively aware of this influence. We stand in relations of influence to our children and we cannot claim ignorance of this fact. We know that we cannot not influence our students. So the question is not whether I should or should not influence my students. We always do. And this influence is osmotically derived from our entire being: the way we are, feel, act, understand, as well as our reflexive awareness of our interpretive being. In other words, we are not only responsible for what we do but also for what we know and how this knowledge gives us a view of the world.

The question is not even primarily whether I should influence my students this way or that way. The question is whether whatever I do is appropriate for this or that child or for these children. Indeed, the practice of pedagogy may be defined as constantly distinguishing more appropriate from less appropriate ways of being and interacting with young people. We can only be pedagogically perceptive if we develop our understanding of how the young people we teach experience things, including our influence. Strangely, this question of how students experience their relations with teachers is seldom asked. In the remainder of this chapter I aim to show how revealing it can be when we ask students to share their experiences. Second, I want to illustrate how reflecting on these students' experiences can open up themes, that can serve as the terms of a pedagogical discourse of teaching. This type of inquiry is intended to enhance the sensibility of pedagogical thoughtfulness and tact in teachers (van Manen, 1991).

Student Experiences and Student Voices

When we ask students to describe their classroom experiences with teachers, it becomes immediately evident how students often see teaching in terms of style, personality, and qualities such as fairness, patience, commitment, and kindness. In a project aimed at discovering how students experience the interactive dimension of teaching, the narratives collected from these students are strongly suggestive of pedagogical qualities that students admire or criticize in their teachers.

Students were asked to write a simple 'anecdote,' a short story, about a single classroom event. Before this assignment was given, students learned how to write vivid accounts of personal experiences. Next they were provided with the following suggestion:

> Think back to one teacher and describe, in an anecdote, a particular experience with this teacher. In your anecdote refer to how the teacher talked, acted, behaved, or used certain gestures. Describe the kinds of things that were said, showed, taught,

or learned in this lesson or school situation. What manner of speaking, choice of words, personal demeanor, or way of behaving may have been part of this situation? What was this experience like for you? Describe, for example, how this particular teacher in this particular moment seemed to help you understand something, to make you feel interested in a topic. Describe how in this situation you felt secure or insecure, capable or incapable, challenged or bored, smart or dumb, good about yourself or self-critical, and so forth. (This event may have happened recently or several years ago. Do not use real names of teachers or students.)

Students were also taught to edit the anecdotes. For the purpose of anonymity and plausibility some further editing was sometimes done. The following suggestions were given to enhance the narrative power of the anecdote:

1 an anecdote is a very short and simple story
2 an anecdote usually relates one incident
3 an anecdote begins close to the central idea
4 an anecdote includes important concrete detail
5 an anecdote often contains several quotes
6 an anecdote closes quickly after the climax
7 an anecdote requires punctum for punch line.

Some stories that students tell are straightforward, other anecdotes are more intriguing. But in almost all cases there is a strong sense of relationality involved in the descriptions. The way that the teacher relates to the students is a dominant theme. For example, in the following anecdote a student describes a teacher holding a class discussion; the student implicitly seems to criticize the teacher for a poor instructional style, as well as for a less than encouraging manner of interacting. The student's account creates a strong sense of classroom atmosphere.[2]

'Okay, close your note books,' Mr Lam said.
    The class did so without delay, except for a few students who quickly glanced over their work in an attempt to memorize fast their answers for the 'discussion'.
    'Okay now . . .' he continued slowly while taking his elevated position on the desk. In a relaxed manner he supported his body with one arm stretched behind him while his other arm formed into one huge finger, 'When was Hong Kong returned to Chinese rule?' He looked around with his finger poised to strike like a stinger of death.
    Momentarily each one of us froze, expecting the finger to terminate its searching movement right at his or her person.
    Before the finger came to a stop the teacher already mocked with a grimace of disgust on his face: 'You are going to have lots of trouble on the test.' Then he pointed his finger first at some of the regulars who usually knew the answers. William guessed almost in a whisper, 'Earlier this year?'
    Mr Lam performed a silly laugh. His finger pointed to Darlene.
    'Five years ago?'
    Mr Lam groaned as if in pain. Then his finger came straight at me, 'In 1988?' I offered hesitatingly.

He did not even acknowledge that my answer was wrong too. But his face was disapproving. His finger danced three or four more times from one student to the other. Finally he stopped and said slowly, 'Hong Kong was returned to Chinese rule in 1997.' Then, as if tortured, Mr Lam pulled himself from his comfortable position off the top of the desk and wrote our assignment on the board.

That ended our 'discussion.'

(Grade 8 boy)

The following anecdote also reports on an incident of classroom interaction. The student seems to experience the action of the teacher as causing her embarrassment.

'Mr Jones!'

Mr Jones turned his head slowly. He looked down at me.

'What is it, Jennifer?' he asked. He was now leaning on the counter and assumed a grimace of exasperated waiting. I hated that. Whenever I had to say something he did not seem to want to hear it. As if I were unintelligent and slow. But whenever he wanted me to say something I did not have anything to say. And so again I would feel stupid. Mr Jones was so good at making me feel worthless and like an idiot. I don't think I am dumb, but whenever I tried to prove it he always thought of something to throw me off-guard.

'Well, Jennifer? Did you have some ingenious comment or question to ask me? I have an answer for everything you know.' He smiled smugly while he was demonstratively awaiting my response.

'I . . . no, it was nothing,' I replied. My neck and face grew hot with embarrassment. Again I had made myself look like an idiot in his eyes.

As Mr Jones continued with the lesson I stared at my book, mulling over what I had wanted to ask. Why did I suddenly lose courage to speak up? I felt flustered and defeated as I could not help but focus on my inner confusion.

'Jennifer! . . . are you awake? No time to go to sleep yet!' Mr Jones' mock sarcasm made me sit up with a shock. A flush of desperation made my whole body tremble. Then my feeling of embarrassment turned into frustrated anger. I don't know why but I slammed my book shut. My reaction caused a stir of laughter in the whole class. I felt like exploding.

The next day I stayed home . . . 'sick!'

(Grade 9 girl)

The Pedagogy of Student Experience

Is it fair to take seriously these stinging accounts of classroom lessons? Are the student accounts exaggerated, perhaps? How would these teachers have described the situations? Of course, they may have been dismayed, arguing that they do not intend to cause embarrassment. In fact the teachers may claim adamantly that they care deeply about their students and that they want them to feel successful in their studies. Indeed, we may be convinced that the teachers are very sincere. But no matter what teachers say their feelings and intentions really are, what seems ultimately more important is how the students *experience* them.

Teacher encouragement is often cited as important by young people. In the next anecdote, written by a Grade 9 student, we gain a strong sense of how important it is for a teacher to relate supportively to the student.

> 'Kathleen, your turn!' I heard the shrill voice of Mrs Shean, and could feel my face turn red. This teacher had a way of making you feel just awful by simply giving you 'the look,' or what some kids referred to as 'the evil eye'.
>
> Slowly I stood up, hoping my legs wouldn't give up on me, and partially wishing we would have a fire drill right then. No such luck! 'Kathleen, we're waiting,' I could hear Mrs Shean say.
>
> Very cautiously I began to read the words off the paper I was holding, and hoping I wasn't boring Mrs Shean and the rest of the class to death.
>
> As my hands began to tremble, with fear no doubt, I just barely saw a nice smile spreading across my teacher's face. I continued to read, but now with more flair and confidence. As I was reading my assignment aloud I started to recall the thoughts and feelings I had last night when I was doing this writing. Out of the corner of my eyes I could see how the teacher was slightly leaning forward, paying close attention to what I was saying. Somehow I could now speak with more conviction.
>
> Just as I finished the last few words of my report, I looked up, and was utterly surprised to see a sparkle in Mrs Shean's eyes as she said, 'Very good Kathleen. That's the best presentation I've heard all day.'
>
> I sat down in my desk, hardly able to believe what I had just heard. Mrs Shean hardly ever gave out compliments, and now she had given one to me, me of all people!
>
> Ring! 'Time to go class,' said Mrs Shean. As I left the classroom, I took one last glance at my teacher, who suddenly didn't seem as mean or cold as I used to think she was. As I looked over at her, she gave me a really warm smile, which stayed with me for the rest of the day.
>
> (Grade 9 girl)

In the above anecdote we can see how important it can be for students to be positively acknowledged by a teacher. The teacher needs to demonstrate that he or she believes in the student. The belief that a teacher shows in a student can indeed transform the student. Negative beliefs can weaken and positive beliefs can strengthen the student's actual performance. It is important for teachers to realize that 'belief' has the creative power to actually bring forth what is believed about the other person. Being encouraging, believing in the students, and giving students recognition seem critical pedagogical qualities. A teacher who truly believes in a student can have incredible pedagogical power. These beliefs may strengthen the positive faculties that the teacher presumes present in the student. It is almost as if the teacher lures these abilities out of the young person with his or her belief. If the teacher thinks highly about a student's ability, attitude, and efforts, then his or her belief may actually awaken and corroborate these qualities in the student.

Many anecdotes that students tell have to do with situations of testing or the teacher handing back a test.

As I slowly approached her desk I trembled and my hands shook nervously. I watched her busily gather her material for our class that was about to begin. I could not interpret her feelings or emotions for her face was totally expressionless. This was the one and only person who had hurt me without cause, making me feel insubstantial, incapable, inadequate, and most of all insecure. Yet she was the teacher.

'Uh, um, are we, are we going to get our tests back, Mrs Montague?'

'Perhaps. Do not ask useless questions. Please be seated Cindy.'

As I walked to my desk I felt that pang of uneasiness that occurred everytime I talked to her. During most of the lesson I hardly heard a thing — until, almost at the end of the class, I heard her say '. . . and I'll hand back your tests . . .' I straightened up and my heart started racing a mile a minute — a mixture of hope tempered with fear.

As Mrs Montague began passing out the tests I sat impatiently on the edge of my seat, my fingers drumming anxiously.

When she handed me my test I looked up to meet her glance for a brief moment. Her stern eyes seemed softened with pride — her flaring nostrils still — but the most amazing startle I got was when I noticed her narrow lips: they had curled into a little, tiny wee smile.

She seemed pleased with me.

(Grade 8 girl)

Many teachers feel quite mixed when I read them stories like these. But these texts often seem to stir pedagogical responses in them. Teachers recognize how seemingly routine and business-like classroom practices may nevertheless be experienced by students in a most personal manner. Or better: students tend to experience instructional relations as personal relations. It matters to them how they matter to their teachers.

Expressing approval, warm approbation or compliment would seem to be an easy gesture. But there is another side to this as well. Many teachers, in giving praise, intuitively feel that extolling the merits or worth of a student is a hazardous act. And many of us know — having been students ourselves and recipients of teacher approval — that it can have dubious value and unpleasant consequences. The following student story lets us see this from the inside:

'Jeff, this problem is a real brainer. You think you can tackle it?'

I walked to the board at the front of the class and quickly did the equation. This was a new school for me and I had no trouble with any of the subjects.

The teacher looked at my solution. 'That's a good shortcut,' she said. And as she started to explain the procedure, she joked: 'Aren't we lucky to have an Einstein among us!'

I sort of smiled but as I walked back to my seat near the back I distinctly heard muffled name-calling and hissing. Some of the kids smirked or rolled their eyes, others looked outright hostile. I realized that things were different in this school and that doing well was not considered 'cool'.

I was somewhat taken aback and amazed how in my new school most kids would shun you if you seemed to be trying to do well in your studies.

Gradually I learned the art of pretending to be dumb and dull.

(Grade 10 boy)

It is not surprising perhaps that many stories that students tell have to do with approval, being noticed, feeling special. Giving encouragement and positive feedback is one of the most common gestures that we expect from teachers in classrooms. It means that we recognize, prize and value someone for something. Moreover, supportive commendation is supposed to build self-esteem in students. But obviously giving praise is not without danger.

It is important that teachers understand the positive as well as the possible negative consequences of praising students. A compliment should be meaningful and should not be granted indiscriminately because, if given too readily and too freely it may lose its significance. Yet, many students no doubt deserve commendation for a variety of reasons. And on occasion it is possible that only one student or only a few students stand out for their accomplishments. For this very reason compliments create dilemmas. Teachers would like to recognize all students, especially if they make good efforts but the practice of praising everyone equally in all instances is self-defeating. And sometimes teachers want to praise a single student but they may not always realize that such acclaim may create difficult situations for the student. This is how a Grade 9 student describes such a situation:

> Mr Venn made a big production of his disappointment. He went on and on exclaiming his amazement at the mistakes people had made on the science test.
>
> 'My God, did I do such a poor job at explaining this stuff to you people? I know there is nothing wrong with your brains. And, you Wendy . . . ? Ken . . . ? What happened?'
>
> It was obvious that he did not really expect an answer. And nobody tried. The class was completely quiet. None dared to crack a joke. Most kids got a failing or near failing mark. Only two or three students barely made over 60%. Again Mr Venn blew his cool, uttering his disgust while he walked around the room, demonstratively placing each paper in front of its owner, as if he could not quite believe it, as if he wanted to verify each case. Most students sort of looked sheepish. I feared my turn, feeling already ashamed. A sense of doom seemed to be hovering over the class. I tried to tell myself inwardly that this was not the end of the world. I would do better next time. When the teacher finally reached my desk he stopped and suddenly changed his tone of voice.
>
> The shift was so dramatic that I am sure everyone in class startled. All eyes were on me. But the teacher's face lit up and I heard him say, with an air of commendation, 'Oh, thank God, there is one amongst you who has caught on. It goes to show that there is still hope . . .'
>
> He waved my test paper above his head, like a silly flag, before he placed it solemnly in my hand. 'Good for you, Michael, not a single mistake. A perfect mark!'
>
> I scarcely could maintain my composure. I had expected the worst and was awarded the best. I did not need a mirror to know that my face was blushing red. The class was still strangely silent. No one uttered a word while the teacher walked back to the front of the room.
>
> I kept my face turned down, staring at my test paper. I could not completely suppress a faint smile. Was it relief? Vanity? Embarrassment? I dared not look at my friends. I did not trust my eyes.

Why did I feel so stupid when I was supposed to feel smart?
(Grade 9 boy)

Here again it appears that what seems at first glance a positive gesture on the part of the teacher (to compliment a student on good work) also has potentially ambivalent significance. The above anecdote looks like a story of humiliation (of the whole class) and praise (of a single student). The teacher singles out a student for commendation, but the student feels confused. To reiterate: pedagogy means the study and practice of actively distinguishing what is appropriate from what is less appropriate for young people.

A problem with praise is that it may lead to feelings of inequality. Praise seems to assign special value and special status to the person. And so, a student who accepts the praise thereby may feel that he or she is making a claim to superiority. And, of course, such gesture could easily be regarded again as a sign of vanity for which one should feel shame. Conversely, blushing is a way of showing embarrassment and thus reducing inequality and the effects of praise and pride. Thus, we see that in the above anecdote the student's feelings are quite mixed and mixed-up. Michael seems to feel special and yet also seems to feel embarrassed for feeling special.

Praise, and the feeling it produces — a positive sense of self — are public phenomena. Praise is something that unfolds in the space of relationships. While a teacher may compliment a student privately, the compliment is more strongly felt when it is given by someone we respect and when it is conferred in public, in the presence of others, who are thereby implicated or witness to the feeling of pride that follows from praise.

Here is another anecdote told by students of a teacher handing back a test:

Mr Archer stomped into the room with the usual frown on his face. He carried all our essays crumpled up in one hand.
'Sit down and shut up!'
We sat and quickly turned quiet. You don't mess with Mr Archer. He literally threw the papers on his desk and shouted: 'I am so disappointed. Look at this stuff. It is pathetic. I cannot believe how pitiful this class is.'
No one dared to stir and everyone looked down. I am sure we all thought the same thing: 'I thought I did all right.'
As Mr Archer handed back the papers he singled out everyone for his criticism: 'Horrible writing.' 'I should send you back to elementary school.' 'Poor effort.' 'Not worth the paper it is written on.' 'You do not belong in this school.' 'Look at this garbage!'
Every student paper looked bloodied from the huge red markings. I quickly noticed that, like usual, these were mostly punctuation and spelling markings. At the bottom a nasty mark in a big red circle. No scribbles in the margin to comment and assist us with ideas. Too soon it was my turn. But instead of handing me back the paper he only pointed and said: 'Ellen. Stay after class today.'
For the rest of the period I could not concentrate. I must have done so badly. But why did he not embarrass me in front of all the others?

> After the class had filed out I slowly shuffled to his desk. He looked up at me, smiling. I was utterly confused. You rarely saw Mr Archer smile. Then he said in distinct cheerful words that still echo in my ears: 'Ellen, you seem to be the only one that can write in this class. Here!' He gave me my paper, with '97%' and 'excellent' written on top. 'Get along now,' he said in a happy but brusque tone, trying to act his usual grumpy self.
> I stumbled out of the room, feeling mixed, flustered, ambivalent.
> (Grade 10 girl)

Teachers obviously have the power to mark or grade the students, and thereby they appear to have great power to affect the students' concept of themselves as worthy or unworthy of respect. Blessed are those teachers who are able to somehow make many if not all kids they teach feel special, unique. But the student, Ellen, who is singled out by the teacher as deserving of praise, does not seem to feel special in such a positive manner. The teacher seems to lack the pedagogical qualities that bring out the best in each student, in such a manner that these students indeed recognize their personal achievements as special.

One problem with commending a student is that it must be done at the right time and in the proper manner. Just because a well-intentioned teacher compliments a student, and thereby places this student on a pedestal elevated from the others, that does not mean that the other students will accept this exalted position. They may feel that the compliment is unjustified, coming from a false source or that the demonstrated respect is false — and now the recipient of praise may even be regarded as vain, conceited, or narcissistic: in possession of false pride.

Conclusion

What the above samples from student descriptions of classroom experiences seem to urge is that we need to be attuned to the ways that students experience things, including our teaching practices. What is needed is the development of a discipline that can be attentive to the manner that students experience their lives in classrooms. I have tried to show that this discipline is pedagogy; and I have sketched how 'pedagogy' has become a term of discourses that have little to do with educational concerns of what is good for children. We need to rescue the language of pedagogy and develop its practice in the service of our children, for the sake of our children, the students we teach.

Notes

1   It should be noted as well that the term pedagogy has a history in the Freirean critical theory tradition. For many North Americans, pedagogy automatically means critical pedagogy, and its agenda is more dedicated to social change than to the educational lives of young people. Of course, North Americans have always seen their school system and its children as the prime engine for social improvement, economic progress, and cultural

evolution. Thus there is a heightened inclination to place the societal agenda above the educational (i.e. pedagogical) agenda.

2   In reproducing these anecdotes I may have slightly edited and changed the gender of the teacher or student.

References

APPLE, M. (1990) *Ideology and Curriculum*, 2nd edition, New York: Routledge and Kegan Paul.

FREIRE, P. (1970) *Pedagogy of the Oppressed*, New York: Seabury Press.

GALLOP, J. (1988) *Thinking Through the Body*, New York: Columbia University Press.

GIROUX, H.A. (1981) 'Pedagogy, pessimism, and the politics of conformity: A reply to Linda McNeil', *Curriculum Inquiry*, **11**, 3, pp. 211–22.

GOODLAD, J.I., SODER, R. and SIROTNIK, K.A. (eds) (1991) *The Moral Dimensions of Teaching*, San Francisco: Jossey-Bass Publishers.

GRONDIN, J. (1994) *Introduction to Philosophical Hermeneutics*, New Haven: Yale University Press.

HANSEN, D. (1995) *The Call to Teach*, New York: Teachers College Press.

JACKSON, P.H., BOOSTROM, R.E. and HANSEN, D.T. (1993) *The Moral Life of Schools*, San Francisco, CA: Jossey-Bass Publishers.

McWILLIAM, E. and JONES, A. (1996) 'Eros and pedagogical bodies: The state of (non)affairs', in McWILLIAM, E. and TAYLOR, P.G. (eds) *Pedagogy, Technology, and the Body*, pp. 127–36, New York: Peter Lang.

McWILLIAM, E. and TAYLOR, P.G. (1996) *Pedagogy, Technology, and the Body*, New York: Peter Lang.

NODDINGS, N. (1992) *The Challenge to Care in Schools: An Alternative Approach to Education*, New York: Teachers College Press.

SHULMAN, L.S. (1987) 'Knowledge and teaching: Foundations of the new reform', *Harvard Educational Review*, **57**, 1, pp. 1–22.

SIMON, B. (1981) 'Why no pedagogy in England?' in SIMON, B. and TAYLOR, W. (eds) *Education in the Eighties*, London: Batsford Academic and Educational Ltd.

SOCKETT, H.T. (1987) 'Has Shulman got the strategy right?' *Harvard Educational Review*, **57**, 2, pp. 208–19.

SOCKETT, H. (1993) *The Moral Base for Teacher Professionalism*, New York: Teachers College Press.

TOM, A.R. (1984) *Teaching as a Moral Craft*, New York: Longman.

VAN MANEN, M. (1991) *The Tact of Teaching: The Meaning of Pedagogical Thoughtfulness*, London, ON: Althouse Press.

VAN MANEN, M. (1994) 'Pedagogy, virtue and narrative identity in teaching', *Curriculum Inquiry*, **4**, 2, pp. 135–70.

VAN MANEN, M. (1997) 'Pedagogisering en ontpedagogisering in Noord-Amerikaans perspectief', in B. LEVERING (ed.) *Hoe gaat het eigenlijk met opvoeding in Nederland?* (pp. 11–22) Utrecht: NVO.

3 The Genesis of Effective Scientific Explanations for the Classroom

David Treagust and Allan Harrison

Introduction

Explanations of any type are usually framed in ways that reflect the style and individuality of the speaker or writer. In this sense, the 'teacher as an artist' simile (Stenhouse, 1988) succinctly describes what may happen when a creative teacher crafts an elegant and concise explanation in a challenging situation. How do expert teachers draw creative word pictures that both appeal to and inform a diverse group like a class of students? Artists and craftsmen are readily distinguished by their styles and it is likely that expert teachers use artistic styles and creative formats within which they develop their explanations, arguments and questions.

As well as being creative and interesting, effective science explanations must obey the rules of scientific discourse. To do this, Solomon (1995) reasons that a good explanation not only takes account of the audience and context, it also satisfies the rational demands of the scientific community. To illustrate this latter point, she writes:

> In science the explanation will not satisfy if it is, for example, in terms of human agency. When Bohr produced his famous explanation for the lines in the spectrum of hydrogen, which had been observed but not explained for half a century, it would not have done to attribute them to impurities in the hydrogen, nor to how the observer had carried out the experiments. A suitable explanation would need to start from Rutherford's sun-and-planet image of an atom which was familiar and acceptable to his scientific audience. This is just what Bohr did. Then he added to this his new concept of electrons in stationary orbits. The existence of spectral lines followed from the application of well-known principles of energy and frequency. The whole argument of the explanation fell comfortably within the context of contemporary physics. (p. 16)

In attempting to delineate the features of an effective scientific explanation, there are constraints on the devices that can be used to explain ideas — concepts, examples and questions all need to be customized for the chosen audience (see for example, Gilbert, Boulter and Rutherford, 1998a). Thus, when crafting explanations, scientists, teachers and students cannot arbitrarily choose any type of explanation to depict a concept; acceptable explanations should be compatible with the scientific consensus on the subject. Another important feature of an effective scientific explanation is its holistic agreement. Bohr satisfied both of these conditions by applying his new ideas to the previous scientific consensus and, out of it, synthesized a powerful new theory.

Solomon also explains that metaphors, analogies and models are important components of effective explanations. Explaining unfamiliar concepts by comparing them to familiar objects and processes is the very basis of analogy (Duit, 1991; Hesse, 1970) but an analogy will only be an effective explanation if a genuine systematic similarity exists between the analog and the target (Gentner, 1983; Gick and Holyoak, 1983; Zook, 1991). Many scientists have supported their explanations by analogy (e.g. Lorenz, 1974; Oppenheimer, 1955) and other scientists (e.g. Huygens, Kepler, Pasteur, Van't Hoff) even used heuristic analogy as a source of scientific discovery (Watson, 1968). Science regularly uses models as analogies; indeed, it is often difficult to differentiate between metaphors, analogies and analogical models in scientific explanations.

Expert Explanations and Teaching Explanations

There also are important differences between experts explaining for experts and experts explaining for novices (see, for example, Gilbert, Boulter and Rutherford, 1998b). At one extreme, experts can use all the technical knowledge and language at their disposal to explain complex ideas to expert audiences. At the other end of the continuum, school science teachers are denied this luxury. Primary and secondary science teachers need to know how to effectively use analogies, anthropomorphisms, and even teleologies, because students do not know the correct scientific terms and have limited science experiences to call upon (Ginossar and Zohar, 1995; Taber and Watts, 1996; Tamir and Zohar, 1991; Treagust, Harrison and Venville, 1998; Wong, 1993). In order to investigate how science concepts are explained to novices, Dagher and Cossman (1992) observed 20 teachers in junior high school lessons and identified and described the use of 10 types of verbal explanations that they labelled as analogical, anthropomorphic, functional, genetic, mechanical, metaphysical, practical, rational, tautological and teleological. These 10 types were seen to be conceptually related to each other and all except the tautological and practical explanations could be incorporated into an organizing framework that indicated how the facts are rationalized and are rendered intelligent to the intended learner.

Similar research into teachers' explanations by Ogborn, Kress, Martins and McGillicuddy (1996) used a communications analysis to show how an explanation could simultaneously be described on several dimensions. They claim that 'we need an account of how teachers create a need for explanation — in communication terms, a difference to be bridged or resolved' (p. 137). These ways include opening up differences, constructing entities, transforming knowledge and making matter meaningful. For Ogborn et al., a school science explanation 'is necessarily a carefully versioned form of scientific knowledge, transformed rather than merely simplified' (p. 137).

Richard Feynman (1994) faced a similar dilemma when he was asked to explain complex physics ideas to college freshmen. As a result, his physics lectures were liberally illustrated using metaphors, analogies, models and teleologies. It is not coincidental that Feynman's lectures are now regarded as classic physics explanations, although there are also some critiques of how he failed to notice his changing audience — from first year undergraduate students to faculty and graduate students — as his lectures progressed (Bartlett, 1992). According to Bartlett, this situation arose because Feynman allowed his 'pedagogy to be guided by the perceived standards of [his] professional peers rather than by realistic understanding of the needs of society and the abilities of [his] students' (p. 67). Nevertheless, we claim that much can be learned from the pedagogical content knowledge of experts like Feynman in providing explanations to less knowledgable minds. This chapter argues that expert explainers use imaginative and expressive devices to make sense of abstract, difficult and non-observable science concepts; in so doing, providing explanations that accommodate the explainer, the audience, the content and the context.

Explanations and Descriptions

At the outset, a distinction between explanations and descriptions is needed. Horwood (1988) illustrates with examples that, in junior high school at least, students often consider the two terms to be synonymous (see also Wong, 1995). According to Horwood (1988), '[f]or teachers, "explain" and "describe" are used loosely, sometimes interchangeably and sometimes jointly ("explain and describe") apparently for emphasis' (pp. 43–4). Explanations are systematic arguments that address the issues of 'how', 'why' and usually include cause-and-effect statements. Descriptions, on the other hand, are statements that concentrate on superficial details like number, size, time and place. At higher levels of secondary education, there is an expectation that a question asking for an explanation of mitosis, for example, will include some of the underlying causal mechanisms. Indeed, as the secondary science curriculum unfolds, the expectation increases that teachers' and students' explanations should become more process-oriented and less dominated by material facts.

There are important philosophical and epistemological differences between science explanations and science teaching explanations, a distinction made insightfully by Martin (1970). Even science teaching explanations differ in many ways such as rigour, length and detail, involve varying degrees of 'explain how' and 'explain why', are sometimes open-ended, include human agency, and can raise new questions as they answer previous questions. Still, explanation has a single purpose and that is to share knowledge and meaning.

The essence of a science explanation is to communicate understanding about the phenomenon under investigation. Numerous books, policies, models and teaching strategies are devoted to this end of improving understanding about science (Fraser and Walberg, 1995; Glynn and Duit, 1995; Treagust, Duit, and Fraser, 1996; Waxman and Walberg, 1991). However, despite the ubiquity of explanations in every form of teaching and learning, until recently the research literature has paid little attention to the role of teacher's pedagogical content knowledge (Cochran, De Ruiter and King, 1993; Grossman, 1991; Shulman, 1986, 1987) and teacher explanations (Dagher and Cossman, 1992; Ogborn et al., 1996) in helping students understand the phenomena under consideration.

Overview of the Chapter

The explanations available to teachers likely depend on a host of theoretical and practical considerations and some of these are considered in this chapter. Whenever experienced teachers decide to explain a difficult concept in a particular way, they are usually influenced by a variety of factors. While teacher and student factors are generally recognized as very important for learning and often are discussed in the literature, the content and epistemology are afforded much less attention. Consequently, in this chapter we concentrate more on the content and the ways that it can affect science teachers' explanations.

In the second section, Philosophy and Explanations, research on the philosophy and epistemology of explanation shows that there are different types of explanations depending on the status of the knowledge and the processes being used to frame the explanation. The third section, The Role of Content in Science Explanations and Teachers' Pegagogical Content Knowledge, identifies the important role that science content plays in framing effective explanations (White, 1994) and describes some of the interactions between the science content, the expert teachers' knowledge and explanatory preferences, the science classroom life, the broader educational context and student characteristics that also influence explanatory outcomes. The fourth section, Explanatory Physics Explanations, examines the way in which an expert scientist-teacher, Richard Feynman, made science content accessible to students and, as Bartlett explains, also to his peers. The final section, Effective Science Explanations for Teachers, is designed to inform teachers about effective explanations in schools and promote reflection on the effectiveness of their explanations.

Philosophy and Explanations

Explanation has rules or philosophical considerations that have been discussed for almost 50 years by science philosophers from Craik (1943) to Ruben (1993). According to Ruben (1990) 'many writers on explanation fail to make the "ground rules" of the discussion of explanation at all clear' (p. 2). For example, at the philosophical level, there is ongoing debate as to whether an explanation includes the product or is just the process. In other words, is an explanation the process, that is, the act of explaining, or is it just the syntactic product? If the product is an important part of the explanation, we should ask whether or not product explanations stand alone, viable because of the agreement between their content and argument, or are they only worthwhile in context? Despite much debate and disagreement

Figure 3.1   Categories of explanations with types and/or characteristics

Categories of Explanation

Scientific Content Explanations	Effective Pedagogical Content Explanations	Everyday Explanations
Deductive-nomological Deductive-statistical	Human action Anthropomorphism	Vague/incomplete Folk theory-driven
Inductive-statistical	Teleology	Intuitive
Complete/comprehensive Causal Empirical	Analogy Metaphor Vignette	Idiosyncratic Tautology Anecdotes

on these issues, most philosophers insist that explanatory coherence and viability depend on the quality of the product. The position taken in this chapter is that in schools, it is likely that both the product and its process are equally important for helping students better understand the explanation of a phenomena.

Explaining scientific phenomena to school students involves both process and product because an explanation's viability is determined by its context. For instance, a Year 8 class discussing kinetic theory may be told that 'air molecules are like tiny elastic balls that continually move around in a random fashion and bounce off each other and the walls of their container'. While acceptable for Year 8, the explanation that molecules are like 'tiny elastic balls' would be classified as incorrect when the structure of atoms and molecules is the topic in a Year 11 chemistry class. Context is important and so is the topic and the age of the students. Indeed, the viability of an explanation depends on whether the concept is central or peripheral to the topic. In Year 11 chemistry, describing molecules as 'tiny elastic balls' could be tolerated as a supporting comment but not when the structure of molecules is the teaching focus. Explanatory legitimacy in the classroom depends upon the students' interest and prior knowledge, the subject level, the teacher's knowledge and the science content. Classroom explanations cannot rest solely on the quality of the product; the act itself is influential in learning because science education is as concerned with thinking processes as it is with content knowledge (Nickerson, 1985; Prawat, 1989).

Categories of Explanations and Types or Characteristics

Based on our reading of the literature, we have divided explanations into three categories that we call: scientific content explanations; effective pedagogical content explanations, and; everyday explanations — the types or characteristics of each category are listed under the three headings in Figure 3.1. According to Ruben (1990), three significant scientific content explanations are deductive-nomological, deductive-statistical, and inductive-statistical. Deductive-nomological explanations use deductive reasoning and are constrained by known general laws (e.g. Newton's Laws, Avagadro's Law, etc.). This is a rational, law-driven, step-by-step generation of knowledge where the applicable scientific laws are preserved and obeyed. In these situations, laws are often more powerful than theories. Deductive-statistical explanations use deductive reasoning that is applied to probabilistic law-driven situations; however, the relevant laws do not hold incontrovertibly. It is the law(s) that is probabilistic. The interpretation is not induced from the data, rather the data are interpreted in a rational and logical step-by-step way to derive the best-fit knowledge. Likely examples are the patterns (or 'laws') of Mendelian genetics and quantum mechanics. For inductive-statistical explanations, the interpretation is the most consistent pattern or generalization that can be derived from the empirical data. If the generalization is found to be valid in every case (no exceptions) the relationship may become a law. It is called statistical because of the lack of a deductive cause–effect links between the relevant law(s) and the outcome; therefore, the interpretation is probably true in most cases or most of the time (i.e. there is a high probability of the law holding but it is not certain). Meteorology and weather forecasting appears a suitable candidate; indeed, chaos theory points to law-like cause-and-effect relationships in weather patterns.

Effective pedagogical explanations, which are described in more detail in the next two major sections of the chapter, are designed to share knowledge and meaning to those who do not have a sophisticated knowledge and understanding of the phenomenon or concept under discussion. An effective way to do this, as we explain using an analysis of Richard Feynman's teaching, is to use language that makes sense to the audience by means of metaphors, analogies, anthropomorphisms and stories or vignettes. However, each of these modes of expression is not without its drawbacks and these need to be identified. For example, analogies have been called double-edged swords because they can give rise to alternative conceptions when not used correctly (Glynn, 1989, p. 199).

In contrast to scientific content explanations, everyday explanations are dynamic and are mostly unconstrained by the rules of evidence and argumentation. Student explanations often fit this category as they are intuitive, incomplete and idiosyncratic (Osborne and Freyberg, 1985) and are based on students' own experiences and peer discussions. Gilbert, Osborne and Fensham (1982) called these explanations 'children's science' and Vosniadou (1994) described them as 'synthetic models'. When used by teachers, everyday explanations were classified as tautological, metaphysical and teleological by Dagher and Cossman (1992). The boundary between teachers' effective pedagogical content explanations and everyday explanations is often blurred. Indeed, whether everyday explanations are effective and acceptable depends on the context (e.g. student age, importance of the explanation in the overall order) and the qualifications that teachers and students apply to these explanations.

Epistemology of Explanations

From an epistemological viewpoint, all explanations should be holistically consistent (Thagard, 1992). Thagard's theory of explanatory coherence claims that viable explanations emerge over time from the dynamic interaction between all the relevant hypotheses, propositions and evidence belonging to a concept. Indeed, Thagard's computational simulation of major theory changes in the history of science argues that holistic explanatory coherence is an essential prerequisite for strong knowledge restructuring or strong conceptual change. Some cases where the theory of explanatory coherence successfully modelled historical conceptual revolutions were Lavoisier's oxygen theory (Thagard, 1992, pp. 39–88), Darwin's theory of natural selection (pp. 131–56) and Wegener's continental drift (pp. 157–90).

Epistemology and philosophy share similar problems in explaining explanations. Causality is a regular theme in the philosophy of explanation (e.g. Lewis, 1993) and causality assumes law-like status in epistemological explanations of events like the acceleration of a car. A car's observed acceleration is caused by the force applied according to the relationship $F = ma$. However, the car's observed acceleration is always less than that predicted by Newton's law and we explain the discrepancy in terms of friction. All sorts of friction cause the acceleration to be less than expected and we invoke other laws like the conservation of energy to support this argument. The more one analyses the features affecting an accelerating car, the more factors need to be included as the explanation unfolds. Such a case conflicts with the reductionist explanations that are all too common in science textbooks. Indeed, Lewis (1993) claims that the causal history of any event is never complete because there is always something more to find and include. While this philosophical open-endedness drives science by suggesting new research avenues and opportunities, it compounds the epistemological aspects of the pedagogical problems facing teachers. How much explanatory information is enough? If explanations can never be absolutely complete, how complete must an explanation be to be satisfactory for school science? Or as Horwood (1988) puts it 'should teachers' explanations to pupils be fully congruent with the accepted research explanation?' (p. 43). We have already argued that the explanatory context is pivotal in answering this question and this issue will permeate the rest of this chapter. Context, however, must be qualified. Context severally means the science content, the time, the place, and the resources. But it also includes all the stakeholders: the teacher, students and society at large.

The Role of Science Content in Scientific Explanations and Teachers' Pedagogical Content Knowledge

In this section, we focus on White's (1994) 10 properties of school science content (see Table 3.2) that can influence the types of explanations used by teachers. Here the teacher's and the students' common experiences, interests, preferences and culture interact in determining which explanations are most appropriate in any given situation. For instance, everyday concepts like force pose problems at two levels: the everyday and scientific meanings of force are quite different and most students hold preconceptions that clash with the scientific concept. At another level, non-observeable concepts like atoms and magnetic fields involve a high proportion

Table 3.2   Properties of content that influence teaching procedures (from White, 1994, pp. 256–62)

Property	Examples
Openness to common experience	force and light (common — has many alternative experience conceptions) compared to atoms (uncommon — has fewer alternative conceptions)
Abstraction	speed is common and tangible while acceleration is abstract
Presence of alternative models	the fluid model of heat transfer is concrete, the kinetic with explanatory power theory explanation is abstract and theoretical
Complexity	density only involves mass and volume but sound includes many contributory concepts
Presence of common words	words like animal, flower force and work have different meanings in everyday and scientific contexts
Mix of types of knowledge	e.g. propositions, images, analogies, episodes, and procedures — when should each be used?
Demonstrable vs arbitrary	differences between flowering and non-flowering plants are demonstrable, physical/chemical changes not so obvious
Social acceptance	creation vs evolution, population control, conservation of forest resources, fossil fuel consumption are contentions
Extent of links	cellular respiration and photosynthesis are closely linked but are often taught separately
Emotive power (interest)	hydrogen pop tests are far more motivating than gas law calculation

of abstract concepts that are most often presented as analogical models and images. Also, multiple and mixed explanations are often needed to cater for the social needs and individual differences that are present in any one class. Explaining difficult science concepts is extremely challenging for teachers. What is most surprising, then, is that many science teachers consistently produce elegant and satisfying explanations with little notice and few resources (Shulman, 1986). The genesis of the nature of some science teacher explanations may be explained by the range of properties of the content being taught.

How teachers' explanations that impart knowledge and promote student understanding can be analysed in a meaningful manner depends, to a large extent, on the theoretical analysis of the content of the science. In this regard, we contend that an investigation into the relationship between the content being taught by teachers and the manner in which they go about explaining it has important outcomes for improving classroom practice and students' learning (see Table 3.2).

In an interesting discussion on the process of developing science content in constructivist teaching, Carr et al. (1994) show how teachers can use constructivist principles to enable them to explore the nature of the science content with their students. Carr and his colleagues debated five questions: 1) Does nature contain a definition of the focus concept which can be uncovered through appropriate experiences?; 2) How does a scientist develop a statement of a concept?; 3) Is there a single explanation for a phenomenon which teachers should aim for?; 4) Can science always provide an answer to a question?; and 5) When a 'better' explanation is proposed, how do scientists decide to accept it? (p. 151). Answers to these questions illustrate the complexity of the task at hand in providing explanations in the science classroom. Also, these questions highlight the challenges facing science teachers because school science can only at best be provisional knowledge leading towards the scientist's construct. In most cases the scientist's constructs are so inaccessible to students that transitional concepts need to be developed and addressed in a comprehensible manner (Ogborn et al., 1996; Gilbert et al., 1982).

In responding to their third question, Carr et al. propose that the level of explanation depends on the purpose of the explanation and the background of the students for whom the explanation is provided. They also emphasize that it is 'inappropriate for classroom interactions to convey the impression that there is a single correct explanation of any phenomena or a single definition of any concept' (p. 156). Likewise, in responding to the fifth question, Carr et al. point to the need to let students know 'the rules of the game' for the development of ideas in science. Teachers should encourage students to evaluate whether or not a proposed explanation is better than available alternatives. The better explanation has features that are related to the notions of elegance, parsimony, and greater connectedness as well as those of intelligibility, plausibility and fruitfulness (Posner, Strike, Hewson and Gertzog, 1982).

The important factors relevant to the student, teacher, content, and context that may contribute to or influence particular explanations are listed in Table 3.3. As a checklist, the factors in the table may help teachers identify influences that they had not previously considered when framing explanations. We expect that readers will add factors to this list and thoughtful reflection of this kind is productive. Indeed, reflection is part of good teaching (Bell and Gilbert, 1996; Kemmis and McTaggart, 1991) frequently leading to expert teacher knowledge (Chi, Glaser and Rees, 1982), a very special form of knowledge that transcends content per se because it is highly adaptive and is elegant, parsimonious, highly connected and fruitful. Beginning teachers often despair of achieving expert teacher knowledge and although many expert teachers cannot explain their expertise, researchers have identified and described expertise in various case studies (e.g. Shulman, 1987; Tobin and Fraser, 1991). This kind of knowledge, referred to as pedagogical content knowledge (Shulman, 1986, 1987), appears to fulfil all the criteria of expert knowledge because it transcends both subject content and pedagogical knowledge and it is consistently and innovatively used to solve classroom learning problems.

While partly agreeing with Shulman (1987), Cochran et al. (1993) contend that the label teacher's 'pedagogical content knowing' is more appropriate from a constructivist position because teachers' expert knowledge is a process or disposition more than a fixed entity:

> [The] central question concerns the transition from expert student to novice teacher. How does the successful college student transform his or her expertise in the subject matter into a form that high school students can comprehend? When this

Table 3.3   Factors that may influence teachers' explanations

Content Factors	Context Factors
• importance of the concept • is the idea central or general? • importance of the concept in the course • is the concept a process or an object? • is the concept a law, a theory or hypothesis? • is the knowledge relational or instrumental? • alternative conceptions (present or expected) • relevance to the topic in hand	• school type (elite, normal, TAFE, alternative) • curriculum and the subject syllabus • course type (examinable, non-examinable) • textbook, worksheets used in the classroom • available time and resources • parental and societal expectations • school accountability structures
Student Factors	Teacher Factors
• student age and ability • student's attitude to learning • student's conception of science • student knowledge in other areas • potential source of analogies and metaphors • preferred personal learning style • group dynamics • motivational and interest • cultural influences • student's language skills	• teacher's conception of science • teacher's pedagogical expertise • teacher's target and non-target knowledge • teacher's rational preferences • teacher's subject matter expertise • teacher's explanatory style • teacher's aesthetic preferences • the education-control dilemma

novice teacher confronts flawed or muddled textbook chapters or befuddled students, how does he or she employ content expertise to generate new explanations, representations or clarifications? What are the sources of analogies, metaphors, examples, demonstrations and rephrasings? How does the novice teacher (or the seasoned veteran) draw on expertise in the subject matter in the process of teaching . . . how does learning for teaching occur? (Shulman, 1987, p. 8)

Our own experience with seasoned teachers offers some insights. Expert teachers in our postgraduate courses repeatedly make statements like, 'I didn't really understand the physics [or biology, or chemistry] content until I taught it'. Comments like this come from teachers who invariably were successful in their undergraduate studies. At some point or other, all good teachers realize that they have to craft new levels of understanding in order to teach their students (Prawat, 1989).

Shulman (1986, 1987) reports various studies showing that teachers possess quite amazing levels of pedagogical content knowledge. Cochran et al. (1993) claim that 'working directly with their students provides teachers with the optimum opportunity to construct a version of reality that fits the experiences of that context' (p. 267). Pedagogical content knowledge (or knowing) is knowledge that is constructed from 'knowledge of environmental contexts . . . knowledge of students . . . knowledge of pedagogy [and] knowledge of subject matter' (p. 268). Pedagogical content knowledge is genuine content knowledge but it is not scientists' content knowledge nor is it idiosyncratic content knowledge. It is content knowledge that has been specially crafted by the teacher to suit the schooling and personal needs of his or her students. Like the teacher's knowing, this knowledge evolves as courses and scientists' knowledge changes. This knowledge is so flexible that an expert biology teacher, for instance, can teach cell structure to Year 9 one period and Year 12 the next with the confidence that the content knowledge in each case will be appropriate to the students' level. Scientists are rarely called upon to develop and apply such explanatory flexibility but experienced teachers do so intuitively every hour of the school day. This is their calling and their unique expertise enables them to tailor their explanation to their audience.

Exemplary Physics Explanations

An examination of an expert scientist-teacher, Richard Feynman, indicated how he made science concepts accessible to his students and others (Treagust and Harrison, 1997). The data for this analysis are physics lectures at Caltech in 1961–63 taken from *Six Easy Pieces* (Feynman, 1994). The analysis was restricted to Lecture 1 entitled, Atoms in Motion.

Six Easy Pieces gives 'general readers a taste of Feynman the Educator by drawing on the early, non-technical chapters of that landmark work [Lectures on physics]' (Davies, 1994, p. xiii). Calling early chapters, like Atoms in Motion, 'a primer on physics for non-scientists' may be too simple because that chapter encapsulates what Feynman believed to be the single most important idea in physics, the atomic hypothesis. Atoms in Motion exemplifies Feynman's teaching; his explanatory style and simplicity may actually be the hallmark of accessibility and relevance. This was Feynman's way. He believed that explaining complex and abstract concepts in everyday terms was his test of understanding.

We contend that the in-print lecture Atoms in Motion is a classic example of an expert teacher's pedagogical content knowledge. It is a macro-explanation composed of many micro-explanations that use physics axioms to develop an holistic explanation (Thagard, 1992) of atoms, molecules and ions. The individual micro-explanations come in many forms: as scientific explanations, they are deductive, inductive, law and statistically driven; and, as effective pedagogical explanations, they include many examples, metaphors, analogies and models and use, where appropriate, anthropomorphic and teleological explanations to make the concepts seem commonplace. Still, the explanatory devices are never arbitrary, capricious or idiosyncratic. Why do we assert that the macro-explanation is an excellent example of pedagogical content knowledge? Because it sensitively accommodates the students' characteristics and needs, it is consistently true to the science, Feynman's personality and knowledge are evident, and the explanation satisfies the requirements of the freshman physics course for which it was designed. As the introductory commentators in *Six Easy Pieces* point out, it is not a textbook; rather it is a friendly invitation to explore physics in terms that fit the hearers' and the readers' world.

A feature of the macro-explanation that quickly captures the reader's attention is the large number of analogies and metaphors comprising all or part of most micro-explanations. Some of the metaphors are anthropomorphisms (e.g. 'jiggling and bouncing, turning and twisting'); a few are teleological (e.g. 'stuck together and tagging along with each other'). While terms like these would be anathema in strictly scientific explanations, these are the devices that distinguish scientific content explanations from pedagogical content explanations. Effective teachers purposely employ these strategies to bridge the gap between the science laboratory and the classroom, and this purposeful aspect is crucial. Shulman (1986) argued that teachers cannot craft knowledge and explanations until they are content experts and expert pedagogues. Feynman's explanations in *Six Easy Pieces* epitomizes this point. Chapters like Atoms in Motion also satisfy Chi et al.'s (1982) expertise criteria because explaining non-observable and abstract entities like atoms, molecules and ions is a solution to a problem. And like all expert problem situations, Feynman elegantly crafts the explanation-solution by emphasizing the pivotal issues while ignoring the noise or unimportant content. Observations of novice teachers indicate that they tend to provide all the information in a linear fashion; on the other hand, Feynman, the expert scientist and teacher, parsimoniously and creatively deduces or induces his answers from but a few axioms.

Feynman carefully avoids the notion of scientific certainty; indeed, he later talks about 'invented' ideas and explanations (p. 9). At the close of the lecture, he returns to imagination by, in the last two paragraphs, musing about wave patterns in water, the patterns and variations in natural phenomena, questions like 'Are we just a pile of atoms?' and, 'How much more is possible?' The explanation is not an end in itself, even though it coherently explains particles and atomic processes; for the student, it is an open-ended invitation to imagine and further explore science.

Feynman's adroit use of effective pedagogical explanations with metaphors, analogies and models fosters a sense of realism throughout Atoms in Motions that motivates learning. The realism induced in the reader is actually a dynamic and fluid mental model (Harrison and Treagust, 1996; Norman, 1983) that grows as the argument proceeds. And this is what good teaching explanations do: they interweave axioms, examples and experimental evidence with ideas and theories using relational ideas like analogies and stories. The sense is made by the hearer or reader, but it is a coherent and orchestrated sense that draws essential life from the explanation. Davies called Feynman 'the Educator' but, as other records show (Feynman, 1992; Mehra, 1994), he also was an actor and an artist and all good teachers, to some degree, possess this artistic quality (Stenhouse, 1988).

Effective Explanations for Teachers

This brings us to the discussion of the title of this chapter — the genesis of effective scientific explanations in the classroom. We have shown by reference to the extant literature and by an analysis of an expert pedagogue, Richard Feynman, that effective explanations need to obey certain rules, thereby transforming scientific knowledge into student-friendly terms. This apparently simple process is surprisingly complex because each effective explanation needs to be customized not only for its audience but also for the context in which it is taught.

While the scientist needs to be knowledgable about the scientific content explanations, as described in Figure 3.1, the science teacher or science educator needs to be knowledgable about science content explanations as well as effective pedagogical content explanations to enable the content knowledge to be accessible to students. To attend to these two categories of explanations effectively, we propose that teachers need to be able to take into account factors relevant to the students, to their own knowledge and perceptions, to the context in which the explanations are made, as well as to the content.

By focusing on the content of these explanations, we have indicated how the nature of the content is central to what is to be explained. It is precisely because so much science content is not available to everyday experiences, as illustrated in Table 3.1, or because everyday experiences are not useful in understanding the underlying scientific concepts, that explanations are needed that take into account the student's current knowledge and connect with this by means of analogies, metaphors and anthropomorphisms. We do not claim that the incorporation of these pedagogical skills into a teaching repertoire to be a foolproof activity; indeed, the dangers of using analogies or metaphors inappropriately have been described in the literature (see, for example, Glynn, Duit and Thiele, 1995). Rather, our argument is that without a repertoire of pedagogical content knowledge to recognize how the content can be explained appropriately to less informed people, teachers will be less equipped to do their work effectively.

Our analysis of exemplary explanations in the science literature, namely, in Richard Feynman's lecture on Atoms in Motion which introduces *Six Easy Pieces* (1994), identifies striking differences between purely scientific and science class-room explanations. The former are characterized as strictly theory and evidence-driven where only the correct scientific terms are allowed. Conversely, classroom explanations allow rich and creative metaphors, analogies and models containing anthropomorphisms and teleological expressions. Classroom science explanations are not scientific explanations per se; rather, they are a unique form of explanation that amalgamate expert scientific and expert pedagogical knowledge. These ex-planations are severally known as teacher's pedagogical content knowledge or pedagogical content knowing. The latter expression emphasizes the fluid, dynamic and adaptive nature of teacher's expert teaching knowledge. This knowledge should be prized in its own right for its capacity to generate scientific understandings in students' minds. In other words, teacher's pedagogical content knowing and the student mental models it stimulates are constructivist in content and process.

Lest any feel that we are trivializing science, one only has to read Feynman's *Six Easy Pieces* to appreciate our point. We claim that the knowledge occupying the interface between the teacher and his or her students is always a special form of knowledge that, in the hands of an expert teacher, is tailored to the needs of each student group. In fact, expert teachers often craft a series of explanations to suit individuals and small groups within their classes. An intended outcome of this chapter then, is to sensitize teachers to the existence of the many influences that may enhance or limit their in-class explanations. Teachers who are conscious of the constraining influence of the science content, the educational context, the students and their own teaching and content knowledge limitations are more likely to recognize the challenge posed by classroom explanations. Indeed, teachers who purposefully reframe some of their explanations in light of these factors will likely enhance the quality of their classroom interactions.

References

BARTLETT, A. (1992) 'The Feynman effect and the boon docs', *Physics Today*, **45**, 1, pp. 67, 69.

BELL, B. and GILBERT, J. (1996) *Teacher Development: A Model from Science Education*, London: Falmer Press.

CARR, M., BARKER, M., BELL, B., BIDDULPH, F., JONES, A., KIRKWOOD, V., PEARSON, J. and SYMINGTON, D. (1994) 'The constructivist paradigm and some implications for science content and pedagogy', in FENSHAM, P.J., GUNSTONE, R.F. and WHITE, R.T. (eds) *The Content of Science: A Constructivist Approach to its Teaching and Learning*, pp. 147–60, London: Falmer Press.

COCHRAN, K.F., DE RUITER, J.A. and KING, R.A. (1993) 'Pedagogical content knowing: An integrative model for teacher preparation', *Journal of Teacher Education*, **44**, pp. 263–72.

CHI, M., GLASER, R. and REES, E. (1982) 'Expertise in problem solving', in STERNBERG, R. (ed.) *Advances in the Psychology of Human Intelligence*, Vol. 1, pp. 7–75, Hillsdale, NJ: Erlbaum.

CRAIK, K.J.W. (1943) *The Nature of Explanation*, Cambridge: Cambridge University Press.

DAGHER, D. and COSSMAN, G. (1992) 'Verbal explanations given by science teachers: Their nature and implications', *Journal of Research in Science Teaching*, **29**, pp. 361–74.

DAVIES, P. (1994) 'Introduction', in FEYNMAN, R.P. *Six Easy Pieces*, Reading, MA: Helix Books.

DUIT, R. (1991) 'On the role of analogies and metaphors in learning science', *Science Education*, **75**, pp. 649–72.

FEYNMAN, R.P. (1992) *Surely you're joking, Mr Feynman: Adventures of a Curious Character*, London: Vintage.

FEYNMAN, R.P. (1994) *Six Easy Pieces*, Reading, MA: Helix Books.

FRASER, B.J. and WALBERG, H.J. (1995) *Improving Science Education*, Chicago: National Society for the Study of Education.

GENTNER, D. (1983) 'Structure mapping: A theoretical framework for analogy', *Cognitive Science*, **7**, pp. 155–70.

GICK, M.L. and HOLYOAK, K.J. (1983) 'Schema induction and analogical transfer', *Cognitive Psychology*, **15**, pp. 1–38.

GILBERT, J.K., BOULTER, C. and RUTHERFORD, M. (1998a) 'Models in explanations, part 1: Horses for courses', *International Journal of Science Education*, **20**, pp. 83–97.

GILBERT, J.K., BOULTER, C. and RUTHERFORD, M. (1998b) 'Models in explanations, part 2: Whose voice? Whose ears?' *International Journal of Science Education*, **20**, pp. 187–203.

GILBERT, J.K., OSBORNE, R.J. and FENSHAM, P.J. (1982) 'Children's science and its implications for teaching', *Science Education*, **67**, pp. 625–33.

GLYNN, S.M. (1989) 'Explaining science concepts: A teaching-with-analogies model', in GLYNN, S., YEANY, R. and BRITTON, B. (eds) *The Psychology of Learning Science*, pp. 219–40, Hillsdale, NJ: Erlbaum.

GLYNN, S.M. and DUIT, R. (1995) *Learning Science in the Schools: Research Reforming Practice*, Mahwah, NJ: Lawrence Erlbaum.

GLYNN, S.M., DUIT, R. and THIELE, R.B. (1995) 'Teaching science with analogies: A strategy for constructing knowledge', in GLYNN, S.M. and DUIT, R. (eds) *Learning Science in the Schools: Research Reforming Practice*, pp. 247–273, Mahwah, NJ: Lawrence Erlbaum.

GINOSSAR, S. and ZOHAR, A. (1995) 'Withdrawing the taboo regarding anthropomorphism and teleology in biology education — Heretical suggestions', Paper presented at the Annual Meeting of the National Association for Research in Science Teaching, San Francisco.

GROSSMAN, P. (1991) 'Mapping the terrain: Knowledge growth in teaching', in WAXMAN, H.C. and WALBERG, H.J. (eds) *Effective Teaching: Current Research*, pp. 203–15, Berkeley, CA: McCutchan Publishing Corporation.

HARRISON, A.G. and TREAGUST, D.F. (1996) 'Secondary students mental models of atoms and molecules: implications for teaching science', *Science Education*, **80**, pp. 509–34.

HESSE, M.B. (1970) *Models and Analogies in Science*, Milwaukee, WI: University of Notre Dame Press.

HORWOOD, R.H. (1988) 'Explanation and description in science teaching', *Science Education*, **72**, pp. 41–49.

KEMMIS, S. and MCTAGGART, R. (eds) (1991) *The Action Research Planner*, Melbourne: Deakin University.

LEWIS, D. (1993) 'Causal explanations', in RUBEN, D-H. (ed.) *Explanation*, pp. 182–206, Oxford: Oxford University Press.

LORENZ, K.Z. (1974) 'Analogy as a source of knowledge', *Science*, **185**, pp. 229–34.

MARTIN, J.R. (1970) *Explaining, Understanding, and Teaching*, New York: McGraw-Hill.

MEHRA, J. (1994) *The Beat of a Different Drum: The Life and Science of Richard Feynman*, Oxford: Clarendon Press.

NICKERSON, R.S. (1985) 'Understanding understanding', *American Journal of Education*, **43**, 2, pp. 201–39.

NORMAN, D.A. (1983) 'Some observations on mental models', in GENTNER, D. and STEVENS, A.L. (eds) *Mental Models*, pp. 7–14, Hillsdale, NJ: Erlbaum.

OGBORN, J., KRESS, G., MARTINS, I. and MCGILLICUDDY, K. (1996) *Explaining Science in the Classroom*, Buckingham: Open University Press.

OPPENHEIMER, R. (1955) 'Analogy in science', Paper presented at the 63rd Annual Meeting of the American Psychological Association, San Francisco, CA.

OSBORNE, R. and FREYBERG, P. (1985) *Learning in Science*, Auckland: Heinemann.

POSNER, G.J., STRIKE, K.A., HEWSON, P.W. and GERTZOG, W.A. (1982) 'Accommodation of a scientific conception: Toward a theory of conceptual change', *Science Education*, **66**, pp. 211–27.

PRAWAT, R.S. (1989) 'Teaching for understanding: Three key attributes', *Teaching and Teacher Education*, **5**, pp. 315–28.

RUBEN, D-H. (1990) *Explaining Explanation*, London: Routledge.

RUBEN, D-H. (ed.) (1993) *Explanation*, Oxford: Oxford University Press.

SHULMAN, L. (1986) 'Those who understand: Knowledge growth in teaching', *Harvard Educational Review*, **57**, 1, pp. 1–22.

SHULMAN, L. (1987) 'Knowledge and teaching: Foundations of the new reform', *Educational Researcher*, **15**, 2, pp. 4–14.

SOLOMON, J. (1995) 'Higher level understanding of the nature of science', *School Science Review*, **76**, 276, pp. 15–22.

STENHOUSE, L. (1988) 'Artistry and teaching: The teacher as focus of research and development', *Journal of Curriculum and Supervision*, **4**, 1, pp. 43–51.

TAMIR, P. and ZOHAR, A. (1991) 'Anthropomorphism and teleology in reasoning about biological phenomena', *Science Education*, **75**, pp. 57–67.

TABER, K.S. and WATTS, M. (1996) 'The secret life of the chemical bond: Students anthropomorphic and animistic references to bonding', *International Journal of Science Education*, **18**, pp. 557–68.

THAGARD, P. (1992) *Conceptual Revolutions*, Princeton, NJ: Princeton University Press.

TOBIN, K. and FRASER, B.J. (1991) 'Learning from exemplary teachers', in WAXMAN, H.C. and WALBERG, H.J. (eds) *Effective Teaching: Current Research*, pp. 217–36, Berkeley, CA: McCutchan Publishing Corporation.

TREAGUST, D.F., DUIT, R. and FRASER, B.J. (1996) *Improving Teaching and Learning in Science and Mathematics*, New York: Teachers College Press.

TREAGUST, D.F. and HARRISON, A.G. (1997) 'Effective science explanations in schools', Paper presented at the annual meeting of the Australasian Science Education Research Association, University of South Australia, Adelaide, July 4–7.

TREAGUST, D.F., HARRISON, A.G. and VENVILLE, G. (1998) 'Teaching science effectively with analogies: An approach for pre-service and in-service teacher education', *Journal of Science Teacher Education*, **9**, 1, pp. 85–101.

VOSNIADOU, S. (1994) 'Capturing and modelling the process of conceptual change', *Learning and Instruction*, **4**, pp. 45–69.

WATSON, J.D. (1968) *The Double Helix*, London: Penguin Books.

WAXMAN, H.C. and WALBERG, H.J. (eds) (1991) *Effective Teaching: Current Research*, Berkeley, CA: McCutchan Publishing Corporation.

WHITE, R.T. (1994) 'Dimensions of content', in FENSHAM, P.J., GUNSTONE, R.F. and WHITE, R.T. (eds) *The Content of Science: A Constructivist Approach to its Teaching and Learning*, pp. 255–62, London: Falmer Press.

WONG, E.D. (1993) 'Self generated analogies as a tool for constructing and evaluating explanations of scientific phenomena', *Journal of Research in Science Teaching*, **30**, pp. 367–80.

WONG, E.D. (1995) 'Challenges confronting the researcher/teacher: Conflicts of purpose and conduct', *Educational Researcher*, **24**, 3, pp. 22–8.

ZOOK, K.B. (1991) 'Effect of analogical processes on learning and misrepresentation', *Educational Psychology Review*, **3**, 1, pp. 41–72.

4   Bridging the Gulf Between Research and Practice

Ian Mitchell

Introduction

It is almost a platitude to assert that there is a gulf between educational research and teaching practice — that there are a lack of structures to communicate research to teachers; few incentives for, and many barriers to, full-time teachers engaging in research; and that the great majority of published research has little or no influence on teaching practice. There are a number of reasons for this: some research is not intended to directly influence classroom practice and some (sadly too much) is not worthy of influencing teachers' practice — it does not deal with problems that matter to teachers or does not suggest approaches which teachers find useful and flexible. However, not all educational research deserves criticism of these kinds; over the past 20 years there has been much research which, when shared with teachers in ways which they find accessible and meaningful, is seen as relevant, interesting and at least potentially useful. Unfortunately, opportunities to connect regularly with relevant research are rare or absent in the working lives of most teachers.

Written accounts of research or research-based advice suffer from (at least) two types of problems with respect to their perceived irrelevance to teachers: how the ideas are communicated; and the type of ideas and advice that the academic literature tends to offer. Important aspects of the first type of problem are well known. For example, papers in academic journals are inaccessible to most teachers, both in location and in style of writing; they are littered with references to other literature and to constructs which are unfamiliar and threatening to teachers, and the teacher-reader is dumped into the middle of a conversation whose origins and earlier exchanges are unknown to the teacher, but assumed as familiar by the writer. It is difficult, if not impossible, to form rich meanings in such circumstances.

The type of idea and advice that one gives to teachers depends in part on how one views teaching. Teaching has elements of a craft, a science and an art, each of these has different implications for attempts to improve classroom practice. Much has been written about the conflict (or apparent conflict) between what student-teachers are told in universities and the teacher culture they find in the practicum. The traditional teacher culture frames teaching primarily as a craft, with new teachers needing craft knowledge about what to do and how to do it in a range of common classroom situations. This culture is suspicious of attempts to turn teaching into a science by grounding practice in empirical research and developing theory which explains and predicts successful practice. Much of the research of the 1960s and 1970s that attempted to do this is now seen as simplistic, however, as mentioned earlier, more recent research on learning provides insights and advice that can be of real and substantial value to teachers. Unfortunately what is commonly missing in the accounts in the literature is the craft knowledge needed to make the scientific knowledge work — the classroom wisdom that is so essential for any intervention or change to be successful: How and when is this best introduced? What are inappropriate times and ways of doing this? What do students' initial reactions and attempts look like? Are there common misunderstandings or negative reactions that can be anticipated and avoided? What refinements, extensions and variations can be added later? This wisdom may not be known to the academic writer — it is a type of knowledge that is best generated by teachers operating alone in normal classrooms — but even if it is known it is not highly valued in the race for tenure and promotion and is not included in most papers.

Improving classroom learning requires both craft and scientific knowledge, but the complexity of classroom teaching means that it also has elements of an art. There are some aspects and examples of skilled teaching that are highly creative and cannot be codified and taught in advance. There are often only very subtle differences between a lesson which was intriguing and inspiring for the students and one which was boring or confusing. As Cochrane-Smith and Lytle (1993) pointed out, teachers in the classroom are constantly reacting to complex events using very complex analytic frames. Consider, for example, a well-planned teaching program with a series of closely linked activities that follows a general sequence as originally suggested in the literature. In the intended program, the third activity flows naturally and logically from the second, but any experienced teacher could easily construct a number of common (and hence likely) scenarios which would require an instant and radical change to activity three. Some of these scenarios could involve unexpected management problems, but changes of plan could equally flow from unanticipated student misinterpretation of a task, the revelation of hitherto unsuspected prior views which render invalid some of the assumptions underpinning activity three — a brilliant student question, a request from excited and interested students to extend activity two in a different direction, or an interruption from another teacher which suddenly removes half the class. Incidents such as these should not be regarded by academic writers as bothersome and abnormal sources of noise or error. They occur constantly, probably daily, during most teachers' working week and skilled teachers are constantly accommodating them, usually with only a few seconds of available reaction time, while attempting to stay generally on track in a way analogous to a white water kayaker using her paddle to cope with unexpected eddies and rocks as she stays near the centre of the current sweeping her along.

One implication of the artistic nature of skilled teaching is that accounts of research should be rich with short-term contextual detail. From the perspective of teacher-as-artist, the teacher-reader's need for rich classroom detail is much more than just a call for examples, rather it flows from the fact that a decision about whether or not a particular course of action is sensible can only be made in the context of all the other things occurring at that moment.

There is another, related reason for arguing that including short-term contextual detail will help bridge the gulf between research and practice. Teachers want ideas and advice that resonate with their own experiences and their own problems and concerns. They need to be able to locate new ideas and advice within their own practice and artistry. The complex and tacit nature of what teachers do means that they need to be able to see the classrooms from which data is being reported.

The above arguments could be taken to conclude that every successful classroom event is totally idiosyncratic with no generalizable lessons for other classroom situations. There would thus be little or no value in conducting classroom-based research (except perhaps for the practitioner researching their own classroom). Fortunately the situation is not so bleak; while there are unique features of every successful (and unsuccessful) classroom event, there are also recurring features which can be clustered into generalizable insights and pieces of advice: 'If x occurs then y is often appropriate because of z'; 'The following teaching sequence is likely to be successful in teaching content type x'. Unfortunately, descriptions of generalized teaching sequences that attempt to ignore short-term contextual factors can appear naive and simplistic from the perspective of the teacher-as-artist. I am not claiming here that a generalized sequence may not be a valid summary of a lot of excellent practice, only that, by itself, it does not do a convincing or effective job of communicating that practice. It has taken me many years to realize this.

The gulf between the teacher's world and academic research is a multi-faceted problem with no single, simple solution. In this chapter, I draw on 14 years of experience in trying to tackle several aspects of it. The interconnected nature of these aspects mean that I comment on several of them, but my primary focus here is on the problems of capturing excellent classroom practices, analysing and framing these in ways that allow them to be applied in more than one context and communicating these insights to other teachers in ways that are accessible, credible and interesting. In particular, I discuss some roles that cases can have both in doing and reporting research.

The PEEL Project

The insights and suggestions which follow have not emerged from a single, neat research study, but rather from 14 years of trial and error. Accordingly, I have organized this chapter as a case-study. The story begins in 1985 with the founding of PEEL (the Project for Enhancing Effective Learning) by a group of teachers and academics in a working-class high school in Melbourne, Australia. I taught half-time at the school and half-time at a university. In 1984 I had heard John Baird present a paper on his doctoral research on enhancing metacognition (Baird and White, 1982). I felt that John's research both resonated with and extended mine, and I suggested to him that we collaborate using my classroom. John's experience in collaborating with only one teacher (Baird, 1986) led him to suggest we call for a group of teachers. Nine other teachers at my school, of six different subjects, eventually volunteered to give up a free period to meet with Baird, myself and two other academics on most weeks in what was planned as a two-year, collaborative action research project. Our primary goal was to develop and research teaching approaches that would stimulate and support metacognitive learning (Mitchell and Baird, 1985; Baird and Mitchell, 1997).

PEEL was essentially unfunded and the teachers were taking on a significant extra commitment in time and energy. They did so for three reasons. Firstly they had existing concerns about passive learning in their apparently successful class-rooms. Secondly, they felt that John's ideas on metacognition and his description of a list of what he called poor learning tendencies (Baird and White, 1982) offered a framework for tackling these concerns; although they reported that it took them several months to become clear about the detail of these pieces of theory. Thirdly, they were attracted to the idea of an opportunity to reflect on and extend their practice in a collaborative manner.

From the outset, control over all aspects of the project, including the research questions and design, was shared. We all began with the view that it was essential that the teachers came to lead the research and accept the role of researcher — a process that took about three to four months.

The first three months proved extremely difficult and stressful for the teachers (Baird and Mitchell, 1997). The initial changes to teaching practice (suggested by the academics) contained what turned out to be some serious flaws and the students became quite hostile to PEEL. After nine weeks of these very negative experiences, I was concerned for the project's future and spoke to each teacher individually about their attitude to it. To my considerable surprise, eight out of the nine other teachers reported that, in spite of the pain, they were now more committed than they had been at the start. The main reason for this was the professional and intellectual stimulation of the weekly meetings in which, up until that time, they had spent most of their time in sharing, analysing and learning from failures. The cross-faculty nature of the group forced all of us to look for and discuss aspects of learning, teaching and change in terms that were not subject specific. The teachers valued a forum where this unusual interplay between specific incidents and more general frames was the norm. About three months in, we had a memorable meeting that was dramatically different in that three big wins were reported. From that moment we never looked back, with the teachers, one by one, becoming highly innovative, independent and confident. The meetings were now characterized by a steady flow of exciting teaching ideas as well as increasingly sophisticated analysis of events.

We learnt a great deal about teaching, learning and student change over the next 12 months and, by early in the second year of PEEL, the teachers were reporting significant changes in students' learning behaviours. These improvements continued and, in intensive studies of five classes between 1987 and 1989, I found that these changes in behaviour were substantial and were accompanied by cor-responding changes in students' beliefs about teaching and learning (Mitchell, 1993; White and Mitchell, 1994). An example of, and some evidence for, these changes is provided by the following case which was written by a student-teacher in 1993.

What Do I Do With All These Questions?: Donna Fox

I am sitting in a Year 11 chemistry class at the beginning of my third and final teaching round. My supervising teacher is tying up a few loose ends and I am due to 'go on' in a few minutes. I am also less than a heartbeat away from quietly putting down my notes, standing up and walking out of the classroom, out of DipEd. and out of teaching forever.

I am using all the techniques I have at my disposal to overcome my nervousness. 'Just take it a step at a time, get through the beginning, stand up, introduce yourself, hand out the notes, pray for a miracle. If that doesn't work, then you can run.'

I have not had a recent soul-shattering teaching experience. I know the students are not lurking monsters as I have taught many of them physics during the week, and they are as genuine and pleasant as any students I have met. It's not even my supervising teacher, the bane of many student-teacher's existence, although Dr Ian Mitchell, researcher and co-author of '*Learning from the PEEL Experience*' and part-time education lecturer at Monash University, could be seen as a horrifying and intimidating supervising teacher. It's none of the usual things that make the palms of a student-teacher sweaty, it's as simple as these notes in front of me.

This is a PEEL classroom, PEEL being the Project for Enhancing Effective Learning whose major aim is the promotion of independent learning by students through changes in teacher's attitudes and teaching methods. So these notes are class handouts — text covering the material I had been assigned to teach, but also interspersed with 'thinking tasks' designed to encourage student processing, further questions and comments, and connections to other content. I write the notes, several drafts of each page. This exercise is hard enough, but the notes themselves cause a greater problem.

The difficulty is that I don't know what to do next. The students have all the information they need in front of them, and there doesn't seem to be much left for me to do. I feel obsolete, unnecessary, superfluous. I wish I'd learnt to tap dance.

To make things worse, I've seen these guys in action. They take nothing for granted. I feel that if I make a suspicious sounding statement, they'll question it, or if I make a reasonable sounding statement, they'll question that too. I'm beginning to feel that they will question absolutely everything I say.

I find, for all my excellent training, my subconscious view of the role of a teacher is still purely to stand up and impart irrefutable truths. When the students have all the content on paper, that role seems challenged and diminished.

I feel like a kitten that's been tied up in a bag and thrown in the river. I'm drowning and I don't even know what water is yet. But I don't walk out. I stand up, introduce myself and begin.

Luckily these students have been well guided and nurtured. They define my role for me, by generating discussions, questioning content and making associations with other theory and their own experiences. Their behaviour allows me to fit into the classroom. The very things I had feared make this class work. I become a mediator, a clarifier and a learner. Often I feel an observer would be hard pressed to identify the teacher from the students. I am learning I have a lot to learn from these students. The image of a diagram discussed in a Diploma of Education tutorial session springs to mind — two circles, a teacher's knowledge and experiences represented by one overlapping but not encompassing the circle denoting the know-ledge and experiences of the students.

As I become more at ease with this type of role and class organization, the students become more relaxed and this makes things easier for me. The discussions become more free flowing, the students begin to answer their own and each other's questions and make more links to their own experiences. Many times the direction of a discussion is dictated by the type of questions that are asked and answered by the students. My presence is often only necessary to keep the lesson channelled in the right direction. It's not chaos, they are considerate and respectful of me and one another. This is not to say this style of teaching is easy. It is a difficult and demanding format in which to teach, but it is also very satisfying.

The confidence of this class is supreme — confidence in themselves, confidence in each other. No idea seems too silly or far-fetched for them to broach. If there is laughter it is always good natured. The discussions are wide ranging, often slightly off the track, always interesting and for the first few lessons at least, quite horrifying for me. They move very quickly from one idea to the next, often far more quickly than is comfortable for me.

But it is surprising how quickly my initial fears are allayed. For example, I am well into my first lesson, beginning to relax and almost enjoy this different classroom organization. I am sitting on one of the front desks trying to answer a question concerning the different layers of the atmosphere. My explanation is beginning to become necessarily complicated and Laurie says, 'Wouldn't a dia-gram be better?' A diagram hadn't even occurred to me, and it was with relief that I said, 'Oh, thanks, what a good idea,' and moved up to the board. I didn't think twice and took the comment in the manner it was given, as a helpful suggestion. It did not occur to me that this might be a threat to my teaching expertise, until Ian pointed it out after the lesson.

I quickly lose the feeling I have to know everything. It is necessary for survival, as I feel these students would be better at picking falsity than most. The conversations and questions these students come up with are unpredictable, but always sensible and legitimate. I learn to sometimes rely on an underused class-room asset, the students. We are discussing steel-making and Robert seems to know a great deal more about it than I do, as he completed an assignment on this topic earlier in the year. I have no hesitation in handing the class over to him, and he gives a beautiful explanation. I also learn to cope with saying, 'I don't know, but I'll try and find out'. I don't feel less knowledgeable, just more sincere. I think they realize and appreciate my honesty. I find that I really have nothing to prove and nothing to lose. I do my very best and this seems to be enough.

Obaidullah was a fabulous student to have in this type of classroom situation. He is very good at chemistry and also a very understanding and tactful person. At times when he sensed I was struggling with an answer to a particular question he would direct a helpful suggestion or statement towards me in a questioning tone of voice, or answer the question himself if it was appropriate. His answers were often far better than ones I could have made.

We are discussing the 'Greenhouse Effect', a topic that at first seems quite straightforward. Laurie is asking about radiation heating the atmosphere. Whatever my answer to his question is, it is not satisfactory, and he keeps asking. I keep re-phrasing my answer, but I'm obviously missing the point. Finally Obaidullah answers in a far more satisfactory manner. In hindsight, I realize that I was not actually listening to what Laurie was saying. This meant that I was answering without understanding or addressing the reasoning that had led to the question. Obaidullah had listened to Laurie and recognized what he had not understood.

The discussion continues with the types of comments and questions that give an indication of how the students are progressing and what misconceptions they have. We are speaking of infra-red radiation. Leonil asks during this discussion, 'Does that mean your television remote control heats up the lounge room?' This one takes me completely by surprise, and I have to say that I've never thought about it. (Those words are now also very familiar.) We decide as a class that it probably does, but not very much.

Incidents of this sort could be seen as undermining my control or authority, or as a threat to my role as a 'teacher'. Ian raised a number of these during post-lesson discussions, but I must admit I did not perceive them as such. This might very well be due to my inexperience, as a student-teacher you need all the help you can get!

This class format and organization is one that is challenging and demanding, but also one I find desirable. At Monash we had spoken many times about approaches like this, but they often seemed abstract, or suited only to experienced teachers. It was a welcome feeling to realize that these things are quite attainable and workable. I would be interested to observe the beginnings of these classes, and what Ian did when the students were fresh from other types of teaching methods, and had yet to learn how to question and discuss in such a thought-provoking and mature manner. (from Mitchell and Mitchell, 1997, pp. 45–7.)

PEEL was planned as a two-year project, but at the end of that time the teachers refused to let it end. There were three reasons for this: firstly, we knew that there was still a lot more to learn; secondly, PEEL worked — many other teachers were seeing or hearing about classes such as Donna describes and wanted to get involved. The third reason was that the process of collaborative action research and the weekly meetings were very rewarding for the teachers. They felt affirmed, recognized and much more professional, purposeful and innovative (Baird, 1995). Although the full-time academics, for various reasons, could no longer get to the weekly meetings, PEEL continued at its original school and in 1988, to our surprise, other schools began to set up PEEL groups. There are now PEEL groups in several dozen schools in Victoria and many more in Sweden and Denmark, where systemic factors have provided fertile ground for its spread. The initiative for these other groups came entirely from them, and ownership and control over all their actions has always remained with each group. Nevertheless, after consultation with the convenors of these other groups, I set up a PEEL Collective in 1989 to provide support for them, to facilitate communication between schools and to provide a structure for continued interaction between academics and at least some of the teachers.

With hindsight, the loss of regular contact with academics led to some changes in the perceptions that the full-time teachers (i.e. I am excluding myself here) had about their role and in the nature of what and how they were prepared to write. During the first two years of PEEL, while meeting weekly with academics, the teachers wrote most of one book (Baird and Mitchell, 1986) and planned and made significant contributions to a second (Baird and Northfield, 1992). Two of them wrote a set of textbooks on writing (Jones and Mitchell, 1987, 1988, 1989); one was first author to a paper (Mitchell and Baird, 1988). Over this time, the teachers became comfortable with the role of researcher, and were prepared to engage in planning data collection and writing in substantive ways to an audience that included academics. With hindsight, this growth in confidence and the acceptance of new roles required (among other things) regular affirmation from academics who constantly made it clear that they had much to learn from the teacher. It took several years before we fully realized the importance and multiple roles of this regular affirmation and teacher–academic interaction. One reason for this delay was that many of the teachers in the different schools that formed PEEL groups after 1988 were willing, with some encouragement, to contribute new teaching ideas to a teacher journal (*PEEL SEEDS*) that we established in 1989. However, what could be described as the more formal research and writing behaviours of PEEL teachers did not survive the loss of regular teacher–academic interaction.[1]

The PAVOT Project

In 1993, I became aware of the above issues and used the PEEL collective and *PEEL SEEDS* to ask if there were some teachers interested in engaging in more formal research (and writing) on projects of their own choosing, using a structure that would include regular meetings with (two) academics. Several teachers responded and we founded the PAVOT (Perspectives and Voice of the Teacher) Project. Apart from stimulating and supporting teacher research, the PAVOT participants are also engaged in researching the process of teacher research and researching ways of communicating research findings to other teachers. One reason for including this last goal was our own mixed success in this area.

With hindsight, we have faced three interrelated problems in communicating the findings of PEEL teachers, all of which became more serious as PEEL continued. The first problem is related to differences between the way most teachers and academics talk about educational practice. As indicated earlier, over the past 14 years the PEEL and PAVOT teachers and their academic colleagues have developed a very substantial body of wisdom about a number of aspects of classroom practice. Codifying this wisdom is essential if it is to be communicable, however this continues to present major challenges. There are several reasons for codification. One is the sheer volume of information: at the time of writing, PEEL has published 4 books and 41 editions of *PEEL SEEDS*; collectively these contain over 1700 pages — some grouping and sorting is needed if these ideas are to be accessible. Another reason for codification is that the findings and pieces of advice variously relate to different people (teachers and students of different ages), to different aspects of classroom practice, to different areas of content and have different levels of specificity.

Reasons such as those just listed exist in all domains; they are so obvious as to seem not worth arguing. However, the processes of collapsing and distilling classroom practice — of looking for underlying themes and unifying principles involve mindsets and types of discourse that are common to academics, but which are not part of school staffroom culture. This lack of daily contact by teachers with more general (and hence abstract) frames provides one reason for the formidable problems of communicating them. Teacher knowledge is structured differently from conventional knowledge (Northfield, Mitchell and Mitchell, 1997).

A second problem that has become progressively more acute over the years flows from the highly interconnected and holistic nature of classroom practice. When I first suggested PAVOT, I assumed that the teachers would choose small-scale, manageable projects that dealt only with one or two aspects of classroom practice. This assumption proved incorrect (Mitchell, Northfield and Mitchell, 1996). It is easy to focus on only one aspect of practice when one is writing about it in an office, but teachers must deal all the time with all (or most) aspects and even PAVOT projects which did begin with a relatively specific focus soon drew in a wide range of other issues. The result was that PEEL teachers, who originally set out to promote more metacognitive learning, found themselves with things to say on a long list of issues: the nature of quality learning and of good learning behaviours, tactics for promoting a metacognitive awareness of learning, the nature of student change, risks associated with quality learning, trusts that needed to be developed, the role of student questions and student talk, how to promote quality learning in contexts such as laboratory exercises, library research, class discussion (and many others) and the role of assessment in promoting student change is only a partial and randomly selected list. Researching the nature of high-quality teaching has been like peeling the proverbial onion with each issue and insight revealing more factors and aspects that require further exploration. To write about all these things in a style which analyses and describes the issues and presents general advice enriched with specific examples runs a very high risk of overwhelming and intimidating the teacher-reader. No-one can think about so many things at once so the safe option is not to try and to remain in the comfort zone of familiar practice.

The third problem relates to the constant need for skilled teachers to react to and, where possible, incorporate unexpected classroom events into their general strategy and tactics. As I argued at the start of this chapter, sets of general principles and general teaching sequences, no matter how well grounded in practice, appear rigid and formulaic when disconnected from practice. We have faced a serious dilemma here. The general frames and principles were not imposed on the PEEL teachers, indeed the teachers played an active role in their generation. The frames were collaboratively developed as ways of making sense of practice and to meet the changing needs of groups whose discourse and type of analysis developed over a period of years. The frames and verbal shorthand were useful, often necessary, for those groups as they moved beyond the (very important) sharing of practical advice to develop deeper understandings of their data. Over the years, teachers have consistently reported that one significant benefit from PEEL is that their teaching becomes more purposeful, varied, innovative and successful as they base it on more explicit and detailed understanding of learning and change.

Part of this third problem — that one group's useful verbal shorthand is jargon for a wider audience — has been known for a long time (e.g. Fullan, 1982) and we were aware of it from the outset. However, it is only very recently that we have realized the danger of taking a rich set of practice, developing frames that are very useful in making sense of that practice and then using these frames as an advance organizer for advice to a wider audience.

How much you try and say at once is important here, as is the opportunity for dialogue and interaction. In inservice situations, we routinely find teachers respond very positively to more general statements when we deal in detail with only one or two aspects of practice. One reason for this success is that the problems of over-whelming and overloading are not present. A second reason is that many examples, in different contexts of the frame, can not only be presented but, even more import-antly, drawn from the experiences of the participants. We can thus recreate the experience of the frame emerging to make sense of practice in the half-to-one-day periods that are commonly available for inservice activities. Unfortunately, when dealing more comprehensively with practice the approach just described does not work. Even when illustrated with as many examples as is feasible, the advice appears static, rigid, formulaic, simplistic and overwhelming.

A dilemma for us has been how to avoid the above problems while still allowing teachers to draw on the lessons and findings of the PEEL teachers. This dilemma is particularly acute when writing a book, which inevitably is a more comprehensive and summative exercise. We did not face this dilemma when we wrote the first PEEL book (Baird and Mitchell, 1986) at the end of our first year; we had much less advice to give and, somewhat fortuitously, we chose a format which avoided these problems. Each teacher (and one student) wrote a chapter which was a case-study of a year of attempted change. The teachers were very reflective, but the results of these reflections were embedded in what one reviewer called 'a very teacherly account' of their year. When measured against the criti-cisms of academic papers listed at the start of this chapter, this teacherly style has several strengths. The accounts are holistic not atomistic, they are rich with what I defined earlier as classroom wisdom and they allow the reader to see the class-rooms and assess the wisdom of the teacher's decisions in terms of the students' actions and reactions. Evidence of these strengths is that this first book is now in its third edition and eighth reprinting; teachers (and academics) report that they find it an easy and interesting read.

The strengths of the case-study format is also its greatest weakness: the advice it has to offer on many issues is fragmented, scattered, and requires quite a lot of synthesis by the reader. When the original PEEL group planned a second book (Baird and Northfield, 1992) with far more to say about how to stimulate and support better learning, we felt we needed a more thematic approach to chapters that would allow readers to find more easily the advice they needed on any specific issue. We were careful to make substantial use of the voice of the teachers and the students, but, with hindsight, the teachers' comments did not include the short-term contextual material referred to earlier. The result has been successful in capturing and communicating important short-term tactical advice about when and how to use a wide range of teaching procedures, but, again with hindsight, the discussion of the more fundamental insights that provide a basis for strategic planning contain some of the weaknesses discussed earlier.

Table 4.1   Some cognitive strategies that result in quality learning

Monitoring
– meaning of a communication (e.g., What is the main point?)
– personal understanding (e.g., Do I understand this?)
– analyse task and generalize intended solution (e.g., How shall I order my arguments?)
– performance against intent (e.g., Why did I calculate x?)
– performance against instructions (e.g., Have I done everything asked?)

Linking
The ideas/activities in today's lesson with:
– each other
– the ideas/activities in the previous lesson
– an idea/activity in an earlier topic
– different subjects
– the outside world/personal life
– the student's existing conceptions/explanations

Cases

In 1993, while becoming aware of some of these issues, I had the privilege of spending two days in a workshop run by Judy Shulman on cases. Judy had made extensive use of cases to capture aspects of teaching for use in preservice education programs and to stimulate discussion and reflection by practising teachers during inservice activities. Her cases were short (2–4 pages) and crafted to focus on particular issues or aspects of teaching practice. Nevertheless they were contextually rich, retained the complexity of real practice and allowed the reader to see the classroom. I was attracted to their potential for communicating newer ideas and outcomes of teacher research to teachers.

For example, Table 4.1 contains a list of cognitive strategies that provide one way of describing quality learning. It is typical of the frames that have emerged from PEEL. It is based on Baird's earlier list of Poor Learning Tendencies (Baird and White, 1982) and subsequent research by myself and other PEEL teachers. The case by Donna Fox describes students engaged in the first two forms of monitoring and all of the forms of linking except linking to other subjects. The case also brings out some important issues of teaching and teacher change that are direct consequences of promoting quality learning. Table 4.2 contains four questions that I regularly put to teachers (typically a whole school staff) who have asked for an introduction to PEEL. The teachers invariably generate impressive and detailed responses to all four questions.

As just illustrated, any one case contains multiple issues — they reflect the interconnected, messy and holistic nature of teaching. Their short length gives them another important use in communicating new ideas to other teachers: the same issue can be examined in multiple contexts. For example, research on student interest (Mitchell, 1993) revealed that one key source of interest, and consequent intellectual engagement, was a sense of shared intellectual control over the teaching and learning transactions in the classroom. Sharing more intellectual control has been a

Table 4.2 Questions on Donna Fox Case

Learning
Which cognitive strategies were these students displaying?

Class Dynamics
In what ways did Donna think that this class was different?

Teaching
What changes in teaching approaches were associated with this classroom?

Achieving Teacher Change
What difficulties/concerns/fears did the above changes create for the teacher?

recurring theme in the reports by PEEL teachers of how their classrooms have changed as they promote more metacognitive learning. If I mention this phrase to a group of educators (teachers or academics) they will all form a meaning for it; however, the meanings will vary and will commonly be narrower than or different to mine — for example, many will associate it with practices such as negotiating the curriculum or classroom rules (I would describe the latter as sharing management control). These mismatches in meaning can easily remain invisible to all parties.

Another problem in communicating to many teachers is that generalizations such as 'share intellectual control' are regarded (negatively) as 'theory' which is divorced from the 'real' world of practice. Examining several cases through the same lens (sharing intellectual control in this case) has proved very helpful in building shared meanings for what PEEL teachers have done in this and other areas. Donna's students, for example, had no influence on the topics or tasks to be done, but nevertheless had (and perceived) a high level of shared intellectual control through the regular influence of their questions and contributions on how and for how long the various chemical ideas were presented and discussed. There are other, quite different, methods of sharing intellectual control (including negotiating curriculum) that are described in different cases. Discussion of a selection of these cases moves this phrase ('share intellectual control') from a recipe with a relatively prescribed implementation to a strategic principle that can be enacted in a range of ways which vary with content and context. It also foregrounds practice rather than theory: the theory (the generalizations) emerge as ways of clustering and making sense of good practice. This is empowering for teachers, it promotes the independent innovation which is so essential to action research.

PAVOT has attracted two large Australian Research Council grants and we have used some of these funds to release teachers (for a day) to write cases. The third PEEL book (Mitchell and Mitchell, 1997) uses the strengths of cases to avoid the (different) weaknesses of our first two books described above. Each chapter consists of a small group of cases that shared the theme of the chapter followed by some short commentaries on issues of learning, teaching or change that were present in the cases. This structure is more teacherly, less dense, more readable and has theory emerging from practice, but also gives the frames that have emerged from PEEL teachers' research a more visible and locatable presence.

Table 4.3   Case writing tips

1	Be clear in your own mind about the themes and issues that you see in your case. This step often comes *after* the first draft.
2	A case generally starts from a critical incident (or series of closely connected incidents) that readers will engage with. Ensure that this incident is a focus of the case.
3	Drop the reader into an incident; the case may begin in the middle of the story you are telling.
4	Make your intentions/goals/purpose clear. Allow the reader to analyse what happened against what you were trying to do.
5	Include problems or dilemmas or both; weave some tension into the narrative.
6	Include your thinking, your 'subtle judgments and agonizing decisions' as you reacted to events.
7	Give the students a voice: keep their specific comments, actions, reactions, etc., visible.
8	Stay in the case as long as possible rather than dropping into analysis and reflection after a few paragraphs. Try and convey some of your reactions and insights via the (often very rapid) decision-making you engaged in at the time.
9	You do not have to have a happy ending, nor do you have to provide answers to any or all of the questions raised. You may end with new questions.
10	4 pages maximum, preferably 3.

Our case writing began as a way of capturing and communicating teacher research, but it soon became clear that the process of writing cases was a valuable part of the research process. There is no clear boundary between good teaching practice, which is reflective, analytical and constantly evolving, and teacher research. Crafting a case has proved very helpful in encouraging and skilling teachers into a more formal research role. The case writing days are structured to include a lot of collaboration and sharing. The teachers have read a number of cases before the day, which begins with a short discussion of where to start and a number of case writing tips (see Table 4.3). We have found it important to emphasize Tip 9 at the outset; to reassure the teachers that there is no need for them to have solutions to problems that they raise.

The teachers spend about an hour and a half writing a draft which they discuss for another hour and a half in a group of about two other teachers plus one academic. This discussion provides the basis for the second draft. Although the two processes are interconnected, we have found that teachers tend to begin with an incident from their practice and then look for why it was important to them rather than beginning with an issue and searching for incidents which illustrate it. This usually means that the first drafts are not well-crafted around the issues and are commonly rather flat. We tell the teachers to expect this in our introduction and the discussions focus on identifying what issues are, or could be, present in the incident and what the case is a case of. Everyone in the group contributes to the discussion of each case; a process which stimulates teachers to apply existing frames to practice and to develop new frames and insights.

The second draft of a case may have a very different structure from the first as a result of the discussion about what the case is a case of. Tips 3 to 7 are stylistic and help make the case richer, more interesting and more likely to stimulate reflection and discussion by the reader. In a good case, the reader can see both the classroom participants and the teacher's thinking: reasons, purposes and reactions. Some of this advice is borrowed directly from Judy Shulman (Shulman and Colbert, 1987) who, as mentioned earlier, stimulated all our work in this area. Other tips emerged or evolved from our case writing days. The advice in Tip 8, for example, only became clear to me after a (fortunately) close colleague went through seven drafts of a case. She was a very reflective and analytical teacher and drew a number of insights and conclusions from her incident. These were all of interest, but they were much more effective when woven into what she did and why at the time, rather than extracted at the end. Embedding the writer's conclusions in the case, apart from making the case more readable, makes it easier for the reader to decide whether or not they agree with the writer.

Our case writing experiences have highlighted another important problem in trying to capture successful classroom practice. One of the problems for a researcher in identifying what works in a classroom and why it works is that much teacher knowledge is tacit and implicit — some of the critical aspects of what a skilled teacher does can be done so tacitly that they never appear in the teacher's explicit descriptions and advice. The process of case writing can expose these hidden, critical aspects. This was brought home very powerfully to me in the incidents described in the case below. I was overseas for the first week of Term 2 in 1997 and arranged that one of the science teachers in PEEL would take my classes. The outcome of this resulted in the following case plus sequel.

Gorgeous, Smoothie and Snowball: Debbie Baulch

I arrived at school and went straight to the extra's board to look at my classes for the day. It was a Tuesday, when I occasionally do relief teaching at the school over and above the two days I already teach there. I saw that I had two of Ian Mitchell's classes and found out that work had been set. I was looking forward to seeing how the students responded in the classroom after being fortunate to have Ian for their teacher. Odile, one of the teachers at the school caught up with me: 'Debbie, you have Ian's classes, I have the work for you.' The bell for form assembly was about to go and so Odile gave me a very quick run down of the work, telling me that she had been on the phone to Ian last night for ages. The work was Year 10 genetics. Four POE[2] exercises. Not a problem I thought (why was Ian on the phone to Odile so long, this is easy?). I have used POE exercises in my classroom and being a biology teacher meant that I was comfortable with the subject matter. The part of my brief that perplexed me a little was the instruction that I was to have the students work through the prepared sheets but I was not to 'close' on the exercise. In other words I was not to give the students the answers. With five minutes to prepare for the class I still went in feeling confident.

The first of Ian's classes was 10C. They were already well into the exercise and did not really need me. As I was to find out later the really difficult part of the activity had already been covered by Ian and they used me just to verify a couple of points but were mostly happy to go it alone.

After recess I headed off to meet 10D not in the slightest bit concerned that I was to have them for a double class. On entering the classroom, I recognized some of the students and felt even more secure. Not for long. 'Do you give marks for questions that we ask?' called out one of the girls. 'No,' I replied, 'but I welcome any questions you may have.' 'Good,' the same girl replied, 'You will have to excuse us because we ask a lot of questions.' 'Great,' I responded. Inside I was thinking to myself that this was terrific, what a motivated class and made a mental note to bite the bullet with my own class and try to introduce marks for questions raised. I said to the class as the first sheet was handed out that we were going to work through the sheets together (four sheets, one POE exercise on each page, one following on from the other). I asked them to read the first exercise and then predict the result. The activity needed them to predict the outcome of the mating of two Guinea Pigs, one with a smooth coat (Smoothie) and the other with a curly coat (called Gorgeous). The students also had to give reasons for their prediction. Afterwards, we wrote up the possibilities for the four offspring produced and tried to discuss their reasoning. At this stage most were just guessing and had no real reason. 'Don't know,' were some of the replies. 'Maybe one is stronger?' suggested one girl. I asked her to clarify what she meant. 'It will beat the other one,' She said. I then asked, 'If that was the case what results would we get?' Another student said, 'Either all curly or all smooth.' 'Perhaps,' I replied trying to be non-committal as I was not allowed to 'close' on the discussion. 'What if they are equally strong?' asked another. 'Well, you tell me,' I said. The student said that there would be a mixture of curly coats and smooth, no pattern. Another sheet of paper was handed out with the results which showed that all the Guinea Pigs produced had smooth coats and so did another set of offspring when the trial was repeated. 'Smooth must be stronger,' called out one of the boys and the rest of the class were happy with this. So far so good.

I handed out the next sheet which asked the students to predict the outcome of mating the original curly haired Gorgeous with one off the smooth-haired offspring (Snowball) that had been produced in the first litter. I had to put up with some of the incestuous comments about the activities of the Guinea Pigs. When I called for their predictions on the board, most of the students decided that the offspring would be smooth coated again. 'Why?' I asked. 'Because smooth is stronger,' some said. Some other students suggested other possibilities but couldn't verify their reasoning. Again the result sheet was handed out, but this time half of the Guinea Pigs had smooth hair and the other half curly. 'How can this be?' said one of the students. 'You told us that smooth is stronger,' said another. I could suddenly feel the dynamics of the classroom start to change. 'Well, tell us the answer,' one of the students said. I said, 'Mr Mitchell has told me that I am not to give you the answer and that you are to try to work it out for yourselves.' 'This is dumb,' called out one of students. 'How are we supposed to get the work done if you won't tell us the answer?' I could feel my stress level start to rise. What was I going to do? Not knowing how Ian would prompt the students I was at a loss. Perhaps this was the reason that Ian had been on the phone to Odile so long! To give the students information could mess up what Ian was trying to achieve. Panic was setting in as I felt the hostility and stress of the students. 'Well have another look at the two examples. What was the difference between them?' 'Snowball is in one, Smoothie is in the other,' replied a student. 'Yes,' I said, 'and what is the difference between these two Guinea Pigs?' 'Nothing, they both have smooth hair,' said another. We were getting nowhere. 'Can't you just give us a little bit of help?' was a student question.

We were all starting to feel really frustrated. 'What has Mr Mitchell told you about genetics?' I asked. 'Nothing,' replied one of the students. 'We have only just started the unit.' 'OK,' I said, 'I will try to give you some information to help you' — hoping I was doing the right thing as far as Ian was concerned. I realize in hindsight that this was giving in and the students were getting part of the answer but in the split second I had to think I could come up with nothing better. I did not think that the students had taken on board the fact that information is passed on from both Guinea Pigs. This was written in Ian's 'clue' at the top of the page. I then launched into a talk about our cells containing a blue print to clone us, briefly mentioning chromosomes and genes. I told them that the human body has 46 chromosomes in every cell in matched pairs. We carry two genes for every characteristic on our body. I then asked about the sex cells, would they have 46 too? A discussion went on and the class eventually decided that they would have 23 so that when the two cells came together, the new individual would have 46 again. I then turned their attention back to our problem. Each Guinea Pig would contain two lots of information one from each parent about its coat. I then suggested that they go back to look at the individual Guinea Pigs so far and try to predict what genes they would be carrying. Finally a break through. 'Gorgeous and Smoothie must be pure bred while Snowball is not pure,' suggests one student. I then had them explain what they meant by pure and unpure as well as why they believed this. 'Pure means two of the same information while Unpure means two different types of information.'

I then asked the students to continue with the exercise. As I wandered around the room some of the students could explain the smooth coat being 'stronger' as the Guinea Pig having curly and smooth information but only smooth was shown. Some could then tell me that to have a curly coat the Guinea Pig must carry two lots of curly information. They were then able to predict accurately the final exercises.

When I walked out of the classroom, I felt frustrated with the way that the lesson had gone. I noted that although the class had progressed from very few people predicting correctly at the start to almost all of the students predicting correctly in the finish, I had not conducted the exercise in the way that Ian intended. It bothered me that I had been manipulated by the students into giving them information that had helped them to get the correct answer without making them really think about it. I have been involved in PEEL and have been trying to change my teaching practice since meeting Ian in 1990. I felt that I had come a long way in trying to implement teacher and student change in my classroom and I was amazed at how easily I had given in and at my difficulty in avoiding giving the students the answer. I realized that I still unconsciously give the students a lot of the answers without making them work for them. The students also are conditioned to respond in a certain way. Their often stressed perspective is that they have work to do and they want to get this done as quickly and easily as possible. This usually involves pestering the teacher for the answer. I realized that in future I needed to somehow get the students to value the process of working out a problem, rather than worrying about whether or not they have got the right answer.

A reaction: Ian Mitchell

Debbie had shared her experiences with Odile including her surprise at how hard she had found it to avoid giving the answers. I found this fascinating, knowing the changes that Debbie had made to her teaching over a number of years and I asked her to write a case about the experience. This has become a significant learning exercise for me about my own teaching.

Over the last 15 years I have run hundreds of in-service activities and had thousands of conversations with colleagues which include me identifying and describing the critical pieces of tactical advice that are associated with making the many procedures that PEEL teachers use, work. I regard myself as very experienced in this area and I had given Odile, a close colleague and very experienced PEEL teacher, as detailed a description as I could of everything I felt was needed for the successful running of this series of four POEs, yet I did not mention four tactics that were critical to success.

One, perhaps the least important, was to delay the introduction of technical terms such as chromosome until the students had invented a need for them. The other three were essential in providing the students with a sense of progress, even though no closure was made and while they were continuing to predict incorrectly (I do not expect correct predictions until the fourth breeding situation). The first tactic was to maintain a list on the board of possible explanations. For example, before the first result is known it *could* be that the hair type will be determined by male genes, female genes, or that smooth will always overcome curly, or the reverse, or that there could be a balance. The first result eliminates several of these and I cross these off creating a visible record of progress in working out how inheritance works. The second tactic involves concurrently building a list of the 'things that we know' (starting with the initial clue). This second list grows as the first list shortens which further heightens the sense of progress. After the second result, the initial list of explanations (or theories as I start to call them) has often shortened to zero, so we use the expanded list of what we now know to generate new theories. The third tactic is to talk about how I intend the learning to occur: looking back and reinterpreting past data in the light of new results is a new form of thinking for some students and the nature of this approach needs some discussion. The general success that I have with this activity when I incorporate these tactics is probably why 10C, who had experienced me using this approach on the first two predictions before Debbie took over, were quite happy to continue with the process.

I did not 'forget' to mention these things to Odile, rather they were still tacit knowledge, in spite of all my experience in making skilled teaching explicit. They were so tacit that only the first two of them came out as I discussed with Debbie her first draft of this case. The last two only emerged as I wrote this piece a week or two later, indeed my description here is slightly neater than what I have actually done. *Because* I have clarified my own practice to myself, I will teach this sequence better the next time round. I am no longer at all surprised at the pressure Debbie felt to give the answers; indeed I now regard Debbie as the fourth Guinea Pig in the story! (Reprinted from Mitchell and Mitchell, in press)

As you can see, I had no idea that I had omitted in my advice such a huge part of what I did. I was astounded to discover this. Identifying the frame of 'maintain a sense of progress' was very important for lesson sequences that have a focus on restructuring or constructing understanding of key ideas rather than completing tasks. During such sequences, it may seem obvious to the teacher that class time has been usefully spent on clarifying or considering the merits and defects of alternative explanations. However, this is not at all clear to many students, particularly those whose intellectual self-esteem is not high. Without a clear sense of progress on a task (e.g. 'I am up to question 8') they lose confidence and interest and refuse to continue to engage in the teacher's game. The lesson disintegrates. On the other hand, if students do perceive that they are mastering a complex idea, their confidence, interest and self-esteem rise sharply and they maintain high levels of engagement. The contrast is stark and there is little middle ground. I had identified this instability of very fluid discussions towards either clear success or failure in earlier research (Mitchell, 1993), however, part of the crucial wisdom that I had also developed about how to maximize the prospect by overtly maintaining a sense of progress of success was only revealed by the sequence of events just reported.

Teaching for Quality Learning

A final use of cases in our research has been looking at a large number which, importantly, were all written by PEEL and PAVOT teachers with relatively common goals and educational values: promoting increased metacognition and the type of learning described in Table 4.1, reported by Donna Fox and desired by Debbie Baulch. We are often asked, and always have had difficulty answering the question, 'What will I see if I watch a PEEL teacher?' The reason for this difficulty is that what one would see in Year 12 mathematics, Year 8 woodwork and Year 3 science will, in many ways, clearly be very different. The teachers' cases came from a wide range of contexts, but a number of common themes emerged when we looked at the whole set. Table 4.4 contains a list of twelve principles of teaching for quality learning. These each describe long-term strategies, which can be enacted in many ways that vary with content and context, but which we believe are probably relevant to all contexts (PAVOT teacher-researchers are currently testing this last hypothesis). The detail, uses and the status of these principles are outside the scope of this chapter,

Table 4.4   *Principles of teaching for quality learning (Mitchell and Mitchell, 1997, p. 114)*

1   Share intellectual control with students.
2   Look for occasions when students can work out part (or all) of the content or instructions.
3   Provide opportunities for choice and independent decision-making.
4   Provide a diverse range of ways of experiencing success.
5   Promote talk which is exploratory, tentative and hypothetical.
6   Encourage students to learn from other students' questions and comments.
7   Build a classroom environment that supports risk-taking.
8   Use a wide variety of intellectually challenging teaching procedures.
9   Use teaching procedures that are designed to promote specific aspects of quality learning.
10 Develop students' awareness of the big picture: how the various activities fit together and link to the big idea.
11 Regularly raise students' awareness of the nature of different aspects of quality learning.
12 Assess for different aspects of quality learning, not for rote learning.

but I stress that I do not consider the list to be definitive and final, we have been exploring its value to a range of audiences in the 12 months since its development.

As discussed earlier, focusing on only one or two of these principles can be the basis of an effective inservice activity. Moreover, anecdotal data suggests that the interweaving of cases and commentaries in *Stories of Reflective Teaching* (Mitchell and Mitchell, 1997) has resulted in a teacher-friendly structure — although we have little data on the specific impact of the list in Table 4.4 on readers of this book. However, our experiences with this list as a handout or transparency brings me back to some of the points made earlier in the chapter about the difficulty of constructing generalized and comprehensive statements of advice that will communicate to teachers.

We never expected the phrases in Table 4.4 to carry meaning on their own and in every case we provide several (quick) examples of each principle. We have found that the reactions of the audience vary substantially with their previous experience in PEEL. For teachers who have been in PEEL, the list, as a list, is affirming — many of the principles are familiar to them, either as phrases they have heard and used or as describing things that they do regularly. The principles helped these teachers organize and make sense of their own practice and provides stimulating, but manageable and non-threatening directions, for future development. Some teachers have reported pinning it above their desks as a reminder and reference. Teachers who have not been in PEEL, however, have a different reaction. While most of the phrases carry some meaning, many teachers are uneasy about whether they understand what is meant and we have found a wide range of often narrow meanings is constructed. Fewer of the principles are familiar as phrases and, while some do, fewer map onto the teachers' existing practice. Although teachers often agree with the general thrust of the list, the number of principles and the substantial implications that each one can have mean that the list is often seen as any, or all, of overwhelming, intimidating, guilt-creating ('there is so much I am not doing') or simply too much 'theory'.

This has been a useful lesson, we had not realized the extent to which, after 14 years of PEEL, we now had two different teacher audiences. It also highlights the potential mismatch between teacher knowledge and academic knowledge. It does not mean that the wisdom generated by relevant and valid research such as the findings of the teacher (and academic) researchers in PEEL cannot be usefully accessed by other teachers, but it does provide advice as to when and how this can and cannot be done. It also suggests that bridging the gulf between practice and relevant research will require changes to the structure of how teachers work. These changes would provide teachers with more and more regular opportunities for ongoing professional development, collaboration, reflection and action research.

Conclusion

In this chapter I have argued for the value of both teacher knowledge and teacher research. I described teaching as having elements of a science, craft and art. The knowledge of many teachers is primarily a mixture of craft and art knowledge.

In no sense is this chapter intended to belittle the value of findings from research done by university-based researchers for teachers (let alone other academics). However, I do argue that much of the 'science' of teaching that can emerge from such research is more accessible and more useful to both teachers and academics when closely linked to relevant craft knowledge. I also argue that teacher-researchers are usually much better placed to generate both the craft knowledge and its synthesis with the science knowledge. Further, that tackling some important problems in education requires the knowledge that flows from research by teachers working (mainly) alone in normal classrooms. This last comment does not preclude the teachers being in a collaborative relationship with an academic, indeed I believe there are important advantages that flow from such partnerships.

As discussed earlier, I seriously underestimated the highly tacit nature of so many crucial aspects of teacher knowledge. Schön (1987) describes the use of phrases such as (teacher) artistry as 'junk categories' which close off further inquiry. I agree that this can be the case, however another positive aspect of teacher research is that it can result in previously elusive art knowledge being identified, explored and codified in ways that enrich the other forms of knowledge.

As was discussed earlier, the mere fact that a particular piece of wisdom was generated from teacher research does not mean that it will automatically communicate to teachers. However, one important advantage of teacher research is that it will generate the short-term contextual detail that teacher-readers demand. It is unfortunate that the current cannons of value used in the academic literature do not place a high value on the art, craft and contextualized aspects of teacher knowledge. It is teachers, not academics, who determine what happens in classrooms and I argue that the literature should place a higher value on types of knowledge and forms of communication that meet teachers' needs.

Notes

1 These issues are elaborated in Mitchell, Northfield and Mitchell (1996) which describes six dimensions of teacher research and the type of support needed for each.
2 POE stands for Predict, Observe, Explain (White and Gunstone, 1992). Students predict the outcome of an experiment, observe what happens, and then try to explain the results, and any discrepancy between their prediction and the actual outcome.

References

BAIRD, J.R. (1986) 'Improving learning through enhanced metacognition: A classroom study', *European Journal of Science Education*, **8**, pp. 263–82.

BAIRD, J.R. (1995) 'Uptake and teacher change', in BAIRD, J.R. and NORTHFIELD, J.R. (eds) *Learning From the PEEL Experience*, 2nd edition), Melbourne: PEEL Publishing.

BAIRD, J.R. and MITCHELL, I.J. (eds) (1986) '*Improving the Quality of Teaching and Learning: An Australian Case Study — The PEEL Project*, Melbourne: PEEL Publishing.

BAIRD, J.R. and MITCHELL, I.J. (eds) (1997) *Improving the Quality of Teaching and Learning: An Australian Case Study — The PEEL Project*, 3rd edition, Melbourne: PEEL Publishing.

BAIRD, J.R. and NORTHFIELD, J.R. (eds) (1992) *Learning From the PEEL Experience*, Melbourne: PEEL Publishing.

BAIRD, J.R. and WHITE, R.T. (1982) 'Promoting self-control of learning', *Instructional Science*, **11**, pp. 227–47.

COCHRANE-SMITH, M. and LYTLE, S.L. (1993) *Inside Outside: Teacher Research and Knowledge*, New York: Teachers College Press.

FULLAN, M. (1982) *The Meaning of Educational Change*, New York: Teachers College Press.

JONES, C. and MITCHELL, J. (1987) *The Writing Path*, Melbourne: Longman Cheshire.

JONES, C. and MITCHELL, J. (1988) *The Writer's Journey*, Melbourne: Longman Cheshire.

JONES, C. and MITCHELL, J. (1989) *Writer's Horizons*, Melbourne: Longman Cheshire.

MITCHELL, I.J. (1993) 'Teaching for quality learning', Unpublished PhD thesis, Monash University, Melbourne.

MITCHELL, I.J. and BAIRD, J.R. (1985) 'A school-based, multi-faculty action research project to encourage metacognitive behaviour', *Research in Science Education*, **15**, pp. 37–43.

MITCHELL, J.A. and BAIRD, J. (1988) 'Teaching, learning and the curriculum — 2: Science and beyond', *Research in Science Education*, **16**, pp. 150–8.

MITCHELL, I.J. and MITCHELL, J.A. (1997) *Stories of Reflective Teaching: A Book of PEEL Cases*, Melbourne: PEEL Publishing.

MITCHELL, I.J. and MITCHELL, J.A. (in press) *More Stories of Reflective Teaching*, Melbourne: PEEL Publishing.

MITCHELL, I.J., NORTHFIELD, J.R. and MITCHELL, J.A. (1996) 'Initiating teacher research and supporting teacher-researchers', Paper presented at the conference Educational Research: Building New Partnerships, jointly organized by the Educational Research Association (ERA), Singapore and Australian Association for Research in Education (AARE), Singapore, November 25–29.

NORTHFIELD, J.R., MITCHELL, I.J. and MITCHELL, J.A. (1997) 'It is interesting . . . but is it research?' Paper presented at the annual conference of the Australasian Association for Research in Science Education, Adelaide, July.

SCHÖN, O.A. (1987) *Educating the Reflective Practitioner*, San Francisco, CA: Jossey-Bass.

SHULMAN, J.H. and COLBERT, J.A. (1987) *The Mentor Teacher Casebook*, San Francisco: Far West Laboratory for Educational Research and Development.

WHITE, R.T. and MITCHELL, I.J. (1994) 'Metacognition and the Quality of Learning', *Studies in Science Education*, **23**, pp. 21–37.

WHITE, R.T. and GUNSTONE, R.F. (1992) *Probing Understanding*, London: Falmer Press.

Section Two

Researching Teaching through Collaboration

5   Researching the Cultural Politics of Teachers' Learning

John Smyth

Teacher Learning through Teacher Theorizing

Teachers worldwide are currently experiencing 'difficult times' as their work is assailed, prevailed upon, reformed and restructured almost beyond recognition by forces bent upon devolution, marketization, de-professionalization, and intensification. Increasingly impoverished enclosures are being constructed around teachers and their work in the form of measures designed to calibrate teaching more, thus supposedly leading to improved productivity and accountability (Smyth, 1995; Smyth, Shacklock and Hattam, 1997). The effects of these new technologies of power, which take the form of competencies, appraisal and effectiveness, is to subjugate teachers' indigenous forms of knowledge through a constant process of the politics of derision (see Smyth and Shacklock, 1998). There are, however, instances of discourses of resistance as teachers find ways of keeping alive dialogue about what works in classrooms and schools as they craft, analyse and test local theories of pedagogy and school organization.

This chapter uses sociological ways of theorizing and thematizing a generic category that has become moribund and under-theorized — it is sometimes called teachers' 'lifelong learning', 'workplace learning', or in situ 'professional development'. In this chapter I use the term 'teacher learning' as a way of describing how teachers make sense of the increasing complexity of their world and their work of teaching. The kind of categories just referred to do not on their own have the intellectual capacity to carry us very far in explaining how teachers survive and thrive (or not) in later modernity. One way into this perplexity might be to 'read' teachers' work against what it is that constitutes the centrality of the work; that is to say, the engagement of teachers with the lives, aspirations, frustrations, experiences, hopes and desires of young people. Understanding, engaging with, and trying to concretely change the life chances of young people is, after all, what teaching is supposed to fundamentally be about. It is far too simplistic to argue that teachers enact a mediating role, although they are certainly a central influence for good or ill in the transition of the young to adulthood and work. But, teachers are also embedded in and constantly learning reflexively about the world in which young people are experimenting, struggling, acting upon and being 'done to'. Herein lies an important intersection (or is it a juxtaposition?) that I want to dwell on for a few moments.

I want to start out by talking about one major research project I am currently involved in, the Teachers' Learning Project, but I will also introduce into the background ideas coming from a second major one, the Students Completing Schooling Project, because of the way the latter is providing us with powerful revelations of how it is that young people make decisions about whether to stay on or leave schooling in the post-compulsory years. It is not possible, in the end, to talk about teachers' work without also making some incursions into the world and experiences of students, despite the fact that much research tries to proceed as if these were artificially separated.

The Teachers' Learning Project came about through the confluence of four things: first, a 30-year personal history of interest in, and having worked as a teacher, and then having intensively studied the cultures, lives and working experiences of many teachers; second, a disturbing personal reaction to discussion in the wider public and political spheres to the work of teaching which is frequently denigrated, trivialized and technicized, in addition to always being misunderstood — that fired a passion within me to correct the misperception; thirdly, success in securing a 3-year grant from the Australian Research Council and the willingness of the South Australian Department for Education and Children's Services to collaborate in the project; and, finally, a feeling that while the academy had expended much energy in studying teachers and teaching over the past couple of decades, that this amounted to very little in terms of clarifying the complexity of this apparently mysterious process.

The Students Completing Schooling Project, another 3-year Australian Research Council funded collaborative project, emerged out of a concern that the dramatic changes in the economy in the late 1980s had produced a situation of 'forced retention' (Dwyer, 1994) that was followed in the 1990s by a dramatic decline in the apparent attractiveness of schooling to large numbers of young people who came to the realization that further schooling was not necessarily a guarantee of entry to full-time, well paid, secure, and meaningful work. In this project we were trying to access the complexities of how students make decisions about leaving school and what is occurring in their lives at school and beyond as they make these decisions.

Clearly, these two projects intersect in crucial ways as young people and teachers work to establish relationships and understand how the culture of the school works to assist types of identity formation that are empowering or disabling. As Furlong and Cartmel (1997) note, contemporary teaching and learning in schools involves embracing 'new scenarios' and confronting 'old barriers' in all areas of social life including schooling, its connection to the labour market, and spheres that appear further removed like politics and consumption (Warde 'Preface' in Furlong and Cartmel, 1997). Both Beck (1992) and Beck, Giddens and Lash (1994) argue that all of us, and even more so the young, live within a 'risk culture' and a 'risk society' where there is a 'growing disjuncture between objective and subjective dimensions of life' (Furlong and Cartmel, 1997, p. 4). Lifestyles have become increasingly individualized, in contexts where social divisions and social inequalities continue to 'exert a powerful hold over people's lives' (p. 4). People are 'progressively freed from social networks and constraints of the old order' (p. 3) but are forced to confront and 'negotiate a new set of hazards which impinge in all aspects of their day to day lives' (p. 3). The wider forces of the social and political economy operate in highly structured ways to continue to shape people's lives, at the same time as they 'increasingly seek solutions on an individual, rather than a collective basis' (p. 4). This 'epistemological fallacy' as Furlong and Cartmel (1997, p. 5) term it, constitutes a situation where social and economic existence is still structured by larger forces (even more so than in the past), but people are increasingly confronted by and experience 'fragmentation of social structures' and the weakening of 'collective identities' (p. 5). What occurs is 'an intensification of individualisation as more people are placed in unpleasant situations which they interpret as being due, in part, to their own failures' (p. 5). While this is not the place to give a detailed treatment of these ideas, suffice to say for the moment that teachers' work is continually being shaped and reshaped by the need to mediate new sets of life chances for the young, working with them to negotiate their inequitable vulnerability to risk, while trying to craft a new pedagogy that takes account of lives and that holds out at least some hope for managing the inversion where 'wealth accumulates at the top, and risk at the bottom' (Beck, 1992, p. 35). I will now turn my attention, in the main, to the Teachers' Learning Project.

It is important in starting this chapter not to underplay the importance of the underlying factors giving rise to the project in the first place because in a real sense they have had a tangible effect on its formulation, enactment, and the way in which teachers have subsequently reacted and responded to what we asked of them. There were three aspects we were especially mindful of:

(i)   teachers' work has undergone some dramatic changes in the past few years and in many respects is barely recognizable from what it was a decade ago; just keeping track of how and in what ways teachers acquire, hold and modify the repertoire of sophisticated knowledge required to be an effective teacher is a major difficulty not least because it resides largely in the private granary of the oral culture of teaching;

(ii)   our capacities as researchers to get privileged access to the complex work lives of teachers is still very crude by any standards. Because most of us do not have the resources necessary to do the extremely detailed ethnographic studies, this has meant that we have had to cut corners, quite severely on occasions with a resultant loss of quality information — this presented those of us in the Teachers' Learning Project with an interesting methodological challenge of how to faithfully capture information about the breadth, diversity, richness, and uniqueness of teacher learning, with finite resources;

(iii)   the increasingly muscular ways in which policy-makers have sought to spot-weld education onto the economy as an engine for economic growth has the prospect of doing considerable damage to the local indigenous ways in which teachers think and operate pedagogically, and how this thinking informs how they act in relation to their own and their students' learning.

What we were interested in at the outset was the phenomenon of teachers as learners, but not of the individual factoid type; that is to say, how lone teachers accumulate contrived repertoires of effective teaching to be paraded when needed. Rather, our interest was in how teachers were able to politically harness the structures of their schools so as to make them work for students in more inclusive and democratic ways. To use the shorthand phrase we adopted, we were interested in the 'dialogic school' in which teaching was construed as a social practice that occurred in interpretive communities, where the intent was to engage others (teachers, parents, students, and administration) in issues of substance around sustaining a culture of learning.

While the quest is by no means complete, it has not lead us down the predictable path of the elusive but largely unproductive correlates of effective teaching. It is true that we were on a mission — searching for the broader set of conditions within which the archetype teacher-as-learner was embedded, but in this instance our investigative journey has produced three interrelated aspects that seem to profoundly pre-form whether teachers will be active learners of the culture and context of their teaching. First, there is the existence of democratic practices and policies that underlie the work of teaching; second, there is the set of coherent school support structures that assist teachers; and third, there is a shared public discourse within the school and its community about teaching and learning.

In many respects these three aspects may appear on the surface to be a fairly unexceptional and common-sense set of ideals, but in reality our experience has shown that they are far from widespread and certainly not universally endorsed or followed in practice. Indeed, they often run counter to recently introduced educational policies that reinscribe hierarchy, that technicize and codify teaching through measurement and accountability, and that foster an atmosphere of competition and distrust among teachers in the quest to supposedly satisfy customer choice, principles of user-pays, and the quasi-marketization of schooling. In this project we have found that teachers reacted differently to these external reforms — from compliance to outright rejection. But, some schools have a more sophisticated process of filtering policies developed at a distance from the school through their existing professional ideologies, perspectives and identities to produce 'resistance within accommodation' (Troman, 1996, p. 473).

Some schools and teachers have quite sophisticated ways of crafting 'visions' about who they are and what they regard as being important, that are markedly at variance with the visions perpetrated by visionaries outside of schools. How schools enact and live out their vision has a lot to do with the way teachers construct a culture of what it means to be a teacher and to 'have a life' as a teacher — making sense of opposition, and moving beyond merely resisting to adopting strategic action with and through the school community. This capacity of schools to create regenerating capacities for themselves — to debate, contest and innovate, even in difficult and turbulent times — seems to have a lot to do with a shared understanding and commitment to the construction of a wider public discourse about the democratic nature of schooling. It differs markedly according to whether the school falls into the archetype of being 'un-renewing', 'collaborative', or 'critically collaborative'.

When one of the case-study schools in the Teachers' Learning Project in effect said to us that they had a vision or a primary purpose of managing social justice within a democratic framework of relationships within the school and its community, we were understandably excited. That a school had somehow found not only the will but also the pedagogic spaces (Macedo, 1994, p. 137) within which to supplant the authoritative discourses of economic rationalism through attempting to recreate a sense of 'civic discovery' (Reich, 1988), seemed to us remarkable, and we suspected fairly uncommon. It seemed to us that this could only be possible through what Bakhtin (1981, p. 342) calls 'internally persuasive discourse' — those ways of thinking and acting on the world that 'engage us from within, rather than impose itself from without'. Compared to the authoritative discourses of schools as engines for economic growth, what we were hearing was an account of how a school had found a way to tackle the wider 'flight from democracy' (Plank and Boyd, 1994) gripping Western societies in general and schools in particular. While the indigenous alternative we were encountering was much more untidy, open to the accusation of being less rigorous, less definitive, less tightly structured and less muscular than the outcomes, accountability driven, pre-formulated and compliant alternative preferred by politicians and policy-makers, what we were witnessing seemed to be much more in tune with the desires, aspirations and realities of this particular school and its wider community. It was true that this grassroots approach was less quantifiable, specifiable in advance, more risk-prone because of its inherent uncertainty and more likely to be hijacked by interest groups, but its redeeming feature was that it was precisely the kind of model that could be fashioned as it went, with all of the political compromises and settlements necessary to make it work because it had extensive and continual ownership by the school itself.

The Dialogic School

I can best draw together this opening section of the chapter by briefly alluding to some of the emerging themes of the dialogic school that presented themselves to us in some of the schools we studied. Again, rather than engage in boring and superficial descriptions of the schools, I will instead sketch out the broad features of the archetype dialogic school. In employing this notion of the archetype, what I am doing is attempting to go considerably beyond the surface facade of the school as it presents itself to us and which are usually captured in observational and interpretive studies. Critical research of the kind we do looks for the deep forms, structures, moulds, models, patterns and themes that pre-figure and underlie what it is we encounter in the fieldwork.

Pedagogy of the Question

When a school is prepared to step out in its policies and its actions and actively promote the importance of questions over answers, then this is a significant statement about the importance it ascribes to openness over closure. This is all the more significant when the philosophy pervades the practices of the school. Contestation, controversy, discussion and debate are considered preferable to certainty, stability, compliance or decree in this school. Questioning the status quo and how it came to be, are never far off the agenda here. Issues of poverty, disadvantage and discrimination are never taken at face value whether in the classroom or the school, but are regarded as social constructions that need and deserve interrogation not only within the school and its community, but society at large.

Resistance within Accommodation

In the current climate of rapid socio-political change in schools in which 'private troubles' are underpinned by 'public issues' (Mac an Ghaill, 1991), there is a lot of institutional pressure on teachers to conform to a particular preferred view of teaching, learning and curriculum. Indeed, the trend toward market-led innovation in education, with schools having to manage image and impression in competing with one another, produces an inevitable tension between what teachers know is best based on professional judgment, and what school systems require, driven by market-led ideological forces. Change is, therefore, not a simple linear process but inextricably bound up with the 'multi-faceted nature of current curriculum change', 'the school's internal power relations, with its multi-faceted elements of control, legitimacy, dominance, accommodation and resistance', and individual's 'careers, ideological commitments and actions' (Mac an Ghaill, 1991, p. 302). In other words, because of the way in which changes are being set up outside of schools, there is bound to be a clash of aspirations especially in schools that have a concern for social justice. These schools continually ask the question of outside initiated activities: 'How will this work to redress the already least advantaged?' There is a continual reshaping of externally derived agenda to make them fit the interests of those in school who are disadvantaged.

Continually Refocusing Change

One of the distinguishing hallmarks of schools that successfully manage democratic processes around a commitment to social justice, is that they are able to continually reposition what they do in the daily life of the school, with an eye firmly fixed on the 'bigger picture'. Change for them is a cascading affair, rather than something that is driven out of mandates, despair, or that even inheres in events. They see change opportunistically — as a way of strategically taking advantage of situations that present themselves to the school. These schools have extremely well-tuned antennae, able to quickly work out what are 'hot topics' and go after them, especially where resources are concerned, but always in ways that enable them to fulfil their bigger vision of improving the life chances of *all* children. They have an almost uncanny ability to keep an eye on the real action, when others around them are distracted by the side-shows. Like most other things in these schools, structures are never fixed; they are always tentative and provisional.

Communicative Competence

Schools of the kind we are concerned with here are talkative places — people continually converse with one another about teaching and learning. Knowledge is not private or closeted — individuals take pride in sharing what they know, and it is a central part of the way the school operates, swapping and exchanging ideas that work, keeping in mind that what works for one person on one occasion may not readily transfer for somebody else on another occasion. Part of this penchant for communication emerges from a need to theorize and re-theorize what is going on, what works, how they know, and how things might be done differently. Teaching is not a solitary or private activity, it is very public, and a major way of breaking down isolationism is to have challenging discussions of teaching and learning solidly located on the official agenda of the school.

Centrality of Enunciative Space

The issue of space, in the sense of room to manoeuvre with ideas (Spivak, 1988), is crucial to the way these kind of schools operate. Because social justice is the central organizing feature, they need ways of working that move them beyond the distressed state increasingly characterizing many other schools. Having space to them means acknowledging that experts generate 'enclosures' (Rose and Miller, 1992), and that they actively close down the spaces in which people can speak. What these schools need are spaces of 'regulated confrontation' (Bourdieu, 1991) where people feel they have an 'entitlement to speak' (Fine, 1992, p. 25). The creation of these radical spaces (Ladwig, 1996) in which the 'moral ascendancy of managerialism' (Inglis, 1989) is able to be challenged and kept in check, means that issues of poverty, discrimination, marginalization and disadvantage are not allowed to 'disappear from the social surface' (Bannerji, 1987) — they are continually confronted and worked through in the 'contours of the [otherwise] oppressive relations of teaching' (Ng, 1995).

Put most directly, because the archetype dialogic schools regards itself primarily as a moral community concerned with the politics of self, school and community enablement, it is continually pushing up against the edges of its 'pedagogical comfort zone' (Macedo, 1994, p. 170) in its naming of inequitable social and economic arrangements.

The Methodology of 'Voiced Research'

Teaching is an oral and storied culture — a feature which has yet to be properly acknowledged by existing research approaches. The account I am representing here starts from the presumption that teachers have important stories to tell about their work, the context of schooling, and the structures that support and inhibit teacher learning.

The term 'voiced research' is a relatively new way of characterizing the bringing into the picture of perspectives previously excluded, muted, or silenced by dominant structures and discourses (Denzin, 1995; LeCompte, 1993; Lincoln, 1995; Fine, 1991; Mac an Ghaill, 1996; Schratz, 1992; Weis, 1990). In the case of schools, they have been relentlessly assaulted over the past several decades by policies, practices and discourses of hierarchy, marketization and managerialism — notions that are not only foreign to schools, but that are anathema to the ethos of collaboration, civility, community and democracy. It may seem strange to be talking about the numerically large group of inhabitants of schools as constituting a subjugated group but, in a real sense, the underrepresentation of their lifeworlds in official discourses of education places them in this vulnerable position. Voiced research starts out from the position that interesting things can be said and garnered from groups who do not necessarily occupy the high moral, theoretical or epistemological ground; they actually may be quite lowly and situated at some distance from the centres of power. As Grumet (1990) put it, the promise of voiced research is anchored in local knowledge in the face of objective, normative, hegemonic forms of knowledge. Shacklock and Smyth (1997) claim that 'In the telling of stories of life, previously unheard, or silenced, voices open up the possibility for new, even radically different, narrations of life experience' (p. 4).

Voiced research is, therefore, political in that it has an explicit agenda of reinserting in multiple ways, opportunities for expression that have been expunged because dominant social visions hold sway. There is always continual struggle over whose views get to be represented and smaller voices, those which are less audible, get 'drowned out by others louder, more dominant, and putatively more epistemically legitimate' (Shacklock and Smyth, 1997, p. 4). In respect of schools, who gets to speak for and on behalf of schools and who gets listened to is an artefact of power and who gets to exercise it. With the growing tendency to regard schools as annexes of industry in the quest for enhanced international economic competitiveness, it is not hard to see how the guys from the big end of town wind up with their ideologies, policies, language and practices being promulgated as being unproblematically good for schools, teachers and children. In these circumstances teachers are treated rather like exiles even in their own pedagogical worksites, frequently disparaged as holding deviant viewpoints, and continually having to challenge and supplant dominant beliefs. This becomes most noticeable when the focus of schools bears upon competencies, outcomes, performance indicators, measurement, testing, and the like, to the virtual exclusion of matters of social justice, the structural features that created and sustained injustices in the first place, critical forms of teaching and learning that unmask wider social injustice, and practices that might make schooling operate to redress inequality and positively enhance the life chances of the already least advantaged students.

What then characterizes a voiced research approach? Because of its epistemological commitment to a more democratized research agenda, voiced research has to be construed in such a way that it provides *a genuine space within which teachers as educational practitioners can reveal what is real for them*. This means that research questions can only really emerge out of 'purposeful conversations' (Burgess, 1988), rather than interviews (whether structured or unstructured). The operation of the power dimension in an interview, where the researcher has the question and he/she is trying to extract data from the interviewee, has all of the wrong hallmarks for a more participatory approach. The notion that what is worthwhile investigating may reside with the research informant and may only be revealed when a situation of trust and rapport is established, can rest somewhat uneasily with some researchers. Not having tightly preformulated questions but being sufficiently confident in the capacity of teachers as research informants to come up with research questions that are sufficiently 'respectable', is a very different game even for many qualitative researchers. At issue is who has the power to determine what is a worthwhile or robust research question, and teachers as informants are in a vulnerable position in this regard. When taken seriously, this represents a significant reversal of the way power generally tends to operate in research projects; the researchers know, and teachers are expected to willingly comply in supplying information. Voiced research reverses those dynamics of power.

Starting from situations of immediacy for the research informants can generate more than a few tensions for the resource-strapped researcher who is usually being propelled by an external funding agency agenda to get the most for the least unit of resource input in a timely fashion. Having discussions stall, reverse, go down cul-de-sacs, and head off on incomprehensible tangents, is a constant and real test of the authenticity of the researcher and his/her democratic commitment to this apparently less structured style of research. Exploring and explicating complexity does not rest at all easily with the requirement of policy makers for rendering simplicity, reduction and utility in research — all aspects that run counter to voiced research with its tendency towards cacophony, multiplicity and idiosyncrasy.

Voiced research can also be argued to have a high level of credibility, at least from the vantage point of school practitioners. This extensive street credibility derives from the embeddedness of this kind of research in the lives, experiences and aspirations of teachers, and it is this feature that makes it so compelling for other classroom practitioners who may choose to read it. At the same time, this feature may be the cause of some considerable loss of respectability with large segments of the academy. It really comes down to the audience question — for whom is the research meant to inform or be useful? Readers of this kind of research are able to resonate with the images, issues, messages, language, and the fact that the complexity, contradiction and struggle of other teachers' lives spills out in lively and recognizable ways into the account, rather than being laundered or leached out. This is what makes voiced research valid — it is believable!

There is an important pedagogical issue in voiced research — it provides a prominent opportunity for practitioner theorizing. Theorizing is something in other forms of research that is the prerogative of qualified outsiders, once compliant practitioners have been conveniently milked. Where voiced research differs is in the way it is predicated on a certain degree of sense-making in situ by virtue of the willing participation of the research informant. The give-and-take of the research opportunity invites a certain degree of identity formation previously out of reach — I call this active practitioner theorizing.

What I am getting at here is that often the question posed by the outsider is the first time the informant has been confronted by the issue and in responding is literally constructing for the first time an inchoate discourse around the issue; in this sense, data are not so much being 'collected' as 'constructed' then and there on the spot. We often witness this in the struggle informants have with tightly structured questions — they are not their questions, or even ones that they have thought about before. There is hence the need to start from a vantage point that leaves them with plenty of scope to sculpt an account more indicative of the terrain they are coming from.

The style of research being described here is interrogative — but not in the sense of boring into the voluntary informants who so graciously put their lives on the line. The kind of interrogation I have in mind is of the contexts and dominant discourses that envelope the everyday lives and experiences of teachers, and that are held in place by hegemonic ideologies, paradigms and world views. One of the aspirations of voiced research is to provide a platform, vulnerable though it might be, by which dominant discourses on the way teaching and schooling are represented might be unmasked and shown as representing 'new management regimes' (Gewirtz, 1997), while denying, denigrating or silencing the 'disruptive underlife' (Gutierrez, Larson and Kreuter, 1995) of schools. In this sense, voiced research makes no pretence to be detached; rather, it is avowedly disruptive and interruptive of the political status quo. Teachers are invited to be socially critical readers of their own biographies and histories and to move beyond 'narratives of denial' to 'narratives of complexity' (Fine and Weis, 1998).

Situating, Locating and Interrogating the Study

One of the distinguishing features of the emergent style of voiced research that we are doing in the context of South Australian schools where we are focusing on how teachers understand, redesign, and reshape teaching and schooling while in the process of doing it, is the notion of being reflexive — both for us and for the teachers we are working with. We are trying to interrogate the lives, the contexts and the circumstances of the participants, but against the background of the broader social, political and economic forces operating to shape those lives and experiences. In this respect the research is pedagogical in the way it is trying to both (re)present voice, but in ways that show that through its very creation there is 'struggle for voice' (Walsh, 1991).

In the earlier parts of this chapter I have spoken at some length of the wider issues and the methodological agenda that have come with it. What I wish to turn to now is some brief speculation about the limitations and shortcomings of this style of research that give me pause for reflection. These ideas are highly speculative at this stage, but it is important that they see the light of day in innovative approaches like this. At the outset, in the fieldwork phase we were, in Foley's (1998) terms, 'trying to rupture the text by depleting it of jargon'. There was a decided element of the 'confessional' in what we were inviting teachers to tell us, with opening gamuts like: 'Tell us what life is like for you at the moment, and how did it get to be that way?' Embarking on this kind of autobiographical approach was a necessary starting point but, as we found out, it was also a process in which the deconstruction of categories was susceptible to either 'over listening' or 'under listening'. Over listening might be characterized as being too attentive to the lives, issues and circumstances raised by teachers, and being blind to the wider forces making things the way they are. In other words, the detail of what teachers say about their everyday lives becomes so absorbing that bigger structural and institutional aspects get underplayed. This can be a real danger when the anecdotal and autobiographical is allowed to operate in an unrestrained way. It ought to be the case that this kind of research is not blind to the wider categories and forces shaping teachers' work, but is concerned about how the researcher and the researched simultaneously construct one another without characterizing or essentializing the other. Categories still need to be present in this kind of research, but in a way in which they can be used to read off lived experience, as well as be reshaped by those experiences. To rework a quote from Inglis (1985) — there is no such things as categoryless lives, only poorly understood categories! On the other hand we need to guard against allowing the theories and categories we bring to fieldwork from becoming the undifferentiated containers into which lives get unceremoniously poured (Lather, 1986). This is what I call 'under listening', in which voices, experiences, lives and aspirations of informants are in danger of being ridden over by the categories, theories, paradigms and the issues of researchers. Trying to maintain a balance here can be a tricky business, especially when trying not to over-romanticize accounts in either direction.

To give an example from the Teachers' Learning Project. We had begun the fieldwork and had retreated to do some writing to make sense of what we were hearing in order to 'build up a picture' (Teachers' Learning Project, 1996). We thought we had done a sophisticated job of sketching out a complete and multi-layered account of the archetype of a teacher-as-learner. We had waxed and waned eloquently about:

- democratic practices and policies that underpin all aspects of teaching and learning;
- coherent structures which support and enhance teachers' learning and pedagogical practices;
- teachers' learning as part of a shared public discourse;
- the importance of social justice;
- the dialogic school and developing discursive communities;
- resistance and competing discourses.

It seemed that in our attempt to provide a sophisticated initial reading of the complexity of what we had learned about teachers' learning, that our teachers' field group (a collection of critical friends that we met with regularly, and who were classroom teachers but not involved in the fieldwork sites), revealed that our account was 'too utopian'! They said that while we had captured an interesting snapshot of the complexity of teachers' lives, we had been short on descriptions of the pathway by which others might advance to the point described in our accounts. In other words, we had done a nice job of getting to the point of a school pre-occupied with the notion of a community of learning teachers, but we had given little thought to how this came to be possible. It seemed that this 'reality check' was an important interruption to the theorizing and thematizing of our work in this project, and it served to alert us to the fact that rendering a case of complexity employing voiced approaches can be more difficult than we think.

Another issue we had to tangle with was that of getting close to the lives of the teachers we were studying through extended periods of fieldwork, but often in ways that brought with it a certain degree of informality, familiarity and requests for reciprocity. This took the form of invitations to provide professional development activities as the school struggled with how to keep professional learning a priority. This was perfectly understandable, but it created moral and ethical choices for us about returning some of the hospitality extended to us, how far we should go, and whether this might blunt the 'critical edge' of our research. How to do this without becoming too heavily implicated in the lives of the people we were trying to study, while not being off-handed by refusing, was something that tested our capacity realistically to draw lines in the sand. While we can make no claim to have definit-ively resolved issues like these and others, we did at least give them a fair airing at regular weekly meetings of our research team, and somehow still sustained amic-able relationships with the school.

The kind of research approach I have just outlined has embedded within it an implicit but passionate commitment to engaging with the wider collapse of dialogic space within schools and the prevailing approaches to educational research which reinforce teachers' loss of entitlement to speak. I have tried to show how, through a different approach to research, it is possible to begin some reversal, particularly when teachers are given an opportunity to theorize the 'crisis circumstances of educational change . . . [through redeeming] "locally" and "particularly" certain events of the problematic situation' (Payne and Hickey, 1997, p. 101). My claim is that when research starts from within the lives, experiences, circumstances and aspirations of teachers — while still keeping an eye firmly fixed on the broader forces shaping the work of teaching — then it is still possible to be hopeful and optimistic. There is indeed a process of reclamation going on, one that is purpose-ful, principled and pedagogical in the dialogue it makes possible between teachers and researchers. A related aspect of this is the restoration these conversations make possible in the increasingly tarnished and contrived arena of collegiality and collaboration (Smyth, 1991; Smyth, 1996; Fielding, 1997). My view is that we can move these notions out of the liberal cul-de-sac in which they have become lodged by arguing that the purpose to which they should be directed is the reinstating of intense conversations around social justice as an educational agenda in schools. If researching teaching is to have any part in this then it has to be around having a critical sensibility to interrogating and unmasking dominant discourses about the way teachers' work ought to be.

Re-affirming the Local, the Political and the Cultural in Researching Teachers' Learning

In this final section I want to briefly draw together the two strands of this paper. In the first instance, I have probably dwelt long enough in the previous section on the reflexive process of 'calling the place of the investigator into question' (Spivak, 1988, p. 271) as a careful reassessment is made of how and in what ways the research method adds to the understanding of a process as complex as researching the lives of teachers. The second part, and here I will be a little more expansive, relates to the substantive revelations of how teachers learn within the cultural politics of teaching. Much has been said and will continue to be said about this aspect, so let me limit myself to the most obvious aspects that have presented themselves to us in the Teachers' Learning Project. They can be best represented as a kind of 'constellation' — a grouping or assemblage of related elements that hold one another in a recognizable relationship.

Firstly, we were surprised (although we should not have been) about the central importance to teachers of the dialogic, or the socially constructed, nature of knowledge about teaching. It seemed that there was a deeply held imperative among teachers to share ideas and ideals and to not back off from having, as one teacher put it, 'feisty debates' about alternatives.

Second, it was also clear to us that while time on its own was an insufficient factor, there was certainly a requirement to build 'conversation time' into schools through deliberate processes of resourcing, even where schools themselves might have to take tough decisions about what had to go or how they were going to work more efficiently for this to happen.

Third, and not unrelated, the school structures had to reflect and support this 'capacity building' (Seddon, 1998) aspect of the dialogical. Without a commitment to democratic decision making, genuine power sharing, and the need to continually (re)affirm and encourage risk-taking, then the kind of inquisitive culture of innovation so central to building forms of teachers' learning simply would not occur. In other words, the creation of a school culture built around 'talking' about the work of teaching was something not to be taken for granted, but rather struggled for at a school-wide level as part of a wider regenerative agenda for all teachers. In short, it amounted to a predisposition towards theory building and theory testing.

Fourth, the schools that we witnessed were not afraid to collect and confront information about what was happening around them, and beyond. But, in particular, they had a single-minded focus on the prominent place of successful student learning in their schema; issues of curriculum, pedagogy and learning were given prominence over government's economic agenda, managerialism, testing, competencies and other skilling agenda. This was a position that required more than a little courage as teachers had to carefully weigh up what they were prepared to take from 'systems directives' which often had a quite different headset. They had to use the 'high trust' settings they had sculpted to work carefully through the perplexity of the daily moral choices of what was to count as learning *for all children* — not just a privileged few. This often required confronting habit, challenging the taken-for-granted, and resisting the nonsensical — often all at the same time. This meant more than adopting some kind of romantic child-centred view of teaching, but having the courage to work through what resourced-based views of teacher-centred learning might look like in an inquiry-oriented culture of inquisitiveness.

Fifth, leadership was not something that was construed hierarchically in schools where teachers were active learners. Rather, it tended to be more 'distributive' or 'provisional' and dependent upon what expertise was required and where it happened to be located at a particular moment. Construed in this way, there were many leaders in schools, and not all of them were accorded the official title of leader!

Sixth, these were sites where the now fashionable notion of the devolved school had taken hold. It was true that this had occurred because the state had unceremoniously backed off from its constitutional responsibility of adequately resourcing public schooling, and schools were expected to dutifully move in to fill the fiscal void. Notwithstanding, these were places where devolution meant, above all, breaking down the shackles of bureaucracy, freeing teachers from isolation and privatism, and where parents and the community had a legitimate role in a coherent school development planning process around devising socially just alternatives to hierarchies of all kinds — managerial, gendered, racist and class-based.

Finally, these were schools where teacher learning hinged very much around a pervading understanding that teaching is an avowedly political activity, and that to take political action by lobbying for a viewpoint was a respectable not a grubby thing to do. To not have a viewpoint and to defer instead to some dominant status quo, was the cardinal sin of being a non-learning teacher.

References

BAKHTIN, M. (1981) *The Dialogic Imagination: Four Essays*, Austin: University of Texas Press.

BANNERJI, H. (1987) 'Introducing racism: Notes towards an anti-racist feminism', *Resources for Feminist Research*, **16**, 1, pp. 10–13.

BECK, U. (1992) *Risk Society: Towards a New Modernity*, London: Sage.

BECK, U., GIDDENS, A. and LASH, S. (eds) (1994) *Reflexive Modernization: Politics, Tradition and Aesthetics in the Modern Social Order*, Cambridge: Polity Press.

BOURDIEU, P. (1991) 'Epilogue: On the possibility of a field of world sociology', in BOURDIEU, P. and COLEMAN, J. (eds) *Social Theory for a Changing Society*, Boulder, CO: Westview Press.

BURGESS, R. (1988) 'Conversations with a purpose: The ethnographic interview in educational research', *Studies in Qualitative Methodology*, **1**, pp. 137–55.

DENZIN, N. (1995) 'On hearing the voices of educational research', *Curriculum Inquiry*, **25**, 3, pp. 313–28.

DWYER, P. (1994) 'Participation or forced retention? Some implications of improved school participation rates', *Unicorn*, **20**, 2, pp. 58–66.

FIELDING, M. (1997) 'On collegiality' Paper presented at the European Conference on Educational Research, Johaann Wolfgang Goethe-University Frankfurt.

FINE, M. (1991) *Framing Dropouts: Notes on the Politics of an Urban Public High School*, Albany: State University of New York Press.

FINE, M. (1992) *Disruptive Voices: The Possibilities of Feminist Research*, Ann Arbor: University of Michigan Press.

FINE, M. and WEIS, L. (1998) 'Writing the "wrongs" of fieldwork: Confronting our own research/writing dilemmas in urban ethnographies', in SHACKLOCK, G. and SMYTH, J. (eds) *Being Reflexive in Critical Educational and Social Research*, London: Falmer Press.

FOLEY, D. (1998) 'On Writing reflexive realist narratives', Paper to the 'Being Reflexive in Critical Educational Research' symposium, Annual Meeting of the American Educational Research Association, San Diego, April 1998.

FURLONG, A. and CARTMEL, F. (1997) *Young People and Social Change: Individualization and Risk in Late Modernity*, Buckingham: Open University Press.

GERWIRTZ, S. (1997) 'Post-welfarism and the reconstruction of teachers' work in the UK', *Journal of Education Policy*, **12**, 4, pp. 217–31.

GRUMET, M. (1990) Voice: the search for a feminist rhetoric for education studies. *Cambridge Journal of Education*, **20**, 3, 1990, pp. 277–82.

GUTIERREZ, K., LARSON, J. and KREUTER, B. (1995) 'Cultural tensions in the scripted classroom: The value of the subjugated perspective', *Urban Education*, **29**, 4, pp. 410–42.

INGLIS, F. (1985) *The Management of Ignorance: A Political Theory of the Curriculum*, London: Basil Blackwell.

INGLIS, F. (1989) 'Managerialism and morality: The corporate and republican school', in CARR, W. (ed.) *Quality in Teaching: Arguments for a Reflective Profession*, London: Falmer.

LADWIG, J. (1996) *Academic Distinctions: Theory and Methodology in the Sociology of School Knowledge*, New York: Routledge.

LATHER, P. (1986) 'Research as Praxis', *Harvard Educational Review*, **56**, 3, pp. 257–77.

LECOMPTE, M. (1993) 'A framework for hearing silence: What does telling stories mean when we are supposed to be doing science?' in MC LAUGHLIN, D. and TIERNEY, W. (eds) *Naming Silenced Lives: Personal Narratives and Processes of Educational Change*, pp. 9–26, London: Routledge.

LINCOLN, Y. (1995) 'In search of students' voices', *Theory into Practice*, **34**, 2, pp. 88–93.

MAC AN GHAILL, M. (1991) 'State-school policy: Contradictions, confusions and contestation', *Journal of Education Policy*, **6**, 3, pp. 299–313.

MAC AN GHAILL, M. (1996) 'Class, culture, and difference in England: Deconstructing the institutional norm', *Qualitative Studies in Education*, **9**, 3, pp. 297–309.

MACEDO, D. (1994) *Literacies of Power: What Americans Are Not Allowed to Know*, Boulder, CO: Westview Press.

NG, R. (1995) 'Teaching against the grain: Contradictions and possibilities', in NG, R., STANTON, P. and SCARE, J. (eds) *Anti-Racism, Feminism and Critical Approaches to Education*, Westport: Bergin & Garvey.

PAYNE, P. and HICKEY, C. (1997) 'Teacher theorising, intellectual resources and praxis intentionality', *Teachers and Teaching*, **3**, 1, pp. 101–18.

PLANK, D. and BOYD, W. (1994) 'Antipolitics, education, and institutional choice: the flight from democracy', *American Educational Research Journal*, **31**, 2, pp. 263–81.

REICH, R. (1988) *The Power of Public Ideas*, Cambridge, MA: Ballinger.

ROSE, N. and MILLER, P. (1992) 'Political power beyond the state: Problematics of government', *British Journal of Sociology*, **43**, 2, pp. 173–205.

SCHRATZ, M. (1992) *Qualitative Voices in Educational Research*, London: Falmer Press.

SEDDON, T. (1998) 'Steering Futures: Capacity building as a new public politics', Discussion paper to the Network of Researchers on Teachers' Work, Adelaide, Flinders Institute for the Study of Teaching.

SHACKLOCK, G. and SMYTH, J. (1997) 'Conceptualising and capturing voices in dropout research', Working Paper: Students Completing Schooling Project, Adelaide, Flinders Institute for the Study of Teaching.

SMYTH, J. (1991) 'International perspectives on teacher collegiality: A labour process discussion based on teachers' work', *British Journal of Sociology of Education*, **12**, 4, pp. 323–46.

SMYTH, J. (1995) 'What's happening to teachers' work in Australia?' *Educational Review*, **47**, 2, pp. 189–98.

SMYTH, J. (1996) 'Evaluation of teacher performance: Move over hierarchy here comes collegiality!' *Journal of Education Policy*, **11**, 2, pp. 185–96.

SMYTH, J. and SHACKLOCK, G. (1998) *Re-making Teaching: Ideology, Policy and Practice*, London: Routledge

SMYTH, J., SHACKLOCK, G. and HATTAM, R. (1997) 'Teacher development in difficult times: Lessons from a policy initiative in Australia', *Teacher Development*, **1**, 1, pp. 11–19.

SPIVAK, G. (1988) 'Can the subaltern speak?' in NELSON, C. and GROSSBERG, L. (eds) *Marxism and the Interpretation of Culture*, Urbana: University of Illinois Press.

TEACHERS' LEARNING PROJECT (1996) *Building Up a Picture*, Research Update No. 1, Adelaide: Flinders Institute for the Study of Teaching.

TROMAN, G. (1996) 'The rise of the new professionals? The restructuring of primary teachers' work and professionalism', *British Journal of Sociology of Education*, **17**, 4, pp. 473–87.

WALSH, C. (ed.) (1991) *Literacy as Praxis: Language, Culture and Pedagogy*, Norwood: Ablex.

WEIS, L. (1990) *Working Class Without Work: High School Students in a De-industrializing Society*, New York: Routledge.

6   Exploring the Labyrinth of Researching Teaching

Peter Grimmett and Maureen Dockendorf

Introduction

Recently, education reform has emphasized 'systemic' approaches. These approaches reflect the complexity and comprehensiveness of the changes that education faces in the last decade of the twentieth century. Examples of systemic attempts to reform education includes the Kentucky Education Reform Act of 1990, the Education Reform Act of 1988 in England and Wales, and the British Columbia *Year 2000: A Framework for Learning* published by the Ministry of Education in May 1990. This general press for systemic reform involves educational leaders in working with teachers to achieve the implementation of new programs and practices. Most teachers, however, view themselves as the primary advocates for students and their learning. Thus, whereas education reformers set out to change schools by making large and striking systemic changes, many teachers attempt to 'think big, [but] start small' (Fullan, 1992) by engaging in researching teaching as a way of transforming classrooms into places of learning. For such teachers, learning is both an individual and social process, students are co-constructors of knowledge and active participants in the process, and they, as teachers, are curriculum makers. How then can leaders work in such a context to bring about systemic change without their relations with teachers degenerating into a what Blumberg (1984) has termed a 'private, cold war?' If practitioner inquiry is to flourish, then we need to know more about the conditions under which teacher research groups operate. We also need to know how teachers transform their practitioner stories and conversations into concerted pedagogical action that leads to rejuvenated learning for students.

In this chapter, we reframe educational leadership around an examination of our practice in facilitating teachers' classroom-based action research. This framing is based on our recent experience with teacher research groups that were established in British Columbia to inquire into their own practice and to construct a learner-focused curriculum in a major province-wide attempt at systemic reform. Maureen worked directly with teacher research groups; Peter worked with teacher research group facilitators. We explore our experiences of facilitating teacher research groups to show the dilemmas and struggles we faced. We also attempt to derive understandings that illuminated the process for us as we battled with our 'monsters' within the maze of practitioner inquiry.

This was a qualitative study of our work facilitating teacher research groups. Data was collected through participants' reflective writing, our own fieldnotes and journal entries, participants' questionnaires, researching teachers' final reports, audio tapes of interviews, video tapes of teacher research group meetings, transcriptions, and teacher and student reflections.

This chapter represents two experiences but one story. Maureen was a teacher-researcher facilitating teacher research groups, Peter was a practising researcher facilitating the facilitators. Maureen was engaged in practice with other practitioners; Peter's practice was engaged with her practice as one of the facilitators. It was not meta-facilitation; just another form of facilitation. Facilitation, we both soon learned, was like stepping into a labyrinth. There were times when we didn't know which way to turn to make sense of what we were experiencing. We were frequently stymied. It was like fighting a monster in the triton-chamber. We felt like Theseus and wanted to call Ariadne to our aid. But there was no Ariadne in our story — only ourselves. If the monster was to be slain, then we had to find a way to do it. Because the monster was of our making, not a wicked king's! The monster was us!

Discovering the Secrets of the Labyrinth

Labyrinth: A vast underground palace, hundreds of rock-carved rooms linked by a spider's web of passages: a labyrinth, a maze . . . Everyone imagined the labyrinth as a horizontal maze, a one-storey honeycomb of corridors . . . instead of being horizontal, the labyrinth was vertical, its tunnels spiralling downwards like the chambers in a triton-shell. To find the heart, therefore, you fastened one end of Ariadne's thread to the opening, put the spindle down and let it roll. It would find its own level, unwinding downwards until it came to the bottom chamber where the Minotaur lurked. To reach the surface again . . . climb up the rock-passages, guiding your way by the dangling thread. (McLeish, 1983, pp. 143, 147–8)

As I drove towards the airport on one of those never-ending winter days, I continued to grapple with my role as the 'fly-in' consultant and the framework, implications and validity of the approaching teacher development sessions I had agreed to facilitate. The framework was based on demonstration lessons followed by debriefing sessions focussed on teachers' reflections, questions and issues. My role was to perform the demonstration lessons and facilitate the discussions. I asked myself many questions. Was I really facilitating conversations or just reinforcing a hierarchical 'telling' model for teacher development? Have the teachers participated in a decision-making process to have me demonstrate lessons in their classrooms or was it imposed by administration without teacher consultation? Are these demonstration lessons inviting teachers into a mode of reflective inquiry or are they placing teachers into a position of feeling coerced into thinking about themselves and their practice? . . . How much of their anxiety or absence of it had to do with yet another professional development session designed by someone else without teacher consultation, decision-making and therefore no ownership by participants? Is my role as a consultant one of authentically supporting teachers or is it permission for districts to add to their resume of yet another claim to empowering teachers? And if so, am I contributing to the façade by agreeing to the performance? (excerpt from Maureen Dockendorf's journal, 1992)

Despite the apparent popularity of the seminars and my own enjoyment at leading them, I was continuing to feel ill at ease in my role as facilitator of learning . . . Of late, one of my important purposes has been to create a space where those directly involved can act and speak on their own behalf. It is my attempt to think and investigate through a struggle of learning from practice. But it is impossible to know anything for definite or become 'teachingly correct' because the struggle is always reconstituting itself. Teacher research reflects this fluidity, celebrating the diversity and ambiguity that contests any totalising attempt to impose a false unity on what is contradictory, fragmented and changing. Why, then, do I still cling to my role as presenter as a way of unifying often contradictory and diverse experiences? (excerpt from Peter Grimmett's journal, 1992)

Amidst this state of questioning whether our own values and beliefs about teacher development existed in our practice as consultant and instructor respectively, we were offered an opportunity to create, develop, and facilitate teacher research groups. This new opportunity appeared to involve processes that were the antithesis of the role as consultant/instructor. As consultants/instructors we were often transmitting information; as facilitators, we were releasing a process whereby practitioners constructed knowledge for themselves. Quite honestly, a major obstacle we had to overcome was our own egos. Within school districts, the Ministry of Education, and the university, we had developed reputations as a theoretical practitioner and a practical theoretician respectively; in short, we were seen as educational leaders. Thus, when we became involved with the teacher research groups, participants thought they were getting 'these educational leaders who had the answers'. We had been competent at transmitting knowledge, giving advice and solving problems. Now we struggled with our reputation, our skills and their expectations.

We became intrigued with the notion of facilitating teacher research groups as a locus for change. Out of these experiences as facilitator, a new set of questions arose for us which guided the inquiry into our practice. How do we step out of the role of presenting and into the role of facilitating? How do we resist problem-solving and facilitate problem-posing? How do we deconstruct our role as presenter in order to reconstruct our role as facilitator? Sometimes painful, sometimes joyous, we began a process of inquiry into our respective practices as facilitator of teacher research groups and as facilitator of teacher research group facilitators.[1]

Prior to facilitating teacher research groups, Maureen had been a teacher for 17 years, and most recently a consultant for a large metropolitan school district and a Faculty Associate (a seconded practising teacher working as a clinical professor in teacher education) at Simon Fraser University.[2] The consultant position involved presenting professional development sessions in school districts, assisting with implementation of British Columbia's Primary Program and developing Ministry of Education resource kits for practitioners. Peter had been a classroom teacher for 8 years and a professor for 15 years (most recently at Simon Fraser University) and had worked closely with the British Columbia Ministry of Education in monitoring the Primary Program and assisting its implementation. We had both worked with teachers, parents, administrators, and superintendents, and had a variety of responsibilities, ranging from school-based inservice sessions to district crisis intervention. At times, we wondered about the effectiveness of this consultant/instructor model for teacher development. We had defined the role of consultant/instructor in linear fashion: we transmitted information, we structured the sessions and we, as distinct from practitioners, owned the process of constructing knowledge. As we reflect on the many workshops we each presented, we question what difference we made to teachers' practice and to student learning. Perhaps practitioners left the workshops with one additional activity to add to their repertoire of strategies; however, we believe these inservice sessions made few contributions to teachers' lives, to their practice, or to the restructuring of schools.

Though our lived experience of evolving from consultant/instructor to facilitator was messy and discontinuous, rather than seamless and chronological, it is possible to unravel some factors and influences which contributed to our transformation. Through reading we became familiar with theory and literature on teacher development and teacher research. As we began to integrate theory with our own practice in facilitating teacher research groups, our assumptions were challenged and our thinking changed. We are struck by the contrast between a linear, transmitting role as consultant/instructor and our mazy, searching role as facilitator. We wondered if we appreciated the diversity in the two roles or just simply longed for some sense of commonality. Initially, facilitating research groups was simply another corridor in our respective professional careers until we each began to define the role as facilitator differently because of doubts about our effectiveness as consultants/ instructors. Although facilitating conversations rather than directing them was a new experience, we presumed the passageway would be straightforward. In reflection, facilitation was more like being a child entering a dark maze at an amusement park for the first time. We remember being that child as our eyes had first to adjust to the claustrophobic darkness of the maze in an effort to make sense of where we were going. It seemed as if the entrance doors were locked solidly behind us; we felt like there was no way out. We remember a sense of bewilderment, frustration and confusion as each door that we opened created more anxiety with the trepidation of what minotaur might exist in the seductive silence behind each gateway. Any notion of fairy-tale romanticism, along with the naive anticipation of a passage through a looking-glass house, dissipated with the fear of what was to come, through the maze of passageways of this 'five coupon' experience. We vividly recall hoping to find a way through the maze to reach the daylight, knowing that only then would the experience come to an end.

Like children, our experiences facilitating teacher research groups drew us in through the maze of mirrors, forcing us to look closely at our own reflection and therefore at ourselves. We did not always like what we saw, as the distortions from the mirror were not always our authentic image; the role as consultant/instructor had been a 'performance' of sorts, now as facilitator both our beliefs about working with groups of teachers and our self-perceptions were being challenged. We experienced confusion and frustration in not knowing where we were going in the maze, and in our fear of the minotaur 'monsters' of the maze: these monsters were the dilemmas that were tangled in our practice, dealing with some of the participants' emotions and actions, our own misconceptions of knowledge, our own insecurities and self-doubts about the role of facilitation, and the very processes involved in teacher research. The metaphor of labyrinth with its difficult, winding passages and mythic minotaur, half human, half beast, encapsulates our experiences in facilitating teacher research groups. This study is both an examination of what lies inside the maze of facilitating teacher research groups, the 'monsters' lurking there, and an outside analysis of the labyrinth practice of facilitation.

Why Tell this Story?

> There has to be a good facilitator, not necessarily the principal or team leader, but there has to be a good facilitator to help that process, and it's the process which is really important here — to make sure people are on task, and that each has their say and to draw people out . . . and to quietly and tactfully make sure that some people don't dominate. (Researching teacher, 1993)

The purpose of this research was to examine our practice as facilitators of teacher research groups. The study was driven by a desire to enhance our effectiveness as facilitators, for the purpose of contributing to teacher change, student learning, and the restructuring of schools. The aim of the facilitation was to engage groups of teachers in theoretical and practical discourse as they reconceptualized perspectives and critically examined their classroom practice. This study also focused on the problematic aspects, tensions, and perplexing questions that emerged in our practice. We examined these numerous dilemmas closely, because it was in addressing these difficulties that our most powerful learning evolved. Some of the dilemmas we experienced were:

- How do facilitators create conditions that minimize the colleague/expert dichotomy?
- How do facilitators reframe information in a way that honours voices but does not validate unexamined practitioners' constructions of knowledge? What defines unexamined construction of knowledge and how, when, and to what extent do these constructions represent misconceptions?
- How can facilitators work with people who believe they have all the answers and have co-opted the language of inquiry, but do not live it?
- When do facilitators intervene with process and content to redirect the conversations while at the same time respecting all practitioners?
- How do facilitators defuse angry participants?
- How do facilitators grasp opportunities to support participants in reframing and reshaping practice for the purpose of making positive changes for teachers and for student learning?

- How do facilitators grapple with fallacious and contestable assumptions brought by some participants without being professionally unethical?
- How do facilitators prod researching teachers to move beyond the seductive peril of merely retelling their own stories to take action towards rethinking and subsequently changing and revitalizing their own practice?

Through inquiry into our practice as facilitators, we discovered ways of supporting teachers as they engaged in collaborative inquiry. To do so, we had to look beneath the rhetoric of effective teaching and restructuring schools to uncover the issues and dilemmas that faced us as facilitators. Thus, we examined difficulties and uncertainties within the maze-like pathways of our practice as facilitators within the labyrinth of teacher research groups. This has taught us more about ourselves, forcing us to look in the multiple mirrors permanently secured on the vertical walls of each corridor spiralling downwards within the maze.

What Can We Learn from this Story?

There is a notable absence of studies published on the role of the facilitator in teacher research groups. Although many scholars have described their work with teacher-researchers (see Lytle and Cochran-Smith, 1990; Cochran-Smith and Lytle, 1993; Bissex and Bullock, 1987; McNiff, 1988; Miller, 1990; Connelly and Clandinin, 1988; Lieberman, 1994; Tabachnich and Zeichner, 1991), discussion of the role of facilitator remains implicit rather than explicit, leaving one to wonder about processes, frameworks, issues, and methodology.

Recently, much has been published that supports teacher research as one way for practitioners to become increasingly vocal, articulate and organized for the purpose of working collaboratively, through disciplined inquiry, to refine, reshape and restructure learning for both themselves and their students. As teachers engage in a process of 'systematic, intentional inquiry' (Lytle and Cochran-Smith, 1990, p. 85), they begin to examine their own conceptions of knowledge and practice. However, little has been published which describes and analyses the process of facilitating this pedagogical, collaborative inquiry. For example, Connelly and Clandinin (1995) have examined the conditions for teacher conversations and the possible relationship to changing teaching practice. They set forth a definition of teachers' personal practical knowledge as a 'particular way of reconstructing the past and the intentions for the future to deal with the exigencies of a present situation . . . a term designed to capture the idea of experience in a way that allows us to talk about teachers as knowledgeable and knowing persons' (p. 25). Richardson (1990) suggests that 'a strong focus should be placed on teachers' cognitions and personal practical knowledge in a teacher change project, and these should be considered in relation to actual or potential classroom activities' (p. 13). Although the importance of teacher dialogue to changing practice is discussed by each of these authors, there is no reference to the use of an external facilitator to support, guide or shape the process of change. Connelly and Clandinin appear to believe that teacher dialogue, or narrative, in and of itself, is enough to effect change in teachers' knowledge. Hargreaves (1996) criticizes this as potentially creating a situation in which teachers' emotional and social needs are being met, but their practice remains unchallenged and thus unchanged. He also suggests that conversations must go beyond the retelling of teachers' stories and be connected to the action of teaching practice.

Connelly and Clandinin (1988) include dialogue journal writing as one of their methods of reflection for teachers working with groups of colleagues. The authors ask teachers to be descriptive of actions and reactions in their writing, with the purpose of thinking differently about their teaching practice. Through these written conversations, teachers are engaged in reflective dialogue with other teachers. Teachers control the dialogue, the issues, the questions and the length of responses. Connelly and Clandinin claim that, through the ongoing dialogue, teachers make sense of new theories from the perspective of their personal practical knowledge and beliefs about teaching. While the written reflections and the ongoing conversations involved in collaborative inquiry are illuminated as an important change force for teachers, there is no reference to the authors' roles as external facilitators in structuring the processes they have described, or in providing external perspectives for change. There is no description of either the framework or the processes that Connelly and Clandinin have created for the purpose of collaborative inquiry. Further, there is an absence of issues or dilemmas which may have existed in their practice of working with groups of researching teachers, an 'empty space' in the research.

Miller's *Creating Spaces and Finding Voices* (1990) is a personal case study of a teacher research group. In her narrative of discussion, reflection and action, Miller describes a dialectical journey taken by six educators who explored and examined possibilities and dilemmas of teacher empowerment and collaborative inquiry through dialogue within their group. Their stories 'centred on individual and collective struggles to explicate sources and effects of underlying assumptions that framed notions of teaching curriculum, research and collaboration' (p. x). Miller stresses the importance of the collaborative process as being a fluctuating one which includes questions, dialogue and writing. Teachers participated in ongoing conversations and continued to redefine conceptions of collaborative research, and of teaching and learning in order to view and review their work. We believe Miller played a significant role in developing and framing the teacher research group she describes, in that she attempted to create the 'kinds of spaces' wherein dialogue can take place. However, she fails to provide the reader with an explicit examination of her role as facilitator despite its centrality to this teacher research project.

Like Miller, Short begins, in her article, 'Professional development through collaborative dialogue' (1991), to frame a set of conditions for facilitating collaborative dialogue within teacher research groups. Whereas Miller's narrative focused on six teachers' conversations about their individual and collective struggles, Short's research is framed around the collegial dialogue of nineteen participants within the context of a 'study group'. Short established a study group which met every two

weeks throughout the school year to explore the potential of groups for supporting teacher learning. The focus of the study group was supporting professional
growth through collaborative dialogue; and this group provided participants with an
ongoing opportunity to step back from their practice and beliefs in order to critique
them. Short's research focuses on, 'how teachers and schools might transform
themselves, why change is possible through this transformation, and the constraints
operating to stifle or inhibit change' (p. 5). She explores the study group as a
context for supporting transformation and collaborative dialogue as a condition
for change. Her research methodology reflected the theoretical belief system of the
study group which was, 'the need to hear all voices and to not prioritize the voice
of the university researcher or facilitator' (p. 6). An integral part of her methodology
was using teachers' voices, both as researchers and in shaping the data analysis.

Although both Miller's and Short's research can be interpreted as substantiat-
ing the belief that there is a role for an external facilitator to effect change within
the context of teacher research groups, the authors do not provide any examination
of their own roles as facilitators. This becomes problematic in that it would be
difficult to replicate their studies because they do not make explicit the methodology, processes and framework used in their sessions. Though one gains a deeper
understanding of the value of the collaborative dialogical process taking place
within both teacher research groups, neither author has elaborated on the specific
details of how this collaboration was fostered and facilitated. We are left with many
questions about their work which have informed the study reported here:

- What are the effects of collaborative inquiry with an external facilitator?
- What are the dilemmas in facilitating groups of researching teachers?
- Is facilitation necessary and, if so, why?
- How were these groups different because of the external voices provided
  by Miller and Short?
- What, essentially, do facilitators bring to the process?

We proceeded on the belief that facilitated teacher research groups could be one
pathway to engendering educational reform. We assumed that facilitated teacher
research groups could have significant implications for teacher education programs,
for teacher evaluation, for education policy, and ultimately for student learning. We
hypothesized that the role of facilitator was important because it could contribute
an external perspective to teachers' dialogue for the purpose of focusing on what it
is that makes a difference to student learning. Within the context of the classroom,
each teacher may have a limited perspective which practice conditions themselves,
may indeed, limit further. Thus, we began by seeing our role as facilitator as
broadening the potential of each teacher's voice through structuring an environment
in which participants had opportunities for exploration and experience.

Although we believe practitioners are the central source of knowledge, we
began with the thesis that, without the external voice of the facilitator, contexts for
pedagogical dialogue have the possibility of becoming nothing more than a retelling of incidents that occur consistently in the dailiness of teaching. Thus, without

the external facilitator, teacher research groups may become rooted in process at the expense of substance. The rigorous conversations and the rethinking of practice may be in jeopardy of being replaced by sessions in which teachers are emotionally and socially supported, but changes in practice are not viewed as vital.

The Story Begins: Entering the Maze of Facilitating Teacher Research Groups

Here we focus on our four-year journey creating, shaping and supporting teacher research groups in British Columbia. These were communities of teachers that functioned to reflect critically on their teaching and rethink their assumptions about schooling. The 'larger mission' for participants was, radically but quietly, to make an impact on school reform[3] and to contribute to the knowledge base on teaching and learning with the ultimate purpose of making a difference to students' learning.

Although we did not realize it at the time, creating teacher research groups led us into exploring our own maze. The maze, for us, was the practice of facilitating teacher research groups. In September 1990, we began conversations to develop a process and a structure for initiating teacher research groups. We worked together as facilitators for the purpose of supporting teachers in scrutinizing and improving their practice through the implementation of a learner-focused curriculum. Our role involved designing a structure for teacher research groups, shaping a way to work together, developing a framework for collaborative teacher research meetings, and facilitating actual inquiry. Each group developed into a different culture woven together by twisted threads of individual and collective experiences as participants created their own stories, continually redefining their relationship to knowledge about teaching and learning. The differences in each such community also created conditions that were uncertain for us as facilitators. The processes and structure for the teacher research groups developed over time and were inevitably rethought, reshaped and recreated as we travelled through the passageways of the labyrinth.

The Context for Teacher Research Groups in British Columbia, Canada

From 1990 to 1994, British Columbia engaged in a radical, systemic restructuring of its education programs.[4] Briefly, the changes involved a reinterpretation of curriculum and the teacher's role in developing an educational program. Curriculum is often interpreted to mean a finely specified, sequentially prescribed body of topics and learning outcomes that all students must address. An important shift expressed in this restructuring was a move away from viewing curriculum as 'ground to be covered', or something to be 'delivered', to a broader concept of curriculum that begins with a focus on the learner. The former view was deemed to neglect the extent to which learning experiences are affected by students' needs, interests and choices and also to ignore the manner in which curriculum is shaped by teachers' expertise and judgments. The change was therefore characterized by the expectation that teachers were to become curriculum builders rather than curriculum deliverers.[5] The restructuring of one of these programs, the primary program, involved 25 teacher research groups throughout the province.

The Nature of Teacher Research Groups and their Participants

Over 300 practitioners participated in the 25 teacher research groups over the four-year project. These were teachers who enrolled classes from Kindergarten to Grade 12; others were resource teachers, consultants, administrators or superintendents. Participants ranged in age from 22 to 63 years old, and in teaching experience from 1 to 33 years of service. Despite the fact that most of the participants were female, there were male participants in all but six of the teacher research groups.

Each group met approximately seven times, typically for three or four hours, over a seven-month period, beginning in October and concluding in May. Initial meetings explored dilemmas, uncertainties or questions within teachers' practice. A framework was devised to provide teachers with opportunities for group interaction but left the individual ownership of inquiry with each participant. This heuristic framework[6] included reflective writing, conversations, developing a research question, working collaboratively, and engaging in consulting/work sessions.

Reflections on the Labyrinth

Possibilities and dilemmas continually fuelled the uncertainties about our practice as facilitators. In our research, we questioned what we were unable to find out about participants' beliefs and values regarding facilitation. What did they *not* write about? What dissonance, or angst did we create that impeded researching teachers in the process of inquiry? What did they honestly feel about the way we practised facilitation that they did not feel comfortable talking about with us? What are the implications of what we do not know about our practice? How would knowing the answers to the preceding questions change our knowledge, our thinking, and our practice? We continued to struggle to understand the basis of our authority as facilitators. Part of that struggle enabled us to see that any fear of disempowering teachers was stronger than our urge to empower them. We had concerns about imposing ourselves on the collaborative inquiry, thereby reinforcing our 'expert' status in the process of guiding teachers' research activities. We worried about placing ourselves, rather than the teachers, at the centre of the research. Had we overstated our responsibility as leader of collaborative inquiry rather than as a co-participant in exploring the messiness of the maze? An excerpt from Maureen's journal illustrates this messiness:

> I am beginning this journal submission with my reflections upon my reflections. I have written about the various perplexing differences in the teacher research groups I am currently facilitating. Out of the differences my dilemmas emerge. Out of those dilemmas powerful learning continues to evolve for me. I can utilise the

same framework, the same structure, yet each group emerges as an entity unto itself. Are the dilemmas and the issues a function of the individuals in the group? Or are they embedded in who I am as a facilitator, as a person? What would happen if a group did not have a facilitator? How would they deal with the unknown when it is not known? Should teachers' systematic inquiry into their own practice be dialectically based? Often I feel the richness of dialogue when there is a multiplicity of viewpoints, when there is something to compare and contrast, when there is a parallel argument, another body of information . . . I continue to grapple with making sense of something mystical that appears to exist within the context of the teacher research groups. Is it about the inner relationships in the groups? Is it what happens in that dialectic over time? What is that tension that exists between the objective, verifiable question we want to unravel and the subjective unverifiable process of self inquiry? Whatever it is — I know it is not reducible to a step by step process . . . The teacher research groups are not without struggle. Is this process I am trying to make sense of bound up in rituals? Is this part of the process that leads to transformation? Is this transformation a mystical, ritualistic, powerful mixture of the known yet rooted in the unknown and the ungoverned? My question continues in . . . the labyrinth of self-inquiry.

The journeys home from meetings provided uninterrupted opportunities for each of us to reflect on what we were doing. We thought about each part of the meeting, and of each individual participant as we wrote in our journals. The constant complexities, the potential conflicts in values and beliefs, and the instabilities that were embedded in the practice of facilitating. We understood implicitly the value of collaborative inquiry as we keenly awaited our next conversation together to reflect upon our most recent experiences.

As we reflect upon the process of writing this research study, we realize that we had procrastinated writing this chapter because of insecurities about our practice as facilitators. These uncertainties were further illuminated as we struggled to put our voice in the text when writing about the perplexities, issues and dilemmas of our practice as facilitators over the past four years. The process we experienced writing this chapter likely parallels the process for many teachers and students as they engage in the process of asking questions and seeking new understandings.

Each of us recalls looking at an untouched computer screen in the quest for a point of entry, a way in, to write about our exploration as facilitators of teacher research groups. When our minds were clearly void of an entry into the labyrinth, we embarked upon the writing process with an analysis of participants' responses, because we felt less vulnerable beginning with their external data rather than our internal analyses. We anguished over the positive responses from the participants' questionnaire and deliberated over inclusion of their voices. We struggled with the dilemma of honouring the positive nature of participants' responses. We believed the nature of their writing to be true from their perspectives; however, we also sought to intrude upon their unequivocal silence. We are making an assumption here, that there is a piece we do not have, a piece they are not writing, a pathway we cannot enter.

The process of reporting this study paralleled the process in which we had supported many researching teachers over the past five years. In fact, many of our dilemmas as facilitators became our dilemmas as writers. What if some portion of our writing contradicted our actions in facilitating teacher research groups? What if we have taken for granted unexamined constructions of some aspect of the framework we developed? What if we have overemphasized our responsibility as facilitators to the detriment of a perspective grounded in researching practitioners inquiring into their own practice? What if our voices are given to transmitting information rather than to searching to know more?

We began writing this chapter in the same way a presenter disseminates information, using the presenter's voice that articulates knowledge, assumptions and conclusions in a comparatively stark manner. As we re-read the chapter we realized we had crafted the writing bereft of our own voices. As the writing progressed, so deepened the authenticity of our uncertainties, our reflections and our voice. As we reshaped the writing in this chapter, we embroidered ourselves back into the tapestry of the text, continuously struggling with the messiness of the maze in a quest to find the center of our labyrinth of self-inquiry.

Insights from Within the Labyrinth

> One person helps another learn to practice reflective teaching in the context of the doing. And one does so through a Hall of Mirrors: demonstrating reflective teaching in the very process of trying to help the other learn to do it. (Schön, 1987, p. 19)

Schön's notion of learning from one another in the context of doing epitomizes the nature of this research study. We have documented and travelled a maze of self-inquiry into the pathways of our practice as facilitators. We have examined uncertainties, dilemmas, tensions, and perplexities within the labyrinth passages in search of the centre of the maze. The process of investigating, analysing and refining our practice has enabled us to identify key components that contribute to understandings in facilitating teacher research. What we have discovered has implications for other educators in the process of creating, shaping, facilitating, and supporting professional communities for teacher research. Further implications are found in the area of student learning as the result of teachers' rigorous examination into their practice.

However, prior to discussing these, there are three factors that contributed significantly to our growth as facilitators. They are: the participants who were involved in the teacher research groups; the collaboration with a colleague; and the dilemmas that existed within our practice. As a result, we have come to new understandings that have changed our practice as facilitators which we will attempt to articulate here.

Participants

To summarize the understandings we have gained from this study, it is important to begin by stating that participants in the teacher research groups were practitioners who chose to be part of this educational undertaking centred upon self-initiated inquiry into their practice. They were often teachers who were 'teaching against the grain' (Cochran-Smith and Lytle, 1993) as they developed a sense of personal and teaching efficacy. They were teachers who recognized teacher research as intrinsic to their professional practice and essential to student learning. They were teachers who abandoned the notion that teaching is just a matter of style; rather, they believed it to be a process of continual inquiry into the details of their practice and its consequences.

Through their participation in teacher research groups, teachers developed a familiarity with, and high regard for, principles and conclusions derived, not just from immediate classroom practice, but also from the thinking, experiences, and observations of their colleagues. They became systematic in their exploration of central issues in student learning. They considered different teaching practices and the improvement of those practices. Their inquiry was thoroughly integrated into daily work, thus it was associated with the accomplishments of all who participated.

Within the context of the teacher research groups, these practitioners grappled intellectually with issues as they worked and learned with colleagues. Through the collective power of these groups, they added to the knowledge base in teaching and played an essential part in school reform as they developed theory through action and reshaped it through further action. The teacher research groups became knowledge generating communities that influenced school, district and provincial policies regarding curriculum, assessment and professional development. Most significantly, these were teachers who cultivated memorable learning experiences for their students and they cared deeply about improving 'life chances for kids' (Cochran-Smith, 1994).

Collaboration with a Colleague

But when the full and complete meeting is to take place, the gates are united in one gateway of real life, and you no longer know through which you have entered. (Buber, 1958, p. 102)

The second key influence upon our learning was that we worked together, thus contributing to our effectiveness in facilitating teacher research groups. We became each other's teacher, mentor, reflective practitioner, and friend while modelling the very conditions necessary for creating and sustaining teacher research groups. We built each other's confidence as facilitators and as learners through ongoing encouragement and validation of our work and, through this process, we both became comfortable with the dissonance of not knowing exactly what we should be doing in the practice of facilitation. We basically had the same needs as the participants for support, encouragement, and collaboration, but could not use the teacher research groups to meet our needs. Yet we could not undertake this journey alone. We reflected into and recreated our own practice, which changed us and how we worked with others. We learned to live with the vexing existence of tension and conflict that is part of the process of change.

Facing the Monsters: Dilemmas Embedded in Our Practice

We highlight these dilemmas because they were the important issues — the monsters in the maze — that we needed to confront as we hurtled through the chambers to find the centre. And, it was in 'meeting the minotaur', as it were, that we then recognized and were able to deal with dilemmas in a way that effected our growth as facilitators. We came to realize the virtue of not knowing, and of how we deal with what we do not know:

> Knowing the right answer requires no decision, carries no risks, and makes no demands. It is automatic. It is thoughtless. Moreover, and most to the point in this context, knowing the right answer is overrated. The virtues involved in not knowing are the ones that really count in the long run. What you do about what you don't know is, in the final analysis, what determines what you will ultimately know. (Duckworth, 1996, p. 47)

Duckworth's words encouraged us as we reflected upon the process of writing this study. We began by infiltrating the labyrinth pathways of the unknown and emerged knowing the boundaries of what we do not know. We discovered that it is hard to know and to not know simultaneously. We began to cultivate a new repertoire of dilemmas, perplexities and tensions that emerged as consistencies in our practice, and constantly reframed our questions. The dilemmas that became embedded in our practice can be framed in the following way:

- How do we reframe information in a way that honours voices but does not validate unexamined practitioner constructions of knowledge?
- How do we grasp opportunities to support participants in reframing and reshaping practice for the purpose of making positive changes for teachers and for student learning?
- How do we decide what defines unexamined construction of knowledge about teaching and learning?
- How can we work effectively with people who seemingly have all the answers and have co-opted the language of inquiry, but do not live it?
- How do we resist the temptation to act on behalf of the silent voices, and to protect their right to be listened to in a way that supports building a discourse community?
- How do we intervene with process and content to redirect the conversations at the same time as respecting all practitioners?
- How do we honour participants' construction of reality but also challenge it?
- How do we challenge participants' preconstructions in a way that simultaneously honours honest and legitimate feelings?
- How do we collect and defuse angry participants' venom and detoxify it?
- How do we grapple with 'the baggage' that needs to be removed from some participants without being professionally unethical?

Tensions threading through these dilemmas became more explicit for us upon further examination. One of these dilemmas emerged when our actions contradicted our beliefs and values about the nature of learning. Each group had its own distinctive qualities and we believed we needed to begin the process of building a discourse community based on where individual participants were in the process of understanding teaching and learning. Although we saw the need to begin meetings at the place, figuratively speaking, where participants were pedagogically, theoretically and emotionally, we sometimes experienced professional anguish when participants were not where we expected or wanted them to be. An example of this was when Maureen arrived at a small, west coast town and was greeted by the district consultant who informed her that the meeting location had been changed to a waterfront restaurant because of lack of availability of space in the school district. As the meeting began, Maureen suspected that this location, with all its melodic sounds of the west coast shoreline, was interfering with her agenda. As participants casually engaged in conversations with one another, admiring the view, seemingly in no hurry to commence the meeting, temptations to direct the process and intervene with content raged from within her. How would the meeting be learner-focused if she intervened with her desperate need to cover her agenda, her content and her curriculum? How was this placing teachers at the centre of the process and not herself as the focus? This particular dilemma acutely mirrored her own experiences in the classroom where she characterized herself as a learner-focused teacher and yet struggled with an external curriculum that she sometimes felt she needed to cover.

A second recurring dilemma was the issue surrounding the colleague/expert dichotomy. In the group that Peter facilitated, many participants had attended workshops he had given in his capacity of an inservice consultant. His previous incarnation, his previous 'successes' as a consultant, returned to haunt him. This monster held him captive to his own history as it put pressure on him to meet the participants' expectations of providing them with knowledge about facilitation. It seemed that he was locked into a narrow corridor, not permitted to move within the complex, tortuous, mazy pathways of teacher research, because some participants' expectations were linear and narrowly based on their experiences of his 'performance' as a workshop-giver. As a result, these participants initially moved away from the more authentic experience of making meaning out of their own uncertainties. They wanted the 'right answer', the magical solution, the recipe for solving their own dilemmas without owning the process. This was the perspective of, 'Tell me what to do . . . tell me which door to open and I shall go through it'. Peter was struggling to be 'within the labyrinth', while some participants wanted him to provide a more comfortable, straightforward road map showing how to pass through the issues without having to live with their messiness.

This colleague/expert dichotomy appears to us to result, in part, from the socialization of teachers throughout the history of education. In the past, teachers' voices have been marginalized, expected to follow directions 'from the top', to not concern themselves with questions of their own practice. A Ministry of Education 'official', administrator or other 'expert' would decide for them what comprised effective teaching and learning. This stance of looking toward an expert 'at the top' has been so reinforced that it has become habitual in the practices of many teachers. At the same time, part of the dilemma lies in the fact that it is also necessary for facilitators to possess expertise. However, having the requisite expertise to facilitate groups is very different from being inaccurately categorized as the 'expert with all the answers'. The practice of facilitation entails searching, listening, and questioning the actions of classroom practice, as distinct from a linear, formulaic model for telling what constitutes effective teaching and learning.

Another dilemma worthy of unpacking arose when well-meaning participants positioned themselves in the role of giving advice or offering answers, rather than asking information-seeking questions within the context of inquiry. Often these voices dominated conversations with personal stories that illustrated their similar experiences with another participant's dilemmas. The stories were often inclusive of solutions which the listening participant could or should apply in his or her own setting. These were participants who had decided to belong to the teacher research group and yet appeared to struggle with seeing themselves as researching teachers. In some cases, these were participants who were not presently teaching classes of students, but rather were in administrative or district positions. Although they were philosophically and theoretically supportive of teacher research groups, they struggled with the notion of researching their own practice. There appeared to be a clash of epistemologies, because they often talked for others, gave advice to others, and attempted to solve participants' perplexities or uncertainties by presenting solutions. The paradox for us lay in our innate desire to direct these voices, just as they were directing others. We wanted to instruct these participants to rethink their actions, and to tell them this was not parallel to their district positions in which the giving of advice and addressing of teachers' concerns might be deemed legitimate and appropriate. We had a strong desire to tell them this was a time to listen actively to other voices, and that they were interfering with the process of discourse. We wanted to tell them they were monopolizing time, controlling conversations, and possibly silencing voices.

We struggled to control those of our actions which would replicate the very behaviour we sought to eradicate. How do we work with people who seemingly have all the answers and have co-opted the language of inquiry, but do not live it? Surprisingly, we interpreted this situational dilemma differently. Maureen felt strongly that she had to resist the temptation to act on behalf of the silent voices, and to protect their right to be listened to in a way that we perceived would support building a discourse community. Speaking for silent voices, she maintained, could end up silencing them further. So, she contended with her craving to intervene in the process and content to direct the participants, the very way in which she is often tempted to direct and control student learning in her classroom. By contrast, Peter believed that this was a situation that called for some intervention by the facilitator but struggled with his innate tendency not to do so even when it became clear to him that the process required it.[7] Thus, we grappled together with the question of how far do we go in managing and directing the group before it impedes the process and disempowers teachers and students? Where is the line? Is there a line?

In the process of facilitating teacher research groups, we experienced all kinds of tensions. Another tension-producing dilemma emerged for us when collaborative partnerships pursued research questions that we felt were trivial. Our stance was that research questions should have a critical edge, that not any question will suffice. This is where our level of trust in the process of reflection, in participants and in ourselves, became severely tested. We had to learn to act on certain assumptions: that, if participants looked closely at some compelling aspect of their practice, if they generated and owned that inquiry, if they cared passionately about their question, and if it was connected to action, then new questions would emerge through the very process of inquiry that would reshape and refine their practice. But it took us a long time and a multiplicity of experiences to develop this implicit trust in the process of reflective practice and in the participants.

Similar tensions created professional anguish for us when we perceived that participants were sharing some potentially unexamined and problematic constructions of the purposes of teacher research groups or of knowledge about teaching and learning. One such dilemma occurred when Maureen met with a group of secondary teachers who were legitimately incensed at the recent changes legislated by the Ministry of Education and sceptical of a project that claimed that classroom-based research would support them in implementing a learner-focused curriculum. They were firm in their belief that action research was not 'real research' and they openly contested her claim that teacher inquiry was authentic research. They voiced their disbelief that any project that involved teachers talking, writing, and reflecting on their practice would be seriously accepted as a source of knowledge about implementing a curriculum. Further, they maintained that, if teacher research was being taken seriously by the Ministry of Education, why did they send a practitioner who is not a university researcher to facilitate this group? Her credibility was further devalued in their eyes because she was not a secondary teacher. This group of participants was in disbelief that the project was an authentic opportunity that would provide them with release time, lunch and a mandate to engage in conversations about the craft of teaching. They were perplexed that the Ministry of Education would sponsor a project that involved teachers in self-initiated inquiry into their practice and they insisted there must be a hidden agenda or a silent mandate in order for the Ministry to fund such a project. From their particular stance, which they articulated fluently, Maureen was not being completely honest in describing the intent of the project. She became perplexed about how to challenge these preconceptions in a way that would simultaneously honour honest and legitimate feelings. She struggled with collecting their venom and detoxifying it. She wrestled with 'the baggage' that needed to be removed without being professionally unethical. She was prepared to honour their voices but not to validate their distorted constructions of reality.

When we began as facilitators of teacher research, we did not even realize that a maze existed; rather, we expected to travel a linear path, as had been typical of our previous incarnation as workshop consultants. However, as dilemmas emerged, we began to recognize the complexities and intricacies associated with facilitation and that we were, in fact, in the middle of a maze. By confronting our dilemmas, we were able to navigate our way and make sense of the labyrinth. We invite others to undertake the journey; for the experience has convinced us that, in a period of school restructuring, leadership needs to be conceptualized as the facilitation of teacher research.

Conceptualizing Leadership as the Facilitation of Teacher Research

Acting as facilitators proved to be much more complex than we initially realized. We wondered how to develop trusting environments and interpersonal relationships to create spaces for teachers to find their own voices. How would we organize time, schedule meetings, determine the size of the groups or develop a framework for the teacher research meetings? How would we support researching teachers in developing a network to make connections and share their inquiry with their colleagues? How would we know when to direct the process subtly or when to provide intervention? Would these teacher research groups even need an outside facilitator to direct their process? Were these not self-directed professionals who would take responsibility for their own learning? Would the role of facilitator create a hierarchy that impedes, rather than fosters, conversations?

Our enactment of facilitation was in constant evolution. Recurrent obstacles, continual dilemmas, and numerous fears elicited anxious yet intriguing complexities as we lived in the dissonance of searchings rather than in the comfort of findings. These issues are woven throughout the following insights which frame the way we conceptualize instructional leadership.

How then can leaders act in ways that value the facilitation of teacher research? Based on our study, we believe that leaders can respond to Goodman's (1995) call to, 'bring teachers, administrators, parents, students, and other interested individuals into the knowledge-making activity of the restructuring effort' (p. 22) by sponsoring and facilitating teacher research groups. In this way, leaders can enable teachers to develop their practice in ways that are framed around the process of learning and the students it serves. What is it, then, that leaders can do as facilitators? Our study suggests that facilitation would involve leaders in building a culture of inquiry, exposing teachers to alternative views and practices, and providing organizational support for teacher research groups.

Building a Culture of Inquiry

Building a culture of inquiry involves sustaining large blocks of uninterrupted time for teachers to talk in teacher research group meetings. The nature of teacher research demands self-disclosure, and leaders need to take time to develop a trusting atmosphere in which teachers feel safe to take risks to disclose themselves and their practice. Thus, the inquiry process in a teacher research group is typically initiated by teachers, not leaders, in response to a particular practical situation or dilemma that teachers face. The leaders' responsibility is to facilitate the group process through sensitive and supportive questioning, to crystallize and focus the collaborative discussion. One of the leaders' purposes would be to ensure that the 'wisdom of practice' (Shulman, 1987) resident in teachers is valued and respected. A further purpose would be to ensure that teachers' real practical dilemmas are elicited in the course of the group discussion. Leaders thus help teachers frame the issues or dilemmas that they face in practice. They listen to what teachers describe and attempt to help them reframe the issue in terms of a phenomenon or problem that they can study in the context of their own classrooms. In so doing, leaders supportively probe, prod, clarify, focus, and generally provoke teachers toward an inquiring sensibility.[8] But what specifically could leaders do to build a culture of inquiry through teacher research groups? Their specific actions would revolve around framing the conditions of inquiry, accepting tension and dealing with conflict, modelling collegiality and experimentation, focusing teacher talk on action, enabling teachers to frame their inquiry, and connecting action with student learning.

Framing the Conditions of Inquiry

Leaders could make use of the framework used in British Columbia — reflective writing, conversations, developing a research question, working collaboratively, and consulting/work sessions — to frame the conditions of inquiry in sponsored teacher research groups. It is, however, important for leaders to realize that each teacher research group will have different dynamics, with its own distinctive qualities. As leaders, it is important to understand and value the different qualities of each group. Leaders could implement a similar framework for teacher research groups' meetings, yet recognize that such a framework can only serve as an heuristic and never as a predictable agenda. Leaders will need to be flexible, responsive and willing to change the focus based on the needs of a particular group of practitioners at any given point in time. Although each teacher research group is distinct, they typically require a similar set of conditions to be effective. It is important for all groups to have a trusting environment, to sustain interpersonal relationships and to focus on collaborative action as primary conditions for healthy teacher research. Individually, researching teachers bring with them a deep reservoir of ideas and experiences and the leader's function is to tap into that. Another necessary condition is that participants feel comfortable expressing the uncertainties and questions inherent in their daily practice. Without this comfort with discomfort, meaningful and compelling research questions rarely materialize. And one of the ways leaders can nurture this condition is by continually modelling the acceptance of tension and conflict as basic to their own and others' practice.

Accepting Tension and Dealing with Conflict

Collaboration between teachers permits the negotiating of the details of research projects. For some teachers this may lead to a conflict between working together and at the same time retaining individuality. In some cases, partnerships might dissolve and new relationships emerge. These tensions could cause anxious moments for leaders who could become caught between their more traditional role in which they essentially forged connections for teachers and controlled situations, and this suggested role as facilitator in which they permit teachers to work through any conflict among themselves and for themselves. One way to enable this is to model collegiality and experimentation.

Modelling Collegiality and Experimentation

In building a professional culture, leaders need to reinforce those beliefs and values that constitute the normative basis for action in a culture of interdependent collegiality (Grimmett and Crehan, 1992) through taking risks and making commitments. They could attempt to become a member of as many groups as is feasible, taking part in the rigorous discussion of teaching and learning that accompanies the observation of classroom practice. Moreover, from time to time, they could bring up their own dilemmas of practice; and their own practice (even their teaching) could be observed and critiqued in a challenging but supportive way. In short, leaders could set out to model norms of collegiality and experimentation in their work with teacher research groups. This then sets the tone for focusing teacher talk on action.

Focusing Teacher Talk on Action

A further way for leaders to build a culture of inquiry is to ensure that the focus of the teachers' talk is on the action of their practice as it affects student learning. This focus facilitates a process that builds shared meaning through action and reflection and ensures that student work, rather than teacher research per se, becomes the agenda for teachers' work. In the initial stages of a teacher research project, many teachers are tempted to begin with questions that revolve around researching other practitioners, other classrooms or aspects of teaching and learning. Here, the task facing leaders is to ensure that teacher research starts from teachers' own experiences and from their own frames of reference in the action of their practice. The closer teachers' research questions are to the action of their classroom, the more compelling their inquiry.

Enabling Teachers to Frame Their Inquiry

When teachers have a question to pursue, the leader's responsibility is to ask questions, provide resources or suggest alternatives for designing the research project. Teacher commitment to the project increases when teachers make their own decisions, not only in relation to the question, but also in relation to the research design. Teachers and leaders need to discuss possibilities for data sources as well as ways to record the data that would essentially address participants' research questions. They can analyse data together by looking for patterns and categories, and refining the questions as new data are gathered. Frequently, the analysis of new data will reshape the original question or raise new questions. Leaders can also bring in professional literature as a resource with which to discuss the research questions and to stimulate conversations that respond to issues raised in previous sessions. In the consulting/work sessions, teachers could be encouraged to bring in articles they have found interesting or controversial. In this way, teachers and leaders alike could begin to discover that research activities are acts of listening and dialogue, a much more reciprocal way of relating than previous, more traditional professional development experiences that were deep-rooted in the 'telling' stance.

Connecting Action with Student Learning

A further task for the leader is to make explicit connections between classroom actions and student learning as teachers engage in a process of identifying issues, dilemmas or questions. This process frequently entails focusing, redirecting, or provoking conversations that connect the action of teachers' research and student learning. Leaders need to ask constantly: Is what we are doing in our practice making a difference to student learning? If it is not, why are we doing it? How do we change the action in our practice so that it is? If this is making a difference, how do we reshape it to continue to improve it? Leaders also need to support teachers as they work with learners to construct knowledge through the process of inquiry, in ongoing examinations of the issues raised by the teachers themselves. This process would enable practitioners to accumulate, evaluate, and disseminate knowledge about teaching and learning. Collegially, leaders and teachers need to examine core ideas, principles and practices. They need to make sense of competing theoretical claims and conflicting evidence to develop practical applications to address the teachers' questions of inquiry.

Exposing Teachers to Alternative Views and Practices

In order to facilitate experimental action in classrooms, leaders can provide teachers with frameworks that sensitize them to examining critically the daily dilemmas of teaching, to reflect on the taken-for-granted societal and personal assumptions that pervade their action, and to reframe problems of practice from the perspective of the learner. Teachers, like all practitioners, are prone to overlook the basic premises that undergird their classroom action. Sometimes these basic premises constitute humanly constructed distortions which teachers have uncritically accepted as valid. At other times, such premises constitute outright biases about teaching and learning that have little justification. Because change in practice is so dependent upon change in beliefs and values, it becomes necessary to help teachers examine collaboratively those beliefs and values that they take for granted.

Teachers do not change their instructional practices nor do they enthusiastically begin collaborating with one another to create a fresh vision for such change without first being challenged to think differently about the daily dilemmas of practice that they face. Such challenge can be provided by leaders who expose practising teachers to alternative ways of viewing practice. The purpose of this is to prevent what Hunt (1987) has termed 'a hardening of the categories', that is, teachers becoming entrenched in a narrow and shallow way of looking at their world and their work. Exposing teachers to alternative forms of practice is one way in which leaders can challenge teachers supportively. These different forms of practice may or may not be part of a leader's repertoire (in the sense that he or she may or may not be able to demonstrate them) but different approaches to instructional dilemmas are usually a vital component of a leader's acquired knowledge. Consequently, leaders can orient teachers to different practices (sometimes evident in other teachers) with which they can experiment in classrooms.

Providing Organizational Support for Teacher Research

Providing organizational support for teacher research groups would involve leaders acting as an advocate at the school, district and state level for the allocation of appropriate resources, both fiscal and human, to restructuring schools through teacher research groups. This advocacy could also include a focus on improving policy so that it supports rather than counteracts the practices associated with such development. Leaders could also set about initiating teacher research networks. Initiating teacher research networks generates both local 'inside' knowledge developed and used by teachers and their immediate communities, and public 'outside' knowledge which can be shared with schools and the larger community. Leaders can facilitate the creation of these networks by linking practitioners' work to larger networks of reform. As the district, state, and national networks develop, teachers both share information and build knowledge that enlarges their vision of teaching and learning. Moreover, as networks evolve, the concept of teachers as researchers becomes recognized as a viable way to add to the knowledge base in teaching and learning (Cochran-Smith and Lytle, 1993). Teachers typically appreciate and value the network connections that leaders create. These networks are important because the outside ideas of others are being worked through the inside knowledge of the various teacher research groups. It is also important for leaders to build networks between the various teacher research groups and the State Departments of Education whose policies support educational restructuring and school reform.

Supporting the continuous investigation of classroom practices, the systematic exploration of central issues in student learning, and the reporting of research findings to a wider community, is one way in which leaders can attempt to bring about social/political, pedagogical and personal change in teachers and schools. By publicizing teachers' work, leaders can establish the conditions under which teachers can become change agents in systemic education reform.

Leadership as Tasks, Not Role

This conceptualization of leadership as the facilitation of teacher research suggests that *it is not a role* involving hierarchical position with its accompanying agendas of power and control *but a series of interrelated tasks* designed to transform the experience into one that sustains a rich conversation about pedagogical possibilities by engaging teachers in classroom action research and observation. Thus, we claim that the primary task of leadership is pedagogical, working with teachers to help diverse learners in a rapidly changing social context by collaboratively addressing the vexing questions and perplexing dilemmas — the monsters — inherent in the maze of practice.

Conclusions

> . . . a labyrinth, a maze . . . When it was finished Minos locked Pasiphaë in the innermost room, far underground, and there she gave birth to her child: the Minotaur, a monster . . . The monstrous Minotaur lived on, still howling and roaring underground, as if the earth itself was bellowing. The islanders devised a ceremony to appease it, in which acrobats danced and leapt. (McLeish, 1983, pp. 142–3)

We have emerged thinking differently about the spaces that we create for both practitioners and students as we are still in the process of unwinding the 'thread of spider's silk' — continuing to explore the lifelong pathways of self-inquiry. We learned that facilitating teacher research groups was more like being in a labyrinth with its vast, intricate corridors spiralling vertically like the chambers in a triton-shell. Our experiences in facilitation drew us in through a maze of mirrors, forcing us to look closely at our own reflection and therefore at ourselves. It would have been easy to run away — to hide from the monster when we got close. We could legitimately have argued that we have to explore the interesting nooks and crannies of the maze. But there was a monster staring us in the face — how to facilitate practitioner inquiry without appropriating the teachers' voices — and we could not condone our cowardly inclination. To have done so would have meant capitulation and teacher research would have been nothing more than a process that made us all feel good but failed to make a difference in the lives of children. It was this urging to connect teacher research with student learning, to avoid the abyss of professional narcissism, that determined our choice.

So, in facing the dilemmas of our practice, we challenged the 'monsters' at the centre of the maze. The monsters within the labyrinth of facilitating teacher research groups were multiple and took on different forms and incarnations, depending upon where we were within the maze. There were times when we were unaware we were amidst a crowd of monsters; at other times we wondered if what we were seeing really was a monster. Or was it just our vivid imagination creating hallucinations of the minotaur, initially brought on by our apprehension, our sense of insecurity, bewilderment, confusion, with being inside the maze, with being new to facilitation. Sometimes, too, there were monsters of our own making. Upon entry, we had no knowledge of the monsters that lurked within the labyrinth. Later, after experience and practice in facilitating teacher research groups, we knew the corners where monsters often lurked, and learned how to deal with them quickly, fearlessly and effectively.

These 'monsters' included the dilemmas of facilitation, dealing with participants' emotions and actions, holding onto our own unexamined and distorted constructions of knowledge, our own insecurities and self-doubts, and the very processes involved in teacher research with its inherent messiness and uncertainty. Although we often wished that the monsters had existed within the labyrinth, they nevertheless served to challenge and provoke us, forcing us to examine our own practice critically and to change our beliefs and actions. The process of creating, shaping and supporting teacher research groups evolved through the discovery of the Daedalian pathways which emerged to shape and reshape our practice. Initially there were many recurrent obstacles as we struggled to live with the messiness, the complexities and with what often appeared to be a lack of direction or possible answers to complex questions. Which corridor do we choose? Which door do we open, and do we truly want to open it? Do we really want to find the centre and encounter the monsters that lie in waiting?

One of the important implications of our inquiry is that facilitators must ensure that practitioners also face their 'monsters', their dilemmas of practice, otherwise the possibility exists that change may not be framed around the needs of learning and the learner. Thus, Maureen claims that without the external voice provided by the facilitator, teacher research groups might not connect to educational reform, nor might they have any focused impact on student learning. Peter, however, sees it differently. While ironically providing the external voice for Maureen in her struggle to facilitate the groups of teachers she worked with, he remains unconvinced that teachers de facto need an external voice to connect their focus de rigeur with students and their learning.

We examined the facilitation of teacher research groups as one pathway to engendering educational change. Because we believe in the importance of practitioner inquiry, we set out to understand more about the conditions under which teacher research groups operate. We also wanted to know how teachers transform their practitioner stories and conversations into concerted pedagogical action that leads to rejuvenated learning for students. Without this, Maureen would claim that teacher research and teacher story-telling run the risk of being criticized as contributing to improving the professional lives and school conditions of teachers but failing to impact on actual classroom processes and student learning. As a result of the inquiry, she has concluded that, without the external voice of the facilitator, contexts for pedagogical dialogue have the possibility of becoming nothing more than a retelling of incidents that occur consistently in the dailiness of teaching; that without the external facilitator, teacher research groups may become rooted in process at the expense of substance; and that the rigorous conversations and rethinking of practice may be in jeopardy of being replaced by sessions in which teachers are emotionally and socially supported, yet changes in practice are not viewed as vital.

Peter, however, contends that this implied narcissism is not warranted when teachers' narratives contain genuine stories of practice. He concludes, by contrast, that there is power in narrative itself; that teachers become absorbed in authentic stories of practice in a way that connects them with students and their learning; and that, whenever this happens, the need for an external voice is moot. The intriguing point here is that Maureen is the practitioner, Peter the academic. Who is right? We cannot say because we do not know enough about how teachers in action research groups connect their instructional inquiry with pedagogical experimentation that addresses the learning needs of students. Thus, we are left with a dilemma, another monster: Is there a need for outsider–insider knowledge? Or can insiders provide one another with perspectives on practice?

Concluding Note

We have reflected upon the nebulous exploration into the labyrinth of our practice. We have entered the darkness of the passages to find a way through the maze. We have struggled both to hold onto, and to follow, the thread that led us downward into the intricate corridors of knowledge. We have faced the dilemmas of our practice as we challenged the mythical minotaur at the centre of the maze. Writing this study has enabled us to understand the maze and its monsters. This was a maze of our own making; and writing this study has brought us through the maze and provided us with the opportunity to view it holistically from the outside, rather than chamber by chamber from the inside. In so doing, we have emerged thinking differently about the spaces we create for both teachers and students. We are also left wondering how to support children in classrooms in understanding their own learning labyrinth. And, although we do not know exactly where the next turn will be, we are beginning to understand what labyrinths are all about as we continue to explore the lifelong pathways of self-inquiry. We are still in the process of discovering the secrets of the labyrinth, and we continue to unwind the 'thread of spider's silk' (McLeish, 1983, p. 143) to find our way.

We have written the two stories as one. What we reported is our story of how we each faced our monsters and got the teachers with whom we were working to face theirs. Peter lost his battle at the policy level (the Premier of the province used his political muscle to stop an experiment in progressive curriculum and pedagogy that had sheltered a good deal of teacher research) but not at the practice level with Maureen. Maureen won her battle, as did the teachers with whom she worked, but a new monster then emerged. The question now becomes one of whether we can slay the new monster, one that is bombarding us with numerous and frequent top–down curriculum changes? We're still in the maze and on our way down to the triton chamber. We hear the monster roaring but we haven't got there yet. Will we slay this one? We don't know. But that's another story anyway.

Notes

1 Although we each practised facilitation at different levels, our story focuses on facilitation as a process and on what we learned from our respective experiences. Only when there are important differences in how the process of facilitation was enacted at the different levels will we make any reference to the different situations in which each of us was functioning.

2 She is now an administrator in the Coquitlam School District of British Columbia.

3 Despite the changes that this systemic restructuring brought about, the government made a political decision in 1994 to reverse the trend and set the province on a more central-ized course of behaviourally oriented school reform. For the teacher-researchers in the province, this proved a difficult pill to swallow. The government decision to disband teacher research groups notwithstanding, they chose to go underground and continue what had become a very meaningful professional pursuit. Their experience since that time suggests that they were and now are engaged in important struggles toward the creation of authentic professional autonomy. For a full discussion of these struggles, see Grimmett (1996).

4 The new programs (Primary, Intermediate and Graduation) were designed to respond to a combination of societal and educational changes. Societal changes included such things as new roles for women, new family structures, increasing cultural diversity, dramatic changes in political and economic patterns at the global level, rapid advances in techno-logy and growing concerns with the environment and sustainable economic development. Educational changes included increased attention to such topics as direct teaching of thinking and learning strategies, fostering student metacognition, promoting creative and critical thinking, tapping the power of social learning, developing social responsibility in students, and the various innovations in education which have addressed these new appreciations such as process writing, whole language instruction, cooperative learning, case study approaches, strategic instruction and the use of new technology. The frame-work of principles and goals proposed to guide the development of these programs and to lead the public education system in British Columbia into the next millennium was outlined in *Year 2000: A Framework for Learning* published by the Ministry of Educa-tion in May 1990. The mission of the school system was newly defined:

> The purpose of the British Columbia school system is to enable learners to develop their individual potential and to acquire the knowledge, skills, and attitudes needed to contribute to a healthy society and a prosperous and sustainable economy. (p. 3)

The characteristics of an 'educated citizen' were delineated as:

> thoughtful, able to learn and to think critically . . . creative, flexible, self-motivated and possessing a positive self image . . . capable of making independ-ent decisions . . . skilled and able to contribute to society generally, including the world of work . . . productive, able to gain satisfaction through achieve-ment and to strive for physical well being . . . co-operative, principled and respectful of others regardless of differences . . . aware of the rights and pre-pared to exercise the responsibilities of an individual within the family, the community, Canada, and the world. (pp. 3–4)

In order to 'enable learners' to develop these characteristics, the framework suggested that the school system focus on three major goals of intellectual development: human and social development, and career development. These goals were to be attained in cooperation with parents and the community. The mission of the school system, the characteristics of the educated citizen and the goals of education were paralleled by a set of five principles for schooling: 1) Learning requires the active participation of the learner; 2) People learn in a variety of ways and at different rates; 3) Learning is both an individual and a social process; 4) Curriculum and assessment should be learner focused; and 5) Assessment and reporting should help students make informed choices.

The educational programs to be constructed on the basis of the defined goals and principles were divided into three separate areas according to the age of the learners. The substance of each of these three programs was defined by a separate 'Foundations' document which elaborated on goals and principles, commented on the nature of learners, described the general characteristics of instruction and discussed the responsibilities of teachers as they related to learners of that age. The foundation documents were, however, not mandated and did not include a scope and sequence of instruction in terms of content or specific outcomes. They were intended only to identify the basic characteristics of the educational program and to assist in making its various elements a meaningful whole for the learner. The *Intermediate Program: Foundations*, for example, stated that it 'is not intended to be a curriculum guide . . . [but it] provides a framework, a philosophy, goals, and a set of principles for designing learning opportunities for all students . . . The Ministry believes that educators, students, and communities can make significant decisions about how to apply the framework to suit their situations, as they select from many different approaches that are best suited to their learner's needs' (pp. 1–2).

5   This change was reversed in 1994 by the direct political intervention of the Premier of British Columbia himself who said that the *Year 2000* educational restructuring initiative had failed the students of the province. He was responding to intense lobbying pressure that certain groups of parents, business people, university academics, and teachers (mainly at the secondary level and the policy-wing of the Teachers' Federation, who saw the restructuring as radically changing the way teaching and learning had traditionally taken place) had publicly launched against the reforms. Needless to say, teachers involved in the primary program, who saw the restructuring as reinforcing what for them was already existing 'good practice', were devastated by this use of brute political force.

6   See Dockendorf (1995) and Grimmett (1996) for a full explication of this heuristic framework.

7   See Grimmett (1997) for a detailed explication of this dilemma.

8   Kohl (1988, p. 57) writes about teachers developing a 'teaching sensibility', a knowledge of student levels of sophistication and how they focus their energy on learning and growth. 'Inquiring sensibility' essentially takes this notion to a different level wherein the primary learners are the teachers and supervisors themselves attempting to discover how teaching can be transformed from the learners' perspective.

References

BISSEX, G. and BULLOCK, R. (eds) (1987) *Seeing for Ourselves: Case Study Research by Teachers of Writing*. Portsmouth, NH: Heinemann.

BUBER, M. (1958) *I and thou*, 2nd edition, New York: Schribners.

BLUMBERG, A. (1984) *Supervisors and Teachers: A Private Cold War*, 3rd edition, Berkeley, CA: McCutchan.

BRITISH COLUMBIA MINISTRY OF EDUCATION (1990) *Year 2000: A Framework for Learning*, Victoria: Queen's Printer.

Cochran-Smith, M. (July, 1994) 'Public Lecture', Burnaby: Simon Fraser University.

Cochran-Smith, M. and Lytle, S.L. (1993) *Inside Outside: Teacher Research and Knowledge*, New York: Teachers College Press.

Connelly, F.M. and Clandinin, D.J. (1988) *Teachers as Curriculum Planners: Narratives of Experience*, New York: Teachers College Press.

Connelly, F.M. and Clandinin, D.J. (1995) *Teachers' Professional Knowledge Landscapes*, New York: Teachers College Press.

Dockendorf, M.E.J. (1995) 'Within the labyrinth: Facilitating teacher research groups', Unpublished MA Thesis, Simon Fraser University.

Duckworth, E.R. (1996) *The Having of Wonderful Ideas and Other Essays on Teaching and Learning*, 2nd edition, New York: Teachers College Press.

Fullan, M. with Sgiegelbauer, S. (1992) *The New Meaning of Educational Change*, New York: Teachers College Press.

Goodman, J. (1995) 'Change without difference: School restructuring in historical perspective', *Harvard Educational Review*, **65**, 1, pp. 1–29.

Grimmett, P.P. (1996) 'The struggles of teacher research in a context of education reform: Implications for instructional supervision', *Journal of Curriculum and Supervision*, **12**, 1, pp. 37–65.

Grimmett, P.P. (1997) 'Breaking the mold: Transforming a didactic professor into a learner-focused teacher educator', in Carson, T.R. and Sumara, D.J. (eds) *Action Research as a Living Practice*, pp. 121–36, New York: Garland Publishing.

Grimmett, P.P. and Crehan, E.P. (1992) 'The nature of collegiality in teacher development: The case of clinical supervision', in Fullan, M. and Hargreaves, A. (eds) *Teacher Development and Educational Change*, pp. 56–85, London: Falmer Press.

Hargreaves, A. (1996) 'Revisiting voice', *Educational Researcher*, **25**, 1, pp. 12–19.

Hunt, D.E. (1987) *Beginning with Ourselves: In Practice, Theory and Human Affairs*, Cambridge, MA: Brookline Books.

Kohl, H.R. (1988) *Growing Minds: On Becoming a Teacher*, New York: Harper and Row.

Lieberman, A. (1994) 'Teacher development: Commitment and challenge', in Grimmett, P.P. and Neufeld, J. (eds) *Teacher Development and the Struggle for Authenticity: Professional Growth and Restructuring in the Context of Change*, pp. 15–30, New York: Teachers College Press.

Lytle, S.L. and Cochran-Smith, M. (1990) 'Learning from teacher research: A working typology', *Teachers College Record*, **92**, 1, pp. 83–103.

McLeish, K. (1983) *Children of the Gods: Myths and Legends of Ancient Greece*, London: Longman House.

McNiff, J. (1988) *Action Research Principles and Practice*, London: Macmillan.

Miller, J. (1990) *Creating Spaces and Finding Voices: Teachers Collaborating for Empowerment*, Albany, NY: State University of New York Press.

Richardson, V. (1990) 'Significant and worthwhile change in teaching practice', *Educational Researcher*, **19**, 7, pp. 10–18.

Schön, D.A. (1987) *Educating the Reflective Practitioner*, San Fransisco, CA: Jossey-Bass.

Short, K. (1991) 'Professional development through collaborative dialogue', Unpublished paper, Tucson: University of Arizona.

Shulman, L.S. (1987) 'The wisdom of practice: Managing complexity in medicine and teaching', in Berliner, D.C. and Rosenshine, B.V. (eds) *Talks to Teachers*, pp. 369–86, New York: Random House.

Tabachnich, R.B. and Zeichner, K. (1991) *Issues and Practices in Inquiry-oriented Teacher Education*, London: Falmer Press.

7 Gretel and Hansel, Research in the Woods: An Alaskan Fairytale in Four Acts

Terri Austin with Patt Caldwell, Bonnie Gaborik, Hannibal Grubis, Shirley Kaltenbach, Cindee Karns, Annie Keep-Barnes, Janelle McCracken, Karen Staph-Harris, Barb Smith

Introduction

Ten years ago, a group of questioning, public classroom teachers came together for the purpose of examining their own practices through the means of teacher research. This is the story of that group of educators. There are two parallel stories in this narrative. The first is the story of the development of the Alaska Teacher Research Network (ATRN), and the second is the story of the Fairbanks ATRN members. There are many voices within the following piece. All have been involved in teacher research for 9 or 10 years, with the one exception of Hannibal, who joined us this past spring.

I (Terri) decided to bring all the voices together to tell these two stories. In constructing this narrative, I have tried to make it clearer for you, the reader, by designating when someone other than myself is talking. Also, since this is an Alaskan fairytale, you will find a few Alaskan terms scattered through out the narrative. I have given brief explanations in parenthesis within the text.

Embedded within this story is a play entitled 'Gretel and Hansel, Research in the Woods'. We wrote this play in 1995 as a way to introduce the idea of teacher research to educators within our school district. We also presented a version of the play at the 1996 International Conference on Self-Study of Teacher Education, East Sussex, England. Writing and performing the play has served as a catalyst for reviewing our history, as well as clarifying our current thinking. The play is contained in the first two acts. Act III is an account of our reaction to our play, and Act IV contains our most recent thinking about ourselves as researchers and the future direction of ATRN. One last note, as a parody of the Hansel and Gretel fairytale, we thank the unknown author for the use of the storyline, and we also beg forgiveness for taking such license.

Prologue

In 1989, Claire Murphy approached the Alaskan State Writing Consortium with the idea of teaching a week long seminar focusing on teacher research. With its support, Claire and Jack Campbell, another Alaskan Writing Project Fellow, invited Marian Mohr to help get everything started. Nineteen Alaskan teachers 'spent five intensive days immersed in the topic of "Teacher As Researcher"' (Anderson, 1991). As a result, the Alaska Teacher Research Network (ATRN) was born.

Modelled after the National Writing Project, ATRN adopted many of the Writing Project characteristics. ATRN believes in the knowledge of the practising professional and the importance of educators sharing that expertise. Like the National Writing Project, ATRN values the knowledge of teachers. Through the growth pains of the past nine years, the valuing of teachers' knowledge has consistently been maintained.

During the first four years, ATRN modelled its structure after the Alaskan Writing Project. We held week long summer institutes to initiate new members to the mysteries of teacher research. Two facilitators coordinated all the state-wide meetings, while local 'chapters' scattered across the state supported and encouraged small groups of researchers. We established a state governing board made of up of one representative from each region of Alaska to oversee the publication of our journal, the summer institutes, and the yearly winter meeting. Adopting a known structure allowed us, as an organization, to focus on the task of developing our research abilities rather than spending energy creating a new association.

The Alaskan Writing Project also supported us financially in the first two years. As ATRN grew in confidence, we struck out on our own. We learned to be creative in financial areas. We make a little money from selling our journal. One year, ATRN sponsored a state research conference which was attended by over a hundred educators. We hold meetings in our schools and in our homes. Realistically we are an independent group of educators who choose to meet outside of our regular teaching day to explore and research questions concerning our practice, and we have found that we need little money to function effectively.

This story tells of our growth, our successes, our shortcomings, and our understandings of ourselves as researchers and as members of a professional community. We invite you to settle back as the curtain opens on 'Gretel and Hansel, Research in the Woods: An Alaskan Fairy tale'.

Act I: Where the Characters and Alaskan Teacher-researchers are Introduced

Narrator: Once upon a time near a great and dark wood, there lived a poor woodcutter, his wife and his two children. The girl's name was Gretel and the boy's Hansel. They had very little to eat or sup, and once when there was a great hunger in the land, the man could not even earn their daily bread. He and his wife hatched a plot that involved abandoning the children in the woods, getting lost and found, mixing with the wrong kind of people and finally arriving home again to find that things would never be the same. But thanks to time and the intervention of caring adults, Hansel and Gretel were able to put their past behind them.

They quickly grew up and attended Pied Piper University with the help of student loans and Pell grants. There they both discovered a love of children and dedicated their lives to the teaching profession. Time passed, and before you could say, 'Rumplestiltskin' they graduated and received teaching certificates from Jack Horner, the Commissioner of Education.

Imagine, no . . . remember, the anxiety and excitement they felt when they secured their first teaching jobs. They were trained professionals ready to take on the challenges of the classroom. And though there was the eensie-weensiest possibility that Pied Piper University had left a few gaps to be filled, they both felt sure that with the help of a clearly written curriculum and well researched text materials they would soon have their students eating breadcrumbs out of their hands.

They dutifully presented themselves at a new teacher orientation session, attended state mandated inservices, collected their curriculum guides and signed up for their 'flu shot. At last they were ready to go to their classrooms. Their school was sparkling and new. It had well lighted parking and head bolt heaters [electrical outlets outside buildings used to plug in battery heaters in cars during extremely cold temperatures]. The 1 per cent for the arts was spent on decorative and culturally appreciative sculptures and murals. The brother and sister walked quickly down the hallway toward their classrooms. Gretel was excited to see her own room. Shortly they came to the door of Gretel's classroom. Gretel turned the key in the lock, swung the door open and switched on the light.

Hansel and Gretel: Gasp! It's the Woods! Not again (they look at each other). We're baaack!

Narrator: Before them stretched a wall of seemingly impenetrable needles and leaves. Gretel stepped inside and peered into the boreal forest [consisting of pines, willows, and poplar trees] letting her eyes become adjusted to the lights.

Hansel: They never mentioned this in our college methods class.

Gretel: No . . . but it might have come up in our children's literature class . . . Hansel, look. I see a path going in.

Hansel: Maybe we're meant to follow it. But Gretel, all I have are a few paper clips to drop on the ground to find our way back.

Gretel: Oh, Hansel, don't be silly. We don't need paper clips. It's all perfectly clear to me. These woods are obviously a thinly disguised metaphor for the uncertainty we are sure to experience as we delve into our teaching. The physical department probably planted them here at the request of the curriculum office. All we need to get through woods is our curriculum guide. Maybe the school board policy manual as well.

Hansel: You think so?

Gretel: Absolutely. Now Hansel, this is where we say good-bye.

Hansel: Huh?

Gretel: These are my woods. You go back and find your way through your own woods. Besides, you need to get out more. Have your own life. No buts about it. You go on now. Shoo! I have everything I need with me. I should be out of the woods by the end of September.

We all started like Gretel, self-confident and self-assured. We've discovered that there is no single ideal path in teaching. The woods are full of extending brambles that cling to our legs and hidden roots that grab at our toes. Most of us became teacher-researchers because we were perplexed with the complexity of teaching. Often, when we get together, we wonder what common element brought us to become teacher-researchers. We've explored philosophies, teaching styles, educational backgrounds and the only common element we've discovered is the fact that none of us have curtains at our windows at home. Maybe that's not highly significant, but it does indicate an element of risk-taking in our individual lives (actually, in Alaska where there is so much space and so few people, it's not that big a risk as it might imply). Even as beginning teachers like Gretel, we've all been willing to set off into strange and unknown places within our teaching, believing that there must be something better.

Narrator: Gretel set off. Having long since abandoned skipping for power walking, she held her district guidelines in one arm while she vigorously swung the other. The forest was dim but not forbidding and while there were many twists and variations in the path from which to choose, the guide said to move forward and so our Gretel did.

 After days unnumbered, Gretel came upon a spruce hen [a rather unintelligent plump bird, similar to a wild chicken] nibbling on a highbush cranberry. The bird looked so friendly and unafraid that when it skittered off the path, Gretel couldn't help but follow it. It led her to the oddest looking house.

Gretel: Whoa, deja vous.

Narrator: But when she looked closer, it wasn't a gingerbread house roofed with cakes or windows of transparent sugar. It was a house built completely of books, shuttered with spiral notebooks and thatched with bright yellow sticky pads.

Gretel: Wow! What a house! I think this is the part where I'm supposed to meet the witch. I'll just ring this bell.

Narrator: (bell like voice) Ding Dong Bell, pussy's in the well. Ding Dong Stout, I may be out.

Which: Ah, welcome to my author abode. You know I just read the most interesting article about houses and how they reflect . . .

Gretel: Gasp! You must be the wicked witch full of evil and doom. I must escape. I must escape.

Which: Wait!! You have me mixed up with my older sister Wicked. She's always been a family problem. In and out of trouble, you should see what happens at family reunions. I'm Which One. You can call me Ms One or, if you'd like to establish a working relationship, Which. What's up, you look a little lost.

Gretel: I think I am. I mean I thought for sure I would find my way through the woods. I mean I have my teacher guides and everything, but I seem to be going in circles. Is there no way out of the these woods?

Which: I know what you mean. You know I read a very interesting book about just that very problem. Have you read . . . I think it's on page 37. . . .

Gretel: I have no time for that. I have to get going. I have things to do, papers to grade, lessons to write. There are so many things I don't know. I don't have time for this. Can you just point me in the right direction?

Which: Are you sure about this? You're sure you don't want to stay and read with me?

Gretel shakes her head.

Finding the time to professionally read is difficult for all of us. For some, it's the last thing to do after teaching all day, grading papers, preparing for the next day, and having a family life. Most of us try to squeeze it in somewhere whether it's right before going to sleep or during silent reading at school. Summer is the best opportunity for most of us.

ATRN meets in some fashion each summer. For the first four years, we followed the Alaska Writing Project model of conducting an 'institute' for five days. Now we manage to squeeze about three days together. We see it as a time to relax in the company of other teacher-researchers, to read, discuss and share readings, and to identify the burning question each wants to pursue for the following year. Our summer get-togethers are fun, but initially there was a hazard as well. Away from the daily work of teaching, we forget how demanding the job really is. Initially we tended to tackle bigger issues than we could realistically handle, but through experience, we now narrow our questions into something we can realistically handle. Also, there usually is someone in the group who reminds us what life is really like for our nine months in the winter. The summer institute provides us with a place to formalize and clarify our thinking through discussions, reading and writing.

Which: All right, try that way.

Narrator: Gretel hurries off, confident that she's on the right track. Directions do help the frazzled sour. She wanders and wanders through the chickweed and horsetail grass [wild spreading weeds that love gardens]. Suddenly, in a clearing just ahead, she sees a chicken.

Gretel: Maybe I took the wrong path. This must be the vocational track. Do I know that chicken? Wasn't it on sale at Safeway last week?

Chicken Little: Hey there little Gretel. Pop on over here and let's roost a bit. I'm Chicken Little and I'm sure you remember what happened to me, don't ya? I thought the sky was falling and ran to tell the King. But do you know what that King did? He looked up in the sky and told me that I had imagined the whole thing. So I went back home and began to study the problem. I knew I had to prove him wrong. There was definitely a problem and it wasn't going to get solved by pretending it wasn't there. So I formed a question to research: 'What is causing the sky to fall?' If I answered the question, I knew I could go back to the King, who by the way is in total denial of the problem, and give him some ideas about how to solve the falling sky problem. I always feel so much better once I form the question. So my advice to you, Gretel, is to figure out the questions you have. Everything can't be perfect in the classroom. There's got to be something that you aren't satisfied with. What is it? What bothers you? What are you thinking about that isn't working very well? Don't just accept what the King says. Form your questions, study it, try different things and then work towards a solution.

Gretel: (thoughtfully) I never thought of teaching like that before. Thank you, Chicken Little.

Chicken Little: Oh, and Gretel? Just a piece of advice. Don't panic like I did the first time I noticed a problem. I went around like a chicken with its head cut off when I thought the sky was falling. I found out that if you just accept the problems as a natural part of life and respond to them, you'll be much happier.

Cindee's Thoughts

That is how I got started as a teacher-researcher. I went to the principal and told him that we were tracking kids and that we had to do something about it. I told him it was hard to motivate those students to learn when they knew they were in the 'dumb' class. His response to me was that we were not purposefully tracking them, it just happened that way. There was nothing we could do about it.

So I went back to my classroom and formed the question: 'How do I motivate an entire classroom of at-risk students?' Finding no great solution to that impossible question, during the next two years my question was: 'What if I give my students more responsibility for their own learning and grades?' I based this on the notion that if students had more ownership, they would be more motivated to learn.

The following year, my questions was, 'Could I create a classroom community of learners who cared about each other, cared about each other's learning, reflected on their learning and reported their learning to their parents?' That year I thought if the students were learning together cooperatively, having fun, and understanding the purpose of learning, the ideas of motivating them to learn would be null and void.

So the next year, my question was, 'How come I'm out here trying all these new things and getting harassed by my fellow teachers? Why don't they ever try anything new and exciting?' And finally, last year's question was, 'How do you motivate teachers to learn?'

> *Chicken Little*: So you can see how important the questions are. Even if you don't have anything else worked out. Forming the question points you in the direction you need to go next. There you are Gretel. That should help you find your way.

ATRN's lifespan has been full of questions. In the beginning we asked ourselves if we could create a network of teachers who would be interested in being researchers inside their own classrooms? We struggled with finding an effective state organization that would support teacher-researchers across the wide expanse of Alaska. We found that having a strong governing board wasn't effective for the organization. The issue of power, decision-making and regional needs caused us to rethink our goals. At the winter meeting in 1994, we decided to emphasize strong local groups and have the ATRN board serve as a central information agency. The ATRN board would continue to publish our state journal and plan the winter meeting. The local ATRN chapters would create their own agendas for supporting and sharing teacher research within their specific geographical region. Now, we have moved away from any sort of state organization and local groups are now the mainstay of ATRN.

Next we wondered if we had enough strength to stand on our own and be an independent entity. After separating from the Alaska Writing Project, we really worried about this, but, in looking back, this element of ATRN was the easiest. This may be due to the fact that we had two years of support where we were able to develop as teacher-researchers. By our third year, we had enough experience and confidence to also assume the total responsibility for the organization.

These questions we were able to answer, but here are some areas within ATRN where we continually ask the same questions. 'How should our community be structured to serve everyone's needs? How do we mentor new teacher-researchers? How do we learn to discipline ourselves to be continuing teacher-researchers? Where do we find the time to do everything? How do we learn to identify and to seek out what we need to grow professionally as researchers? How do we maintain a researcher's frame of mind on top of all the pressures of teaching?' These types of questions continue to follow us even after nine years.

Gretel: But I have so MANY questions and the first one is which way do I go next?

Chicken Little: Head that way (pointing). I love going that way. Great worms over there.

Narrator: Armed with Chicken Little's reassurances, Gretel once again heads through the forest, but tiptoes around the worm area. While she's overcome her wariness of spiders, she hasn't yet developed a relationship with worms. After a short hike through pines and birches, she once again spots . . .

Gretel: That house again. I have been going in circles. What am I going to do?

Which: May I suggest this journal. It has some great ideas on using maps.

Gretel: (stamping her foot) Ms One, I'm tired and I want to get on with teaching. Give me a direction!!!!!

Narrator: Once again Gretel sets off down the path clutching her school district guides. But the longer she walks, the more muddled she feels. Finally she just sits down using her curriculum guide as a seat. Taking deep breaths to calm her rising panic, Gretel notices a tortoise making its way slowly toward her.

Tortoise: H-E-L-L-O G-R-E-T-E-L. Have you seen a hare zip by here?

Gretel: No, I just arrived.

Tortoise: I never seem to arrive you know and when I do finally make it there, it's time to go somewhere else. I'm always working to get there.

We've learned a great deal about teacher research over our nine years. In the beginning, we believed that every teacher-researcher should choose a question to research during our summer institute. Then over the school year, the teacher would collect data, analyse and do a literature search. Then sometime before April 15th, the researcher would write up the findings and mail it off to be published in our research journal. At our next summer institute, we would celebrate our wisdom as displayed in our publication and begin the cycle all over again.

We fervently believed in this model for three years. While we did not make any formal revisions in a written document, our thinking changed. First, we realized that questions are not automatically answered by April 15th. Many of us wanted to continue the quest and not be limited by a date. Secondly, we have changed our view on publishing. We now have a broader view of what it means to publish. This could include sharing at a conference or writing a piece for a journal or for oneself. Also, not publishing did not mean failure as a teacher-researcher. This idea alone eased the internal pressure for many of us. And finally, we realized we did not have to be researching a question all the time to be a teacher-researcher.

We recognized the benefits of resting before setting out on the quest again. Overall, we're more relaxed about the research process itself and our involvement within ATRN. We see now there are places for listeners, readers, researchers, questioners, and writers within our organization.

> *Gretel*: Well, so far, I've gotten nowhere. I rush and rush, but I always seem to go in circles. I can't figure it out.
> *Tortoise*: Like my grandfather, Tortoise Shell, always said: 'Slow and steady wins the race'.

Shirley's Comments

When I'm making my way through the woods of teacher research, I find that slow and steady is just the right pace when it comes to planning the study that will answer my research question. Right now, I'm working on a study of parental involvement in schools. One of the first discoveries I made was the fact that by making a plan for the study, I began to refine the research question. As a result, my current research question now reads, 'What is the range and variation of parental involvement in a third grade classroom?'

This study is made up of three parts. The first part calls for the teacher-researcher to keep reflective records of parent teacher interactions during the year. The second part calls for finding out what others within the school context think about parental involvement at our site. Finally, the third part involves keeping a record of documents that go home to parents. In this way, three types of data sources will help me, the teacher-researcher, to answer the research question. What motivates me to keep going at my slow and steady pace is that I know the process of conducting research itself helps me to improve my teaching practice. This process helps me to reflect more about what it is and anticipate what I can do to make it better. I know that the process of reflection, more than anything else, is what it takes to make teachers better educators.

> *Tortoise*: So, slow and steady is just the right pace for me. Take my advice — stick your neck out and advance slowly. You know if I were you, I might go in that direction.
> *Narrator*: So again, Gretel heads off slightly refreshed from these words of wisdom. But like before, she returns to Which One's book bungalow.
> *Gretel*: Not again. I don't want to hear it! Just point away.
> *Which*: There's this new publication you've just got to see . . . Are you sure you don't want to read it? Okay, that way, girl!
> *Narrator*: Knowing that she will meet another strange character, Gretel hurries off, hoping she'll at least be close to her destination. Around the bend, she spots it. The third little pig. This reminds her that she's hungry.
> *Gretel*: If this were the true story, I'd be stuffed with chocolate porch trimming from the Which's house and feeling quite content right now. Let's see what this little porker has to say.

Pig: Hamming a nice day, Gretel?

Gretel: It's all so very confusing. I thought teaching was going to be so easy, you know. Just read the manuals, keep the room neat and tidy, and record grades. It seemed so simple. Then I began to have all sorts of questions. Plus, I'm meeting the strangest people.

Pig: I thought the same about house building. It's not as easy as it looks. You need to do a couple of things. You've got to have courage. Courage to be messy, courage to try something new, even when those around you are not. You have to be willing to take a chance, just like I did with my house of bricks. Everyone laughed at me, but I kept going. I had a vision and I did it. You have to have a risk taking attitude. Do you take risks?

You have to be playful, because this is play, Gretel. This is hard fun. So remember those three things. You have to be messy, you have to have courage, and you have to be playful.

Karen's Comments

I look and I see and see again. In a recent self-study, I looked at the child who had been disturbing me so much. He was never still. First in his seat, then over by the window and then out the door. I found him extremely disturbing and wondered why he was so unsettled. I decided to do a sociogram to obtain a better picture of his movements. I discovered that he was not the only one that was moving. There are others also moving. That's when the light bulb went on! That was one little clue to the puzzle. I gathered more data by watching him in other situations inside and outside of school. I interviewed him. I talked with his other teachers. It turned out to be a fascinating research question and now I love every movement he makes.

As a researcher, I am learning. I know it takes time and it takes patience, but you can have fun finding out. Data analysis is like the icing on the cake. I was so busy before, I never noticed what was happening. But when I focused on that one question, that one student, everything else became clearer to me.

Pig: Oh! I saw the wolf over there trying to borrow another cup of sugar. Better stay away from him, he's trouble. He hangs out with trolls, dwarfs, and such. Best go that way.

Narrator: Sure enough, Gretel ends back at . . .

Gretel: Which One's . . .

Which: . . . Publication Palace! That's right, welcome back. I have something that you really should take a look at. I think it would help you on your way. Why don't you take this book with you and maybe read it as you go along? There's better light if you bear a little to the left.

Narrator: So our fearless and rather bewildered heroine sets off again. This time reading and walking at the same time. Notice how she's getting better at multiple tasks — the sign of an experienced teacher.

Gretel: Hmmmmm (mumbles to self while reading). Have I been doing this? How effective am I? Why can't I really find my way out of the woods?

Narrator: Suddenly she notices a mirror hanging on a willow tree.

Gretel: (Looks in mirror) Oh, I wonder if I need to add more sunscreen. The ozone depletion is such a bother. Mirror, mirror on the wall . . . Oh, my, now I'm talking to myself.

Mirror: Relax Grets, lots of people have conversations with the magic mirror — even queens! This self-reflection of yours is really quite normal. In fact, as a teacher-researcher, it's an essential part of the research process. One of the reasons you're probably going to become a teacher-researcher eventually is because you can't turn your head off. You're always having a running conversation with yourself. Questioning your latest strategy in the classroom and your students' actions and reactions towards this newest approach.

Bonnie's Comments

One of the things I discovered with the first research question that my co-worker, Annie, and I were working on was that if we sat right down at the computer immediately following an after-school session with a special student group, and quickly recorded our thoughts on whatever we'd observed, we were able to clarify for each other and ourselves what had really taken place during the past hour. In addition, this 'quick write' ultimately generated more questions for us to ponder and quite often would lead us to consider other options which we had not previously thought about. Later, in my own personal journal, I would review the day in regard to my research question. I would record my thoughts, concerns, ideas, questions, excitement, or disappointments. It was a time to be completely honest with myself as to how I perceived my personal research was or was not progressing.

Mirror: For me, self-reflection reveals the process of classroom research and often becomes as interesting to me as the question itself. You might think of it as 'The Rest of the Story'. Speaking of which, you'd better get on with the rest of the story yourself, Grets, old gal. You better move on. Head that way.

Gretel: I know, I know. Back to Which's Volume Villa. Hi ya, Which. You know this book wasn't bad. Do you have something on assessment?

Which: Just so happens I have the perfect thing. Come out back. I have everything from bookmarks to bookworms. Won't you stay awhile and pursue your question through literature?

Gretel: Sorry, I must get on with my travels. I can't quit my job, you know. What do you have that I could read along the way?

Which: Take that, and this is good. The articles are quite thought provoking. When you finish, maybe we could talk.

Attempting to construct an agenda that met everyone's needs was an ongoing task for ATRN. At the state level, our week-long institute struggled with two populations. We realized how important it was to provide stability and continuity for the new teacher-researcher with lots of time for discussion and questions. The experienced teacher-researchers, however, had a different need. Many came with a specific personal agenda. They wanted more insights into data analysis or wanted direct feedback on their study. Their level of conversations were quite different, they shared 'war' stories about data collection and midnight writings.

In the end, our schedule reflected the diverse needs of the two groups. At times, the experienced researchers led introductory sessions for the new ones. At other times, the beginning researchers met together to help clarify a vision of teacher research. The returning researchers also met by themselves to share their experiences and to push themselves further into the process of researching.

We used the reading of teacher research case-studies in several ways. It provided a common thread for everyone throughout the week and gave us all a common frame of reference. Through our discussions, the returning researchers modelled ways to respond to the literature. We used the case-studies as a way to not only gain information about teaching practice, but ways to examine how teacher research was conducted. We learned a great deal about the research process by deconstructing the text. In many ways, we taught ourselves about teacher research in this manner.

In our Fairbanks meetings, we have tried everything from no structure to posting a time schedule on a poster. We have found that we do need some type of framework in which to guide our Saturday mornings, without a framework we tend to float and whims control the mornings.

We still generally follow the example set by the summer institutes and use readings to guide our discussions. In the beginning, I brought the articles to read, now everyone signs up for a specific Saturday and leads the meeting. We have learned to allow 30 minutes for social talk before the meeting begins. For us, this type of talk is going to happen, so we might as well schedule it in and then it doesn't crop up as readily during our later discussions. There is usually a few minutes of book sharing or announcements, then someone passes out an article to read. We read for about 20 to 30 minutes, then stop whether we have finished the article or not. Discussion follows for 15 to 20 minutes. The rest of the morning is spent on some aspect of our own research. This is open and anyone can bring their work. We often consult each other about a problem we encounter or ask others to read a portion of our study. The discussions help clarify our research as well as motivate us to continue.

> *Narrator*: Thinking positively now, Gretel energetically heads west. She considers her adventure and feels virtuous about all her physical, as well as her mental, exercise.
>
> *Gretel*: Bet I can get into that size 8 dirndl now. Hey, I could borrow Snow White's outfit for Open House next week. The white apron would be a hit. OHO! What a mess.
>
> *Humpty*: Hey, you're supposed to empathize. Think of me as being elliptically challenged. One day, I couldn't take it any more and my head exploded and this is the result.
>
> *Gretel*: Oooooh, bad hair day. Bummer.

Barb's Comments

I could empathize with Humpty. One day last June, I gazed at all the pieces of data scattered around me and wondered how I was going to manage to gather these pieces together to form a cohesive, informative paper. The small group of ATRN members who attended a research retreat with me last summer came to my rescue. Without their help I would never have published my paper.

I began by going through my journal and summarizing the information I found. I had no idea where to go from there so I took my paper to Cindee. She read it and showed me how a web might work. I played with that idea for awhile, but could not seem to get anywhere. Another colleague suggested several metaphors, but I did not feel comfortable with that either. Frankly, my writing skills just were not strong in that area. So I showed it to another colleague and she suggested a timeline. That worked for me.

Having found the form I was comfortable with, the paper seemed to flow. Nothing could drag me away from the computer now. After finishing the first draft, I asked both Ruth and Terri to read it. They helped me iron out a few wrinkles in the transitions and two revisions later, I had a paper to share with my fellow researchers.

It wa not until I read this paper aloud to these trusted friends that I realized just how much of myself I had invested in the second grade student in my study and how much he had given me. After that reading, I selfishly did not care if it ever got published. I had learned so much. But the ATRN members reminded me of the importance of sharing our experiences with other colleagues. I returned home and my son edited my paper. Yet another revision!

I followed the guidelines for sending material into *Teacher Research, The Journal of Classroom Inquiry*, and a few months later received a package containing two very positive notes from two reviewers. After a few revisions, it would be published. I made those revisions and it was published this past April.

> *Gretel*: It's nice to know your version of the story turns out well. I better continue on my way. Why don't you take these teacher's guides. Maybe you could use them for something. I have other things to read now. See you later.

Early in our formation, we recognized the importance of sharing our findings with fellow researchers. Fifteen Alaskan researchers boldly published their first year's research studies in 1991. Following Tim Gillespie's observations in 1990, we called our publication, *The Far Vision, The Close Look*:

> Sacajawea, the Shoshone woman who was the guide and translator for the Lewis and Clark expedition to explore the Oregon territory, has always been a heroic figure for me. Near the end of her life she was asked how she found her way through thousands of miles of unexplored territory, through many languages and cultures she didn't know. She said simply, 'The far vision, the close look.' Her words have implications for us in literacy education. The 'far vision' is the theory we construct, our philosophy, and our grand aims. And the 'close look' is the steps we have to take day by day to get there, the classroom realities. We always have to keep both of these in mind. (Alaska Teacher Research Network, 1991, title page)

The Far Vision, The Close Look continues to be our primary medium for sharing our work. We have published three volumes with one currently in press.

We have grown and changed in perspective concerning the purpose of our journal. In our first edition, we accepted anyone who submitted a piece of research as we were glad to have completed pieces of research to publish in a journal. With the advent of the second publication in 1992, ATRN talked about having a jury of reviewers consider each piece to ensure that each piece was truly 'teacher research'. As an organization, we were very concerned about the 'correct' way to conduct teacher research and concerned about having our research accepted by the wider educational profession. In the end, we decided to hire an editor to ensure quality of each piece.

Our views dramatically changed by the third volume, published in 1994. During this time, we were questioning ourselves about what constitutes teacher research, and this edition reflects our widening perspective by including personal narratives, essays, a cooperative research study, and a case study.

Our latest volume of *The Far Vision, The Close Look* mirrors our comfort with the possible variety of teacher research. We are much more relaxed about the whole process. It includes several pieces of varying length. Before, all pieces had to fit within a certain size. It also includes two studies done by one researcher. We only accepted one piece from each researcher in previous editions. We've gained confidence in our work and now publish what fits and reflects us.

Which:　Oh, you're back again. Would you like to borrow a few more books?
Gretel:　I can take a few. I gave my guides away. You know they were great for the biceps, but I found them weighing me down.

Terri's Comments

As I continue in teacher research, I see how beneficial it is to continually read and examine the research of others. I read on three levels. I read to discover their findings. I want to know what they discovered. I also read to see how they conducted their research. I am always looking for new and easier ways to set up my studies. Finally, I read to examine how they wrote up their study. In studying their writing, I become a better writer of my own research.

Once I have identified my question, I begin my literature review. I read to find out what others in similar areas have said, tried or done. As I read, I discover new ways of looking at my question or suddenly see new avenues of thought. In considering the thoughts of others, I continually refine all aspects of my study. I not only read within my field of study, but outside as well. In my latest study of community, I examined research in the fields of business, sociology, psychology, critical thinking, feminist writing and critical social theory.

My reading is my window to the world's thinking. I read journals, newspapers, books, publishing catalogues and research drafts of my colleagues. It keeps me in touch with fellow researchers everywhere. And with e-mail and the world wide web, I have many more opportunities to explore. Through text, I have a world of long distance mentors.

> *Which*:   I would be lost without my books. I'll gladly share what I have.
> *Gretel*:   Great, I'm eager to read AND network. Who else is out there in the woods?

As members of ATRN, we have accepted the responsibility of sharing our discoveries with others. One way is through our publication of *The Far Vision, The Close Look*, but there are other ways as well. Many of us present our research at local, state, national and international conferences, while others prefer to share with the colleague down the hall or next door. Whatever method we choose, we do find that we love to talk about our current study. It is very similar to grandparents pulling out the baby pictures. Once we start, it is hard to stop us.

> *Which*:   Take these journals. I think you might enjoy meeting Snow White. She's just down the path, that way.
> *Narrator*:   Gretel grabs her journals and rushes through the willows. Standing right there on the path was Snow White with blue birds on her shoulders, just like in the movie.
> *Snow White*:   Shoo! Move! Get off me! You know, at first they're kinda cute, but they make holes in my dress. I only have this one you know, so it has to last. Shoo!
>
> I hear you've been a little lost — a little bewildered. Believe me, I've been in your shoes. You need some people you can trust. Because my friends, the seven dwarfs, have sustained me through many confusing events, I've come to rely upon their sound advice. Perhaps their words of wisdom might be helpful to you, Gretel.
>
> Doc, whom many have described as practising medicine without a license, prescribed the following treatment: get out, mingle with others with similar interests, share ideas and mutual concerns and partake of food with colleagues. This can be more rewarding than a vitamin. He highly recommends ATRN as just the right medicine.
>
> Grumpy, who would rather complain than take action, grumbled all the way to his first ATRN meeting. He and Sleepy could not believe that anyone would gleefully choose to arise early on the second Saturday morning of every month for a 10 o'clock meeting.
>
> Bashful was very reticent to join the rest of us. He anticipated feeling very awkward about sharing his ideas with others, and fully intended to sit quietly in the corner passively participating. Imagine his surprise when no one pressured him to contribute his research finding.
>
> Sneezy, although he often suffered from severe allergies during the week, insisted that he somehow felt better after attending an ATRN meeting. Perhaps having a forum to relieve the stress he often endured was precisely the antihistamine he needed.
>
> Dopey was ecstatic. People laughed with him, not at him. Happy was thrilled to be associated with other friendly professionals.
>
> Grumpy, Doc, Sneezy, Sleepy, Dopey, Bashful, Happy and I all agree: ATRN has something to offer each one of us. It's our support group.

ATRN has developed into a professional organization that is built upon friendships and trust. Over the years, we have grown to care about each other. We are often the first to try out each other's research. We volunteer to 'give it a try' in a different grade level. We borrow, adopt and revise ideas and do so openly with encouragement from the researcher.

Gretel: That's just what I need. I'll see you on Saturday. I need to go visit Which again. I just thought of another book I need.
Narrator: Gretel jogs back to Which One's chapter chateau and shares tales of her adventures.
Which: You've had an exciting time. Would you like more things to read? What do you need?
Gretel: Lots! I brought my environmentally correct string bag to carry them all. What do you have on. . . .
Narrator: And so we leave Gretel filling her bag with books and journals and filling her head with questions to pursue, people to meet, ideas to write and most of all, a sense of direction. Sort of . . .

Act II: Where All Fairytales Don't End 'Happy Ever After'

All did not turn out as we expected from our presentation at the Alaska State Reading Conference. We did have many new guests at our next meeting, but the visitors took over the meeting complaining about a reading program adopted by the school district. We were totally unprepared for this kind of happening. We discovered that our group may not be able to withstand instant growth and too much change.

Barb: So, Annie, how do you think the meeting went?
Annie: Barb, how can you ask that? It was awful. Your article was really good. I really enjoyed it, not that we talked that much about it. We did hear more than I ever want to about that particular reading program. Did you see Terri's face? I thought she was going to explode.
Barb: No. . . .
Annie: It was incredibly nervy for those women to manipulate our one Saturday a month in order to complain about a reading program that Terri fought furiously against.
Barb: Well, I. . . .
Annie: I mean I have to admit for a while I was taking a kind of evil pleasure out of their dislike, but then they wouldn't quit. The sad part was that we had new people there who had no idea how an ATRN meeting usually goes, so they walked away thinking ATRN members are disgruntled teachers. I have never been to an ATRN meeting that turned into a gripe session. Who were these people to take what we have worked so hard to create and turn it into something so negative. Why did I let them?
Janelle: There wasn't an ATRN meeting until noon. The morning was awful. There was no conversation, only teacher lounge talk — complaining and gossip. No one quoted from the article or talked about research in any way. I couldn't help but feel I should have stayed home. After all the new people left and we ATRN members pulled up chairs off to the side and started talking is when the ATRN meeting REALLY started. That's when I felt like I got what I always come to ATRN for.

Bonnie: I hated the meeting. I kept waiting for Terri to bring our meeting back into focus. I was tempted, myself, to say something. Terri always has a way of refocusing meetings in a firm but polite manner. I found myself waffling between cringing at comments being bandied back and forth and watching the clock, wondering how much longer the negativity was going to go on. *When* were we going to get back to discussing the article? Most of all, I felt embarrassment — for Terri who was having to listen to an incredibly insensitive group of former colleagues, for you, Barb, who had agreed to lead this meeting, for the reputation of our group, and for teacher research as a whole. This was NOT what we were all about. Reflecting back, I wish I had taken ownership and reclaimed my meeting.

Barb: Terri, wasn't that a great turn out at the meeting? What did you think of it?

Terri: It was horrible. I hated the whole thing. I never want to have a meeting like that again. They completely took over and turned MY ATRN meeting into a gripe session. At one point, I was so mad and upset I had to leave the room. I kept thinking 'Why doesn't anyone take over and bring us back to focus on the article?' Where was everyone? Someone needed to say something. Why didn't an ATRN member step in? Why do they always wait for me? This was such an emotional issue for me, I just couldn't rescue the discussion and take charge.

Act III: Lessons Learned or There is a Moral in Every Story

We have learned so much since our beginnings as teacher-researchers. All our concerns about ATRN and teacher research that continually weave through discussions were brought into focus because of that meeting. We wanted other teachers to join us and then we worried about how to support them in their initial steps in teacher research. We wanted all the external trappings that showed success — large numbers, published articles, bulging professional development classes. In other words, we desired to be a group of significance.

The Saturday morning experience was the signpost that pointed us in a new direction. We have come to the conclusion that size isn't everything. Several years ago, Allan Glatthorn (1995) said that we should love what we're doing and have fun and not worry about who is there or not there. Some of us were not willing to believe this until after that particular Saturday. We also realized that we needed to share the ownership of ATRN. It could not rest on one single person. Now, the person who brings an article to share is also in charge of the entire meeting.

We learned that we could not mandate teachers to be teacher-researchers. That semester, I created discussion groups in five different schools and required the discussion leaders to attend the monthly ATRN meetings. My goal was to encourage the discussion leaders to understand the reflective process and then, hopefully move into the stance of a teacher-researcher. This view was entirely oppositional to ATRN's view of inviting teachers to be researchers. I think we were so caught up in the want to be seen as an official group, that I completely forgot about the underlying values of ATRN and pushed my way forward.

The other realization that emerged from that meeting was that we did not like our research community being disrupted. We attend ATRN meetings for a specific reason and when that was not fulfilled, we felt cheated. We came to the meeting with an understanding of the fundamental aspects of our set agenda. We knew we would read and discuss a thought-provoking article. We knew we had a forum in which to share our current research and would obtain thoughtful feedback. We also knew that we would be in the company of like-minded professionals where nothing needed to be defended or extensively explained. We could get past the surface explanations that we frequently used in our individual schools and dig into examining our practice with the support of others. When that did not happen, we felt a great sense of loss and anger.

Act IV: Teetering on the Edge of the Forest or Which Direction Next?

At this point in time, we again feel like Gretel as she opens the door of her classroom and sees that broad dense expanse of boreal forest. The Saturday morning signpost pointed us to this new section of the woods and we wonder where it will lead us. We feel as though we are in a transition as we reflect on our growth as teacher-researchers and look forward to new possibilities.

I believe the developmental growth of ATRN has mirrored our growth as teacher-researchers. In the beginning, we all needed the specific structure of the research process (Hubbard and Power, 1993; McNiff, 1991) just like we needed the organizational structure of the Alaska Writing Project. The idea of finding a question, gathering data, selecting the research design, analysing data, reviewing the literature, and publishing provided a solid frame for our research actions for about three years. We clung to this as the only 'authentic' way to conduct teacher research and our summer institutes were the vehicles in which to instruct others in this method.

About the time that we began to question the value of such a strong state-wide governing board, some of us began to venture beyond this frame. I remember sitting on the couch in the Schiabble Retreat Center during the 1993 summer institute and looking at the report of my research, thinking that the papers in my hand did not represent the essence of my work with the students. I tore the manuscript in two and proceeded to write a letter of reflection to my students (Austin, 1994b). Later that afternoon when I shared my writing, the institute participants tackled the topic of defining research. A year later, Cindee arrived with no finished paper, but with a stack of books and announced them as 'My bibliography'. These were our examples of our first explorations beyond the initial framework and it has not ceased. We continue to wonder about how to creatively and most effectively share our work with others.

Defining and describing teacher research was a parallel topic. When we began, we studied teacher research accounts found in books by Goswami and Stillman (1987), Perl and Wilson (1986), and Bissex and Bullock (1987) and took those models to heart. Our view of the act of teacher research, as well as the representation of work, was based on those articles. Now, along with our discussion of ways to share our work, we also continually re-examined our beliefs of what it means to do teacher research. Is it a procedure or a way of thinking? What are the variations? Are all research studies valid? The revisiting of these types of questions prod us to continually and critically assess our actions and thoughts.

Gradually ATRN phased out the state governing component altogether and each local site functioned alone. During this particular period, we (the Fairbanks group) decided to host a state-wide research conference. The call for proposals stressed the importance of the conference as 'a place where we, as teacher-researchers, can publicly share our work and learn about others' research. It's a place to orally publish'. The two-day gathering in June 1994 reflected our growing confidence in ourselves as researchers. Our presentations ranged from beginning teacher-researchers sharing the impact of their research on their teaching, to a university and elementary cooperative project. We felt we had much to offer the 50 other educators who attended.

Today, as I complete the writing of this chapter, the Fairbanks ATRN is holding a summer retreat here at my home. It is the second of such gatherings in the past three years. ATRN, as conceived initially in 1989, has changed. There is no state-wide organization, and Fairbanks is the only place where teacher-researchers continue to meet consistently as a group. Late last night, we sat around the dining table and discussed the barriers we found in influencing other educators to become engaged in teacher research. In the end, Karen pointed out that living our teaching life as a teacher-researcher in the presence of others is the most effective:

> I think I've given you my transcendental meditation quote before, where it said something about when there is one mediator in the crowd they will effect six others. And that is the way ATRN is and I've said this before, I'm sure. Others get affected by seeing one teacher-researcher with a clipboard or asking questions, that sort of stuff. I think that's part of it. I think its the nature of it to be sort of small and intimate. It's not a big thing, like everyone gets on the bandwagon sort of thing. It's the nature of the process and people come to it when they need it, like a crisis.

ATRN serves as a community for those of us who choose to be classroom researchers in schools where this is not valued. Our research community provides a stable base of colleagues who encourage, support, and respect each other. We find this extremely important as we struggle to conduct research alongside our teaching.

Another one of our topics late last night was the feeling of incredible learning that occurs among us. In looking back, I can see how the work of the ATRN members in Fairbanks influenced each other as well as other educators. Mary Lou Morton's (1991) research focusing on the integration of special education students in the regular classroom setting provided the beginnings to the conversation that led to the school district re-examining this issue.

The integration model is now being used in many of the local schools. Building on Mary Lou's work, Barb Smith (1996) and Shirley Kaltenbach (1993) chose to examine students who were mainstreamed into their classrooms. Shirley's initial case-study led her to explore the issue of parent involvement. Her work led us to think critically about the role of parents and classrooms. Janelle McCrackin (1994) added another dimension to parent involvement with her study of family nights. Her study showed us the importance of making school an inviting, comfortable place for parents. Our discussions rippled outward to other teachers and administrators and added to an awareness of the importance of parents. For the past several years, one of the school district's goals is to encourage and foster meaningful parent involvement.

During this same time, I was examining the issue of assessment and, learning from Shirley's work, I recognized the need for parents to be an integral part of their students' evaluation. As a result of my research with quarterly student-led parent conferences (Austin, 1994a), within my district these types of conferences are an accepted alternative to the traditional teacher–parent meetings. Most recently, Bonnie created an opportunity for any district teacher to become part of a discussion group. Using our ATRN meetings as a model, she coordinated these many groups throughout the year. Bonnie worked with the school district to allow teachers to participate in a discussion group rather than attend the required inservice. It was so successful, the program will continue this year as well.

In last night's talk, we suddenly realized that, because so many of us become excited about each other's questions, we tend to 'try out' each other's research in our own room. During our monthly meetings, we share our observations and in a sense become a partner in each person's research project. For me, it is this kind of support and enthusiasm for my research topic, coupled with the discoveries I uncover when adopting others' research, that I find mentally invigorating. So how do we share this excitement and knowledge with others? The dilemma of new members continue to haunt us on several levels. How do we welcome and sustain those new to teacher research? How do we maintain the integrity of our monthly meetings?

There are some things we do know. We know that we are no longer worried about the size of the group. We do know that we come to the monthly meetings with the anticipation of learning. We do know that our research has value and worth. We do know that we value our time together. With those things in mind, we realized that we wanted to offer a similar opportunity to other teachers in our district. We talked last night of the possibility of offering a professional development class in the fall on the basics of teacher research. This would be a district-wide invitation to anyone wishing to know more. We, then, could offer our experience and expertise in helping them create their own like-minded community of teacher-researchers.

The second idea we carefully examined was the culture of our ATRN meetings. We have established expectations and purposes for meeting. To help any new teacher-researcher who visits us on a Saturday morning, we decided one of us would adopt that person and become their mentor. Having a personal guide might ease and sustain the new researcher.

We also realized that our meetings have a specific outlook. While we do share concerns, the meeting is not a place for complaints. A few minutes ago as we tried to articulate this idea to each other, we became aware that while we do honour problems, we also see the problems as leading us somewhere. The difficulties are not barriers, but situations to be examined and studied. It is this subtle difference that characterizes our meetings that we value and desire to guard carefully.

We also decided that we are selfish individuals. It has taken us a long time to admit to this. We attend ATRN because it satisfies our need for intellectual and social stimulation. Earlier in this chapter, I wrote about struggling to find a common factor among the ATRN members. I now realize it is the commitment to each other, to research, and to our students that holds us together. We are cautious about sharing it with others who do not have this same vision.

In our reflections over lunch, we recognized that we have shifted in our thinking about research. In the beginning, we viewed our research as a way to look outward upon classroom happenings. Now we see it as a way to be reflective and to look inwards. We now understand that our research changes us as people, which in turn changes our practice. Teacher research is not a thing to do, but a way to be.

At ATRN gatherings, we always use a piece of writing to focus our discussions, and over these three particular days we're reading aloud *Radical Presence* by Mary Rose O'Reilley (1998). With her help as a long-distance mentor, we're considering what it means to create a space that nourishes an inner life. As we read aloud the first chapter, we stopped to chat about her definition of mindfulness:

> . . . the Buddhist practice of simply being there, with a very precise and focused attention, listening, watching. Not being somewhere else, answering some question that hasn't been asked. (O'Reilley, 1998, p. 3)

We decided this is an apt description of us as teacher-researchers. Totally attending to the actions in the classroom as well as being aware of ourselves as reflective learners. It is the interchange between these two positions that keeps us alive intellectually.

References

ALASKA TEACHER RESEARCH NETWORK (ed.) (1991) *The Far Vision, The Close Look*, Juneau, Alaska: Alaskan Department of Education.
ANDERSON, D. (1991) 'Introduction', in ALASKA TEACHER RESEARCH NETWORK (ed.) *The Far Vision, The Close Look*, (p. I), Juneau, Alaska: Alaskan Department of Education.
AUSTIN, T. (1994a) *Changing the View*, Portsmouth, NH: Heinemann.
AUSTIN, T. (1994b) 'Travel together in trust', *Teacher Research*, **2**, pp. 122–7.
BISSEX, G. and BULLOCK, R. (eds) (1987) *Seeing For Ourselves*, Portsmouth, NH: Heinemann.
GLATTHORN, A. (1995) Personal Communication.
GOSWAMI, D. and STILLMAN, P. (eds) (1987) *Reclaiming the Classroom*, Upper Montclair, NJ: Boynton Cook Publishers Inc.
HUBBARD, R. and POWER, B. (1993) *The Art of Classroom Inquiry*, Portsmouth, NH: Heinemann.
KALTENBACH, S. (1993) 'What do you think? A parent–child classroom study', *Teacher Research*, **1**, pp. 49–57.

McCRACKIN, J. (1991) 'Family nights', in ALASKAN TEACHER RESEARCH NETWORK (ed.) *The Far Vision, The Close Look*, pp. 63–8, Juneau, Alaska: Alaskan Department of Education.

McNIFF, J. (1991) *Action Research*, London: Routledge.

MORTON, M. (1991) 'I really am o.k.: A perspective of integration', in ALASKAN TEACHER RESEARCH NETWORK (ed.) *The Far Vision, The Close Look*, pp. 113–24, Juneau, Alaska: Alaskan Department of Education.

O'REILLY, M. (1998) *Radical Presence*, Portsmouth, NH: Boynton/Cook Publishers Heinemann.

PERL, S. and WILSON, N. (eds) (1986) *Through Teachers' Eyes*, Portsmouth, NH: Heinemann.

SMITH, B. (1996) 'Challenges to choices: A year with Michael', *Teacher Research*, **2**, pp. 45–51.

8 Discovering Our Professional Knowledge as Teachers: Critical Dialogues about Learning from Experience

Tom Russell and Shawn Bullock

Introduction

Teachers' knowledge is personal, context-rich, and elusive. This chapter approaches the issue of researching teaching by demonstrating the power of critical dialogue in naming and transforming teachers' professional knowledge. In this instance, the dialogue is made possible by the authors' shared commitment to probing the importance of pedagogy and experience in facilitating learning. Tom is an experienced teacher educator seeking the best ways to identify and encourage the learning of science teacher candidates in a program based on early extended experience; Shawn is a teacher candidate coming to terms with his first extended teaching assignment and his preservice education courses. Each is helping the other identify and interpret his professional knowledge as a teacher by reading and commenting on e-mail accounts of teaching–learning experiences. Sharing our personal experiences of teaching drives the process of naming our professional knowledge as teachers. By grounding our analysis in experiences of teaching and critical dialogue about teaching, we demonstrate how we come to understand our knowledge and our ongoing efforts to extend, refine and consolidate that knowledge.

Setting the Stage and Introducing the Characters

We see ourselves as two actors on the stage in a learning-to-teach playhouse. Tom began teaching in 1963 and has been teaching preservice teachers at Queen's University since 1977. Shawn began the education portion of his Queen's–Waterloo concurrent education program in 1997, after completing the first two years of his Honours Physics program at the University of Waterloo. Shawn and Tom met at Queen's in late August 1997, when Shawn found himself in Tom's course on methods of teaching physics.

Shawn began his first teaching placement at Aurora High School on the first day of the school year in September. After eight weeks, he returned to Queen's for two weeks of courses that coincided with a two-week protest by teachers across the province of Ontario. He then returned to Aurora High School for six more weeks of teaching, until the school closed for holidays in December. In the Winter Term of the BEd program, Shawn spent eleven weeks in courses at Queen's, with a three-week 'alternate practicum' in late February and March. He returned to his science studies at Waterloo in May and is scheduled to teach again for four months in the Fall Term of 1998.

Tom began teaching with no formal training but years of observation as a student, just as Shawn did. Tom taught for two years (in Nigeria) before entering a formal teacher education program, and he has always paid special attention to the role of experience in learning to teach. Schön's (1983) *The Reflective Practitioner: How Professionals Learn in Action* has influenced his research over the last 15 years. The 1997–98 academic year happened to be the first full year of a revised BEd program structure at Queen's University, a structure that can be summarized as 'extended teaching experience first'. In this program, Tom met Shawn in several classes in late August, worked more intensely with him in a group of 11 for 2 weeks in late October, and then continued through the Winter Term in a class of 26. An invitation from John Loughran to prepare a chapter for *Researching Teaching* came shortly after the curtain rose on Shawn and Tom's 'shared adventure' of preparing, exchanging, and commenting on each other's teaching notes.

The Curtain Rises

In a two-hour class on Thursday, 30 October 1997, feeling inspired and empowered by his first three one-hour classes with eleven candidates and their stories of eight weeks' teaching, Tom 'made his big move'. He had been developing an experience-rich approach to teaching science, but the group seemed ready for more. In this class Tom developed links between the new teachers' learning (to teach science) from experience, their students' learning (science), and his own learning (to teach others to teach science). Tom argued that all three categories of learning are more similar than different, and he urged that all three be seen from the vantage point of 'experience first' — a phrase that later evolved into 'the power of experience'. Several people responded positively, and this class set the tone for the remainder of the ten-hours-over-two-weeks block of classes. On October 31, Shawn sent an electronic message to Tom that included the following, and the curtain rose on our shared adventure in dialogue about pedagogy and learning from experience:

> Although I might have been realizing it at the subconscious level, the ideas we talked about yesterday [in class] finally put a lot of things into focus. The idea you mentioned about Experience coming before Theory really makes a lot of sense to me. Last night . . . I started looking at my day book and journal from the past two months. And then the crux of what you've been saying hit me like a tonne of bricks: that experience lays a foundation to learn a concept, and theory cleans up what was floating around in one's mind after the experience. I then applied that to my own learning as a Teacher Candidate: I've been experiencing teaching, and I've had my own successes and challenges, but only by reflecting on it will I truly learn anything from my experience.

These two weeks are helping me come to some important realizations, specifically last night. Now comes the unique part: When I return in January, I, like everyone else, will be learning from experience and consolidating ideas for four months. But what I find exciting is the notion that I get to go back to Waterloo and apply what I've learned about teaching to my own learning, and then, in September 1998, I get to have another four-month 'practicum'. These two weeks are valuable, because they serve to refocus, but I get to do it on a large scale with two four-month blocks next year.

Later that Friday afternoon, Tom sent Shawn a reply that began with the following:

[Your message is] off the scale, Shawn — what pleases me most is that I think I can honestly say I 'heard' (saw!) in your earlier e-mails and writing the potential for that kind of response. One of the beauties of e-mail is that you never quite know when you will get a response (I had thought of sending a 'what's up' note earlier, just because I was truly interested, and then I reminded myself — 'give Shawn time, Tom — he's busy and has lots to do; he'll reply when he's ready!') Now I can just float home for the weekend on the good signals in your note.

With this exchange, the curtain was up and the action began on our stage of pedagogical conversations. We began with no clear purpose beyond exploring the issue of 'experience first' in the teaching of science and in the teaching of new science teachers. John Loughran's invitation to Tom to prepare a chapter for this collection arrived just as Shawn began sending weekly reports to Tom, by e-mail, from his school. Tom extended, and Shawn accepted, an invitation to explore our discussions further by preparing this chapter. Naming our professional knowledge and interpreting its development thus became an important additional focus that fits well with the 'experience first' approach.

Act I, Scene 1: Shawn Writes and Tom Responds

In this scene, Shawn speaks in the first person about the various benefits he sees in the processes of writing about his teaching experiences and engaging in dialogue with Tom about his interpretations of his experiences.

A Journal of Experience

First and foremost, writing creates a detailed record of experience. So much happens in teaching that it is easy to forget things, and a journal allows one to look back and say, often nostalgically, 'I remember that!' It also provides an invaluable record of successes and failures. Each time I look at my notes, the experiences I had in the classroom rush back to me. By keeping detailed records of lessons, student responses, and my own thoughts at the time, I get a palpable sense of being back in the classroom.

There are certain lessons that I conducted over my practicum where I took a pedagogical risk, in the sense that I deviated from a standard approach and took an 'experience first' approach to science teaching. The journal allows me to revisit, with remarkable clarity, the experiential science lessons that I conducted. This proved to be an invaluable tool in completing my action research report.

I think that my detailed notes for the lessons in which I discussed the concept of gravity with my 12A physics class were the best example of my journal of experience. The unit started out with a 'bang', a successful interactive demonstration activity in which I showed that all objects fall to the Earth with the same acceleration. I then set the class the task of designing experiments to determine a numerical value for the acceleration due to gravity. That particular class was one of the highlights of my practicum, in terms of being the science class I envision myself teaching in years to come.

Conversely, my notes for the class when the students conducted the experiments they designed on their own reveal the angst I felt when I 'let the reigns go'. I had hoped to be far more comfortable in an experiential setting than I actually was. The thoughts from this particular entry, upon revisiting, have helped me understand experiential learning on a deeper level, as well as providing a framework from which to shape further experiences.

> Today the physics class carried out their experiments to determine the acceleration due to gravity. I vowed to provide them with as little guidance as possible, since yesterday I emphasized that they would be responsible for writing up their own methods in the final lab report. I let them debate amongst themselves how to minimize error. It was one of the most difficult things I have ever had to do. My every impulse was to point out errors and make suggestions as they performed their experiments around the classroom. Instead, I just walked around and made sure that they weren't totally lost. I was amazed at the diligence with which they worked. Frustration levels were high, but they kept going with their labs. I expect that their frustration was due to the fact that I did not hand out a piece of paper that said 'Laboratory Instructions'. This sort of approach bears further investigation. Sidebar: CONTROL! CONTROL! I craved control . . .

Positive Reinforcement and Encouragement

This is something that teachers do not get very much of in general, and as a student-teacher I found it quite useful to have constructive positive feedback on what I was doing. Students certainly are not the first to come up after a class and say, 'Great Lesson, Sir!' Quite often the dialogue reaffirmed that what I was doing was worthwhile, even when I had little direct evidence.

As a student-teacher, I found positive reinforcement very beneficial to my professional development. Although I usually knew when I could have improved things in my lesson, I often found it hard to identify things that I did well. Tom was able to provide an outside observer's perspective when he read my notes, and as such could identify positive things I was doing based solely on what I wrote (i.e. no classroom observation). To this end, Tom usually commented on different things than my associate teacher(s) identified as being positive. Having another point of view in my journey of learning to teach was invaluable.

I was apprehensive when I started teaching a general math class because I did not have any experience with classes at the general level. (In secondary schools in Ontario, courses are offered at basic, general and advanced levels; courses at the advanced level prepare students for entry to university.) My apprehension came through in my notes, and Tom provided some words of encouragement (below) for the route I was taking with the class. Again, it was extremely important for me to have the support both from an excellent associate teacher and from a faculty member.

> YOU WERE NERVOUS, and that struck you as odd. That's what jumped off the page at me, along with the incredibly creative teaching materials you provided for the class. We so easily think that something is wrong when we are nervous. But isn't it all the anticipation of the unknown? — and you've shown that there are some things that even martial arts didn't completely prepare you for. Welcome to the human race! (I give you credit for recording the nervousness here — again, your comfort in sharing your thoughts with yourself and with me is impressive — and no doubt part of my taking the big risk of suggesting that we write something together.) I think being nervous in a situation like this is incredibly positive and important. There would be something wrong if you weren't nervous. You KNEW that there was much to learn, and much that could be unpredictable.

Issues are Explored and Revisited

One of the themes I notice when I revisit my writing is that I am reminded of unresolved issues that I would like to explore in the future. Many things happened during my practicum to inspire me to think, and there are many teaching issues that cannot be 'answered'. Instead, they must be constantly revisited, which is something I hope to do in the future. One of the dominant themes in my journal concerns the issues surrounding general level education. I did not teach a general class until the last half of my practicum, when I switched into an 11 General math class. After having a lot of experience with the advanced level math students and the senior physics classes, I was amazed at the different atmosphere in a general level class.

The journal record of my first day in a general math class finds me wondering where the 'general = stupid' label comes from. I also wondered how a level whose mantra is supposed to be one of 'experience first' seems remarkably unconnected to the outside world, short of textbook examples. I revisited this issue many times during my work with the math class. I struck gold with a unit on buying a car, and I found myself making connections with the students' self-esteem as it was affected by success in math class. I also managed to develop a technique of interactive note-taking, which involved the students in completing the calculations in examples as we did the 'note'. This technique came about from revisiting an observation I made on my first day, namely that general level students tend to get 'hung up' on mechanical errors.

The experiment came in my so-called 'note' portion of the overhead. Rather than finishing the examples all the way, I would set up the problem and leave the mechanical math for the students. It seems that general students make as many calculation errors as they do conceptual errors. So I ask the class to have their calculators out for the lesson, and I get them to finish up the examples. I emphasize that we need three answers to agree to accept it. The students seem to get more into the lesson, and it partially solves the age-old problem of math class: sitting and mindlessly copying notes.

An Exercise in Metacognition

I am concerned with students thinking about their own learning, and not simply being 'theory sponges'. One of the themes I took back from the on-campus weeks was Tom's statement that 'How we teach IS the message'. I feel that by engaging in metacognition during my practica, I can learn from EXPERIENCE how to encourage students to think about their learning. It is my contention that the act of keeping a written record of teaching experience is an exercise in metacognition. Tom provided a push in terms of organizing my thoughts by suggesting that I sum up key points of each week in a separate portion of my entries. This pushed me into the new realm of reflection-in-action.

I became convinced of the benefits of writing about learning shortly after I began, and I even started including metacognitive exercises in student assignments towards the end of my practicum. I asked the math students to comment on what they learned about buying cars from the unit I created, and I asked physics students to comment on their feeling towards experiential science. I found that asking students to write on their own learning needs to be an ongoing process, much like keeping a journal of experience myself. Perhaps the single greatest moment in metacognition came in the final instalment of my notes. I tried as best I could to sum the philosophies I had developed over the practicum. I formulated a 'big picture' to my placement, and laid the foundation for the conclusions and extensions that would become a part of my action research report:

> I would argue that the nature of science is to construct your own reality of how the world works. I would also point out that most physical tasks performed in a high school laboratory could be performed by anyone (pour this, time that, measure this). High school labs should focus on 'discovering' things, not developing basic motor skills to verify facts that are already known. We as educators should remember that although it is apparent to us that, say, all objects undergo the same acceleration due to gravity near the Earth's surface, it remains a mystery to most high school students. 'Experience first' allows people to discover science rather than be information sponges.

Pedagogical Sounding Board

For me, the fall practicum was a place where I could build my own pedagogy. The writing task forced me to record and reflect on experience, from which I could construct theories and philosophies based on the 'So what?' of my experience. I was able to 'sound my findings off' a colleague well-versed in the subject matter, allowing me to revisit and refine my philosophies based on experiences and comments. Over the course of the writing exercise, I sent Tom 'snapshots' of my teaching experience in the form of detailed descriptions and sample lesson plans and handouts. I usually made some conclusions about how the lesson went, or how effective the material was, based on my own musings and conversations with my associates.

One of the pedagogical issues that I discussed at length with Tom was the place of labs in a science class. We both feel that labs need to be based on an 'experience first' pedagogy rather than the more traditional approach of 'theory first, lab later'. I was able to investigate the notion of labs before theory in conjunction with my action research report. We discussed at length the notion that, when asked, over half of my Grade 12 physics class preferred doing a lab first and then naming their experiences with standard physical theory (in this instance, the Law of Universal Gravitation).

In one entry I hypothesized that the ability of Grade 12 students to function in an 'experience first' approach might be due to the fact that they were used to a very structured approach to labs. I felt that this comfort level could allow them to rely on skills achieved through rote learning, and allow them to function independently. Tom asserted that there was a difference between 'experience first' and 'functioning independently'. To this end, I tried a similar 'experience first' approach with a lab in my Grade 9 class, with the help of my associate. The Grade 9s reacted quite differently to the 'experience first' approach than the Grade 12s did, although I am not sure how much those differences were due to issues inherent in the relative ages of the two groups. Tom helped me unpack much of what I learned from the two classes, and it became clear that this particular topic, like so many others, would bear further investigation.

> I tried the 'experience first' concept with the Grade 9 class. The topic was reflection of plane and curved surfaces (concave and convex). I introduced the equipment, explained very carefully how to use it, and basically turned the class loose. I insisted that they have a piece of paper out when I was explaining things, so that they could write down the experimental method I was outlining — in their own words. It was quite an interesting class, to say the least. I had to intervene more with the Grade 9s then I did with the Grade 12s. I am forced to wonder if I had to intervene more with the Grade 9s because they haven't had the years of conditioning that the 12s have had, thus making it easier for them to function independently.

More Questions, Deeper Meanings

Tom was adept at not giving 'the right answer' on issues and opinions that I raised via electronic mail. Instead he would ask more questions to help me reflect on a deeper level and get to the heart of the matter. I now realize that he was avoiding the pitfalls associated with what our physics methods class came to call 'Answerland'

— the near-universal tendency of teachers and students to focus on the pursuit of right answers. I must stress that I always found it engaging and worthwhile to read his opinions on certain issues, because they were presented as 'a colleague's observations' and not as 'the right answer from a professor'. The questions Tom asked always pointed me towards deeper meanings, with the option to tackle the issue in the next e-mail or to let it sit in the back of my mind until I was ready to deal with it. I still haven't answered many of the questions I was asked, nor do I feel pressured to, because they were presented as 'points to ponder' not as 'questions'. Tom commented on my pedagogical conclusions in an interesting way. Rather than giving his opinion on my conclusion, he asked more questions to help me explore and revisit my findings.

One of the most poignant examples came early in the writing process. After arriving home from school one day, I had a breakthrough in my thoughts on teaching science. I wrote that teaching science is really about exploring everyday notions that we need to explain the phenomena around us, and that 'the role of the science classroom is to quantify our everyday knowledge, and dispel common scientific misconceptions'. I have since amended that assertion, along with many others, in my journey of learning to teach. Tom asked me, 'How quick should we be to label everyday thinking (common sense) as wrong, and how eager should we be to let science have the final word on everything?' He could have just as easily said 'I disagree because . . .', but instead he asked me questions that required me to look at deeper issues. I have since explored the notion of interpreting experiences in different ways.

I ended off the term believing that the role of a science classroom is to help students construct an understanding of the world around them by linking their personal experiences to scientific ideas. I am sure that I will amend this view in the future as a result of asking myself more questions.

Adding Links to My Map of Teaching

Many times during the placement I felt like I was dancing around some central themes or issues, but I could not put my finger on what they were. Initially, I might have said that Tom assisted me in naming my experiences, but I have come to view that as inaccurate. 'Naming' implies that Tom was trying to fit what I was experiencing into a pre-moulded pedagogical genre, which was certainly not the case. He recognized that my teaching experience, like everyone's, was unique and that the key was, as Tom put it in an e-mail, 'constructing understanding from experience first'.

One of the challenges of exploring teaching pedagogy is to be speaking the same language in terms of concept naming. In our particular case, this had the potential to be further compounded by differences in experience: a university professor and a teacher candidate. Very early on, however, we discovered that we did indeed speak the same language. It started out with an 'experience first' pedagogy, something I had experienced both as a Queen's teacher candidate and as a University of Waterloo Co-op student (alternating terms of on-campus study and off-campus work experiences).

Over the course of the writing exercise, all of our writings could probably be grouped under one heading, namely, 'How we teach is the message'. It is a concept I have taken very much to heart. If I want students to construct an understanding of the world around them, I must create an environment rich in experience. Through questioning, Tom helped me create links between various ideas and philosophies that I was discovering. The final instalment of my teaching notes showed the beginning of my being able to name what I was seeing independently, when I was concerned about students being active learners as opposed to 'theory sponges'.

The Road Ahead

Certainly one cannot learn to be a teacher in four months alone, and through 'thinking questions' I was shown many things to explore further, both practically and conceptually, during my next four-month practicum in fall 1998 and, indeed, during the rest of my teaching career. After concluding my writing experience for the Fall Term, I found that I had a clear route defined in terms of what I wanted to accomplish at the Faculty of Education. I saw the Faculty as a place to unpack and explore my experiences with peers and colleagues.

Act I, Scene 2: Tom writes, Shawn Observes and Responds

As our drama continues, the first person voice passes to Tom, who illustrates and interprets the researching of his teaching by recording and sharing with Shawn the notes of his teaching of the chemistry/physics methods class in which Shawn was one of 26 students.

A Journal of Experience

I have always wanted to keep a detailed personal account of my teaching of BEd candidates, much as I had done in my second year (1992–93), teaching one class a day of physics in a local secondary school. Shawn's notes in November–December and the commitment to prepare this chapter finally pushed me to begin. Once started, there was little chance of stopping, thanks to the commitment made to share weekly notes with Shawn. I soon realized that the replies from Shawn were invaluable. After the first six weeks of classes in the Winter Term, all candidates departed for a three-week 'alternate practicum'. While they were away, I worked on replies to questions they had left for me, and it occurred to me to review the notes I had kept thus far. I was stunned by the detail in the notes, particularly by the sense that we really had done more than I could remember doing. While I have always tried to be open about my teaching, the discussions with Shawn had made that openness seem very safe, and so I posted the complete set to a website where members of the class could read them. Education programs are often criticized for their lack of substance, and it seemed important to provide members of the class with a reminder of how much we had done. Two hours later I had the following reply from another member of the class:

> Hi Tom. Wow. I just finished reading your personal teaching notes that you put on the web. I must say I found it pretty mesmerizing. It was neat to see how you perceived things. What surprised me (although it shouldn't have) was how often your perception of how the class went was in sync with ours. For example, I remember being disappointed by our last class before our practicum as well. How quickly it is that I've forgotten how clear it should be to a teacher when a class has gone well or not. Anyway, thanks for sharing your thoughts with us.

The record of experience had already paid rich dividends.

Positive Reinforcement and Encouragement

When Shawn not only comments positively on issues and events in my class but shows me that he is adding to my points, I know that one person is hearing me very well. This encourages me to carry on and continue the points with the entire class, particularly if I feel I am taking a risk. The following notes relate to the class on 27 January 1998, the fifth class of the Winter Term, and they illustrate three types of data available in our conversation about my teaching. Shawn kept notes about each class in his own files. When I sent a file containing my notes for the week, Shawn would return the file after inserting comments. The first entry contains Shawn's notes on the class, and this provides the reader with a small window on my classes. This is followed by my own notes on the class and then by Shawn's comments on my notes.

All three notes require some introduction. The focal point of our work together was a teaching procedure termed 'Predict-Observe-Explain', or simply P.O.E. (White and Gunstone, 1992). Before presenting an observation, predictions are requested and explanations for each are discussed. Students then close their eyes (to avoid being influenced by others) and vote for various predictions before observing what does happen. Finally, the full explanation is discussed. In the class on January 27, two of Shawn's classmates presented a P.O.E. that involved rubbing balloons on one's hair and then observing that they repel (like charges). As Shawn explains, a question about the charge on the balloon prompted me to bring out grass seed to answer the question; someone else in the class later suggested that we observe the effect of the balloon's charge on iron filings. My note records the reaction of K (one of the classmates) to picking up the equipment (a bicycle wheel that can be spun on its axis and then rotated while standing on a platform free to turn) that had been used in a P.O.E. in the previous class. The significance of personal experience of phenomena in science teaching was one of the points I had been trying to develop as pairs of people presented P.O.E. events to the class. I took a few minutes to describe three quite different ways one can 'learn' that a stove is hot (Olson, 1974, p. 12).

Shawn's personal notes on the class of January 27: Sometimes I wonder if this class can keep up with itself. The wheels have been turning at breakneck speed for so long, I wonder if there will ever be a point where people sit back and go 'PHEW!' Frankly, I hope we never have the time to do that.

Another great class. We generated topics that WE want to discuss — again designing our own curriculum. I am again forced to wonder how much learning could happen if students were shown the opportunities that exist in the world, and then ask the STUDENTS to design their own curriculum. Idealistic? You bet. But I am coming to believe that idealism is in the job description.

What a fantastic P.O.E. day. At first, the balloons were repelling each other due to the like charge given to them by hair. Nothing too exciting . . . until someone asked if the charge is spread out over the balloon. I became intrigued. More than that, I HAD to know the answer. You brought out the grass seed and all of the sudden I felt like I did when I was a kid on a field trip to the science centre: pushing this and that, turning levers, all the while filled with a sense of awe. The grass seed jumping towards the balloon summed up another important aspect of P.O.E. I have mentioned before how P.O.E.s can be considered the core of science, but I neglected to mention how they can create a sense of wonder, that question 'WHY?' that humans have been asking for centuries. I suppose it does not surprise me that I hadn't been able to encapsulate this until now. I hadn't experienced it until today!

Tom's personal notes on the class of January 27: O.K., it's not quite noon and for the FIRST time I'm writing immediately after class. I have been dying to get to the keyboard to put down what I can remember of what I overheard K saying when she stepped on the turntable with the bicycle wheel and turned it: 'It's really true. You have to feel it for yourself'. Haven't I always 'known' this? Wouldn't most people agree with it? Is it as simple as the fact that we have become comfortable with school as a place where we are TOLD, and occasionally get to SEE, but rarely get to FEEL? I suppose so, if it makes sense for Douglas Barnes (1976) to draw a distinction between school knowledge and action knowledge. It takes me back to David Olson's (1974) paper that describes three ways for learning 'the stove is hot': being told, seeing someone else touch a hot stove and jump back, and touching the hot stove personally. Content-wise, they appear to be identical. But in terms of impact on future action, they are VERY different. Need I go any further to explain why teacher education has had so little impact, historically, on future action? There has been lots of telling, a little seeing, and very little doing. NOW, after 12–14 weeks of teaching, everything we say and do can be interpreted in light of personal experience. Even so, we have some amazing things happening in terms of immediate shared experience as a class.

Shawn's comments on Tom's note above: The stove is hot. What a powerful example — I wrote it down as soon as you said it. That little phrase encapsulates so much of what I have come to believe about science teaching. Why must science be thought of as an esoteric subject? Why are arts courses disrespectfully labelled 'touchy-feely'? I think that every scientist (myself included) spent a good portion of [his or her] childhood ripping things apart to figure them out — I was fond of radios. Could it be that I was trying to connect my theoretical understanding of things to real-life experiences? I remember ripping the case off of a clock radio and plugging it in to see if I could detect a flow of electrons (I heard about current on some science show for kids). I then concluded, from experience, that electrons have to be really, really small. . . . the power of experience.

I believe any teacher would draw encouragement and support from notes such as these that Shawn shared with me. His return to his own experiences years ago, taking a radio apart, suggest that he has 'caught' the messages I hope people are taking from my classes. His notes give me more detailed indication than I can infer from people's short comments in class of what it is like for someone in the class to participate in someone else's P.O.E. I have described the example of 'the stove is hot' to previous classes, but never has there been the uptake that Shawn describes. While I would not assume that everyone took the example as far as he did, I am encouraged to believe that the time being devoted to the P.O.E. strategy is worth continuing.

Issues are Explored and Revisited

Time and again, the e-mail exchanges with Shawn (and our occasional conversations about this chapter) helped me understand particular features of my teaching more fully, pick up issues that had slipped out of view temporarily, and take points further than I might have on my own. Because I have never before shared and examined my teaching with a student throughout his or her time in my class, it is a challenge to describe just how our relationship developed. Once we were underway, there seemed to be no stopping us. Each of us respected the other's autonomy and independence. The common ground of 'experience first' and the shared pleasure of 'talking pedagogy' were ever-present themes.

In the first week of February, Ian Mitchell (of Monash University and the Project for Enhancing Effective Learning — PEEL) visited Queen's University and participated in my three classes and also presented an evening lecture about the PEEL project. My notes on his lecture and Shawn's comments illustrate the exploration and revisiting of issues that we both consider important in our teaching:

> *My notes about Ian Mitchell's lecture*: 45 people in the audience, including CC and her [evening] class. I think there were 11 from Chem-Physics [our class], and R has already watched the videotape. I wonder how I could find out if that evening talk made a difference. For me, it was an absolutely stunning performance of good teaching practice ABOUT good teaching practices. I need to revisit the videotape myself to take it all in. I wonder about doing a quick on-paper survey of how many times people saw Ian during the week and what insights and further questions they gained from him. I have to assume that more contact meant greater impact, particularly since extra contact would mean there was already a significant level of interest.

> *Shawn's comment closes with an intriguing speculation*: I see that you have gone with your original plan as far as the survey goes. I think it goes without saying that

Ian had a remarkable impact on me as a professional. It is so rare that someone practices what they preach in the Crystal Palace. People do take notice, and that is part of the reason I think ChemPhys has been so successful. I wonder if the reason so many students do not internalize good learning behaviours is because they are not getting 'quality teaching practices'. Practice what you preach . . . hmmm . . .

Pedagogical Sounding Board

This section might also be titled, 'Clarifying, consolidating and refining the "so what?" of my teaching'. Our earliest exchanges about 'experience first' convinced me that I could trust Shawn with any and all thoughts about my teaching. He never let me down, and I hope he can say the same about my comments on his teaching. There are times when Shawn seems to see the big picture better than I do. His comments about what he sees me doing often show me new ways that I can 'drive home the message' with the entire class. The discussion we had following the class on 29 January 1998, illustrates how the conversation with Shawn served me well as a pedagogical sounding board. We were two weeks into a five-week block of classes, meeting for ninety minutes three times a week. I knew, from experience, that the climate established by this stage in the term is crucial, and so I was watching everywhere I could for clues about how each member of the class was responding to our 'class tone' and atmosphere. Focusing on the P.O.E. strategy automatically (and refreshingly) reduces the importance of 'right answers' in the classroom. Yet beginning teachers often look to experienced teachers for long lists of 'right ways to teach' or 'best ways to teach'. Both the events of this class and the position of this class in our course made me particularly interested in how my pedagogical moves were affecting members of the group. After the class I sent an e-mail message to Shawn that I included in my notes for the day, which then evolved into an e-mail message to the entire class. It is convenient to pick up the storyline with Shawn's subsequent comment on part of my message and to continue with the text of my message:

> *Shawn's comment on an earlier portion of my notes*: The simple answer is something that you said at the beginning of the year (and I didn't quite grasp): 'The medium is the message.' How you teach is what inspired me to take on the challenges that I have taken on. I hope that how I teach infects students with a love for science . . . that is my ultimate goal.

> *My notes on the class of January 29*: [part of an E-mail message to Shawn] Thanks for listening. I remember your 'So What?' comment about having someone outside the school to talk to about teaching. I'm feeling it far more dramatically than that at the moment — it makes ALL the difference to know that someone has made a commitment to being an active listener. Teaching really is a lonely profession. Now to my notes. [end of E-mail to Shawn]

> [continuing to write with Shawn as audience] Surprise, surprise, suddenly what I was going to write seemed important to put to everyone. I can't make that an

every-class process, but today turned out, in hindsight, to be incredibly important to me. I think there were several turning points and leaps forward, as well as something of a sequel to that 'experience first' talk in the on-campus blocks last term. Anyway, you'll see it both ways, Shawn. Here you can insert any comments you might have!

[start of E-mail to class] Thanks, everyone, for another class that I will certainly remember (as I rush out to buy beer nuts! [an ingredient in the day's P.O.E. event]). I don't know if I will ever 'sell' anyone else on Predict-Feel-Explain, but it really did come to mind there and then, thanks to your contributions (and nudges!) to our 'The stove is hot' discussion. THANK YOU for the comments on the P.O.E. sheets — at first glance they are as rich and fascinating as I expected them to be. I'll get them typed up right away for all to see.

There are several ways to think about the 'right answer' issue. I think I made one reference today that it is increasingly important to ME that you realize that I do not have right answers that I wish you to adopt as science teachers. My job teaching you is VERY different from your job teaching 9-OAC science [14- to 18-year-olds]. At the same time, if you are enjoying the relief of time to think about practice, after a major 'dose' of it last term, I encourage you to think through how you might adopt (appropriately) features of the environment we are enjoying three times a week in 339 [our classroom]. For me, today's class was very important on two fronts: I started out, from The Stove is Hot, suggesting to at least some that Experience is the Best (and only?) Teacher. Fortunately for me, you brought me back, quickly, and I spotted some of the missing pieces. I had 'Change takes an idea, a challenge, or a puzzle' in my notes, but I didn't say it. Perhaps the extra piece is 'Change has to have experience to build on'. There's plenty of important room for telling and seeing, but both are greatly enhanced by 'feeling' — direct personal experience, whether of spinning wheels or spinning classrooms.

If I have any 'right answers' to offer you, they are about the learning process, not about how Grade 9 density should (or should not) be taught. 'Backtalk' and 'action research' and 'experience first (P.F.E.)' are all general processes that tend to be missing [unintentionally] from most classrooms. You should know that I tend to get very 'nervous' in large-group discussion such as the one that started in response to J's question (which, refreshingly, I never heard!), simply because only one person can speak at a time. But it seemed O.K. today and I loved the way you all kept building on each other's ideas. The climate at the moment is one that I treasure — there are no put-downs. People listen openly and respond honestly (or else I've been fooled!). This is hard to build in a class of teenagers, but if it is one of your two or three central goals from the first day, I think you can make progress.

In reply to my weekly set of notes, Shawn made the following comment: I think that the key point to remember is that teaching is NOT just about curriculum, classroom management, labs and exams. Teaching is a profession, which entails a responsibility to be a reflective practitioner. Action research, backtalk, and thinking about learning are missing from most departments and staffrooms. Talking about teaching, it seems, is quite often left as how to deal with so-and-so or whether something needs to be on a test. These are important points, but there need to be more open forums for teachers to talk about teaching. I think that our e-mail conversations provide that. What concerns me is the resources that go untapped when people do not reflect. The most disturbing thing is that, back in August, I didn't even know what a reflective practitioner was. I certainly did not know it was a part of teaching. Thank you for opening my mind.

It should be self-evident that I was using my conversations with Shawn, and with the entire class by e-mail, as a pedagogical sounding board. The preceding material seems an appropriate passage to extract from our conversation because it reveals what was clearly the case — I was thinking about broader pedagogical issues ('So what?' not 'What?') and Shawn was doing much more than encouraging me. He too kept looking for the bigger picture, linking back to the start of the course in August and its initial phase in 10 hours of classes in October. Shawn's comments about being a reflective practitioner were of particular interest because I do not believe I had encouraged him to use that phrase; he had found it elsewhere (in a transcript of a lecture by Donald Schön) and was using it to point to what he now sees himself doing.

An Exercise in Metacognition

Just as Shawn reports his concern with students thinking about their own learning, so I can report that I am always eager to learn about what my students are thinking about their learning — and learning in the 'teachers' college' setting is always complex. I was particularly successful this year in encouraging members of my class to call the Faculty of Education the 'Crystal Palace', because we are always teaching about teaching and our teaching actions can so easily contradict our words about teaching. Soon after starting to teach in the Crystal Palace in 1977, I made a 'mid-course evaluation' (free responses about strengths, weaknesses, and suggestions) a regular feature of my courses, so that everyone could see what everyone else was thinking about the course and so I could attempt to clarify my purposes for the second half of the course. For the last decade, I have required a final assignment that is the 'story' of one's year learning to teach, and to those who ask 'Why?' I usually say that I want them to have a record of this year to look back to in two or five years, to be better able to judge their progress. On February 19, as they departed for three weeks of teaching, I collected individuals' free responses about our work since early January and posted them to a website where all could read them at their convenience.

Shawn provided a number of personal comments about the comments of the entire group, and this became a very special element in our ongoing conversation about my teaching. I insert in brackets comments about my reactions as we listen to Shawn thinking about other people's thinking about their learning in my course.

An overriding theme on the web page is people's overwhelming appreciation for you to 'talk the talk and walk the walk'. This is a crude way of saying that how you teach is the message. I think that we were all a little confused [when you said it] in August. I remember thinking, 'Is this guy for real? Does he really MEAN all the stuff that he says?'.

The single greatest way that you proved it to us was by throwing out the assignment sheet. That sent a strong signal that you were willing to make the course based on our experiences. The other indicator was generating the topics in the first class. I remember feeling that the class was truly shaping its own curriculum. [These are themes Shawn notices regularly, yet it is additionally helpful to have him speak on behalf of the group.]

It is my feeling that one of the problems with some of the courses here is that people are simply throwing as much at us as possible, based on their experiences. There is so much to cover on the topic of teaching that it is easy to get lost in a sea of pedagogical ideas. One person said it the best: 'Russell's enthusiasm, and particularly his single-mindedness in following the path that he feels, is central (overall strategy/intent/aim/vision of what you, the teacher, are trying to accomplish when you have certain activities done in the classroom) is impressive, sobering (are there teachers, and teachers of teachers, who really do think about, and care about, these ideas?) and even inspirational.' I could not agree more. [By selecting and repeating a comment from the website, Shawn helps me see even more clearly just what he and others are noticing.]

I also note an overall enthusiasm for P.O.E. You are really selling it as a useful tool, but it seems that people are taking P.O.E. at different levels. I think that there is a range of everything from 'a neat way to do a demo' to 'a hook' to a 'pedagogical philosophy'. Some seem to take P.O.E. as a means to an end, and others as an end to a means (if that makes any sense). [P.O.E. is the most powerful teaching strategy I have ever used, and it certainly lends itself to being taken in many ways on many levels.]

The general consensus of weaknesses in our course rides in tandem with its greatest strength, namely the self-directed learning. Some see the lack of structure in the class as a weakness because it seems like we are spinning our wheels sometimes. Others indicate that lack of a 'plan' results in huge tangents in our work (five-minute brainstorming running over a whole class). My opinion tends to be that you have a definite goal in mind for the end of the course, but you are willing to let us take ourselves there. It's sort of like a race where the finish line is definite but there are no lanes. [Shawn's supportive interpretation of the responses under 'weaknesses' helps me see some of the contradictions in my teaching.]

I was dismayed to see one person questioning the use of the story assignment, but I think it is indicative of the atmosphere you have created that someone feels comfortable enough to say it. [This matches my own interpretation exactly.]

The suggestions made seem to point towards the finish line. There is a desire to hear what you think on issues. Many people tend to see our class as an ideal. Now the trick is to apply what we have learned to our own classrooms (maybe even math ☺). Although I did not understand what you meant at first, I think that how you teach is truly the message, and now the trick becomes how you close and leave us with the big picture (or perhaps more tools for us to discover it on our own.). [As he often does, Shawn concludes with a challenge and a direction. I addressed the issue of 'what I think on issues' by inviting questions and then posting responses to the class website.]

More Questions, Deeper Meanings

As one of 26 people in my class, Shawn hears others' responses and compares them to his own. When he comments back about similarities and differences, I gain a better sense of the environment in which, and to which, I am teaching. He shows me his own interpretations, but may also indicate alternative interpretations that others in the group seem to be putting on events. Thus I am reminded regularly that while I may hear only one or two reactions, there will always be 26 responses to my teaching in a class of 26 individuals.

I recall vividly one particular contribution Shawn made. I was puzzling about how to proceed with my plan for the next day's class. Shawn sent me a message that clarified and sorted the 'student perspective' beautifully and pointed me clearly in a productive direction that I would not have seen otherwise. But he pointed rather than defined, always leaving the next move to me as we sought deeper meanings in issues already 'on the table'.

Adding Links to My Map of Teaching

I might also give this section a title such as, 'Making connections I would not see otherwise'. When Shawn names what he sees me doing and what he sees happening in our class, I get a better sense of how to continue to develop perspectives that I believe are important to sustain new teachers through a career of science teaching. As we looked back over my teaching, Shawn was in a special position to point to what may have been unique features of my teaching to the class of which he was a member. Because I invited everyone in that class to read my recent account of how I believe my teaching of teachers has evolved to its present state (Russell, 1997), Shawn was able to draw together features of a number of classes in the following summarizing statement:

> You manage to draw on your wealth of experience without giving us your resume. I was fascinated to see you drawing links in class to your dissatisfaction with [the teaching of] undergraduate physics at university, to your experience first teacher training, to your physics classes in 1966–67 [from which you shared students' accounts of their year in your class], to Queen's Faculty of Education and finally to us. Your teaching practice seems to have come full circle — you teach teachers in the manner that you learned.

How intriguing to have Shawn helping me to see that I have come full circle! I trust that this account supports my hope that I teach teachers as I myself learned to teach, not because I am teaching as I was taught but because I have examined my own learning and extracted a coherent set of premises and practices.

The Road Ahead

My teaching of preservice science teachers has come a long way in 20 years, but most of the significant progress has come since returning to the physics classroom in 1991 and 1992 and since constructing a personal understanding of the pedagogical insights of the PEEL project (Baird and Mitchell, 1986; Baird and Northfield, 1992). Working in an 'experience first' program structure for preservice teacher education took me the rest of the way forward, with Shawn's insightful assistance. In the first half of 1999, a sabbatical leave at Monash University will enable me to explore the PEEL project first hand in Australian classrooms. My challenge is to extract the principles from this year's experiences so that I may enact them more fully with the next group of preservice science teachers. After 20 years it is finally clear: teacher education can only walk its talk when it makes pedagogy its central focus.

The Curtain Falls for the Interval

We expect our pedagogical conversations to continue for some time. We continued to write through the last nine classes in Tom's course in the Winter Term, and we will resume our conversations about teaching when Shawn returns to the classroom in September, 1998. On 4 May 1998, Shawn resumed his undergraduate studies in physics at the University of Waterloo; he will be awarded the BSc degree from Waterloo and the BEd degree from Queen's in May 2000. On 28 May 1998, Tom was one of two faculty members presented with the Education Student Society's Golden Apple Award for Excellence in the Education of Preservice Teachers. This is the first time in 21 years that Tom's teaching has been recognized, and it is difficult for him not to attribute part of his success in the year's teaching to these ongoing conversations with Shawn.

So What?

This closing portion of our chapter might typically bear the heading of 'Conclusions'. In this instance, 'So What?' is consistent with our shared view that every teacher needs to pose this question at every possible opportunity. Brookfield (1995) is one of many who have noted how readily gaps can and do appear in teaching, between what teachers think they are doing and what learners see them doing: 'One of the hardest things teachers have to learn is that the sincerity of their intentions does not guarantee the purity of their practice' (p. 1). Perhaps it is only in this shared experience of supporting each other's efforts to study our professional knowledge as teachers that we more completely understand just how easy it can be for a teacher to lose a focus, misinterpret a response, or put one goal at risk by pursuing another.

We have used the following headings through Scenes 1 and 2 of Act I:

- A journal of experience
- Positive reinforcement and encouragement
- Issues are explored and revisited

- An exercise in metacognition
- Pedagogical sounding board
- More questions, deeper meanings
- Adding links to my map of teaching
- The road ahead

These headings worked well for both of us, and we will probably continue to research our teaching in terms such as these. These headings point more to the process than to the content of our research into our teaching, and they have worked well across two different teaching contexts. While our contexts are different, we are pleased to have confirmed that 'experience first', personal learning from experience, and metacognition help us see the similarities, particularly in terms of learning processes.

We are offering this shared study of two individuals' teaching as a contribution to a collection titled *Researching Teaching*. This provides the inspiration to ask what others may ask as they read this chapter: Is this research? and Is this real research? We believe it is, in terms of the following aspects of our professional knowledge:

- The personal accounts of our teaching, with each other's comments embedded, enable us to revisit our experiences and remind ourselves how we interpreted them at the time.
- We better understand our teaching and the responses of our students to our teaching.
- We better understand the pedagogical perspectives and values that we share, and we are encouraged to pursue them further to understand and enact them more fully.
- We better understand how we think about our teaching and about our professional learning as teachers.
- We realize more fully that powerful perspectives on teaching may take years to understand and develop in our teaching.
- We realize that a shared dialogue such as this involves risks and trust, trust in each other as well as the process to which we committed ourselves. We recommend such dialogue to others willing to take similar risks to overcome the invisible and private nature of most teaching and thinking about teaching.

When we began this research, we put our faith in a process with little sense of the possible outcomes. The risk of unknown outcomes is inherent in all research, just as it is inherent in teaching. While many of the details of our teaching may be unique to our personal classrooms, we are pleased to have discussed both the science classroom and the science teacher education classroom in one piece of research. We will be pleased if others interested in 'experience first' teaching approaches that value personal learning from experience find meaning for their own science or teacher education classrooms. The process we have followed is one that we have tried to illustrate as openly as we revealed the content of our discussions. We both find strong meaning in saying that how we teach *is* the message that we want our students to hear. As we conclude this account of our study of our teaching, we hope that readers will understand us when we say that how we research teaching is also the message.

References

BAIRD, J.R. and MITCHELL, I.J. (eds) (1986) *Improving the Quality of Teaching and Learning*, Melbourne: Monash University Printery.

BAIRD, J.R. and NORTHFIELD, J.R. (eds) (1992) *Learning from the PEEL Experience*, Melbourne: Monash University Printery.

BARNES, D. (1976) *From Communication to Curriculum*, Harmondsworth: Penguin.

BROOKFIELD, S.D. (1995) *Becoming a Critically Reflective Teacher*, San Francisco: Jossey-Bass.

OLSON, D.R. (1974) 'Mass media vs. schoolmen: The role of the means of instruction in the attainment of educational goals', *Interchange*, **5**, 2, pp. 11–17.

RUSSELL, T. (1997) 'Teaching teachers: How I teach IS the message', in LOUGHRAN, J. and RUSSELL, T. (eds) *Teaching about Teaching: Purpose, Passion and Pedagogy in Teacher Education*, pp. 32–47, London: Falmer Press.

SCHÖN, D.A. (1983) *The Reflective Practitioner: How Professionals Think in Action*, New York: Basic Books.

WHITE, R.T. and GUNSTONE, R.F. (1992) *Probing Understanding*, London: Falmer Press.

Section Three

Researching Teaching through Context

9 Teachers' Subject Subcultures and Curriculum Innovation: The Example of Technology Education

Alister Jones

Introduction

This chapter explores curriculum innovation in the context of the developing area of technology education and examines the ways in which teachers' subject subcultures influences the successful uptake of this innovation. The chapter begins by exploring teachers' perceptions of technology and technology education and then considers how these perceptions influence the subsequent implementation in the classroom. The data for this chapter arises from research undertaken before the full implementation of the curriculum but reports the findings from studies where teachers have been involved in some substantial professional development. The chapter will reveal how teachers' perceptions and concepts can be explored and how they are reflected in classroom practice.

The opportunity to explore the introduction of technology education into New Zealand schools arose due to the release of the national technology curriculum in draft form in 1993 and the final version in 1995 (*Technology in the New Zealand Curriculum*, Ministry of Education, 1995). The introduction of this curriculum was part of the major curriculum reforms in the early 1990s (Bell, Jones and Carr, 1995). These reforms were determined by the New Zealand Curriculum Framework (Ministry of Education, 1993), which provided an overarching framework for the development of curricula in New Zealand and which defined seven broad essential learning areas rather than subject areas. One of these learning areas was technology. Although New Zealand has a long history of technical education in the senior primary and secondary school, a framework for technology education for *all* students had only recently been developed (Jones and Carr, 1993). The technology curriculum had the general aims of developing students' technological knowledge and understanding; their technological capability; and their awareness of the interrelationship between technology and society. These aims were to be developed through the technological areas of: materials technology; information and communication technology; production and process technology, electronics and control technology; biotechnology; structures and mechanisms; and food technology.

Teachers' concepts and practices have shown strong links with the initiation and the socialization of teachers into subject subcultural settings (Ball and Goodson,

1985; Goodson, 1985). Teachers, therefore, have a subjective view of the practice of teaching within their concept of a subject area (Goodson, 1985). This is often referred to as a subject subculture, and leads to a consensual view about the nature of the subject, the way it should be taught, the role of the teacher, and what might be expected of the student (Paechter, 1991). Given the lack of a technology subject subculture in New Zealand, other subjects subcultural impact on technological classroom practice becomes very complex. There are a multitude of subcultures impacting on technology education in a variety of ways, as dependent on the teachers' subject backgrounds, concepts of technology, and their concepts of learning and teaching both within technology and generally. Paechter (1991) also points out that the teachers' beliefs about what was important for students to learn in their existing subject were transferred to technology education. Since technology is a new curriculum area, teachers' awareness of their own conceptualizations of technology as a learning area are limited (Jones and Carr, 1992).

This chapter will explore these subcultures and consider how they influence the development of a new knowledge area for teachers. The next part of the chapter considers exploring teachers' perceptions of technology and subsequently considers how these perceptions, even after intensive professional development, impact on classroom practice and learning outcomes.

Exploring Teachers' Perception of Technology Prior to the Curriculum

A total of 30 teachers (16 primary and 14 secondary) were interviewed from three schools, one primary, one intermediate and one secondary school. These teachers ranged in experience, level of responsibility and, particularly in the secondary school, subject specialities. The teachers were interviewed individually and the interviews, which were audio-taped, lasted between 15 to 45 minutes. These interviews were transcribed and analysed.

A schedule of the areas to be explored was prepared but the interviews were a free ranging discussion. To put the teachers' comments in perspective they were first asked about their career history and then their initial response when they heard about technology education. The questions then explored what technology education meant at a school and individual subject level. Later in the interview they were asked about the contribution of existing practice to technology education, how they saw technology fitting into a school program and the management of this subject. The interviews also explored what students should be learning and how a subject like technology education should be taught.

The following analysis first considers secondary school teachers since their subject orientation was revealed to be a major influence on their perception of technology education. Next, primary teachers perceptions are analysed, and, finally, the influence of interests and past experiences of both primary and secondary teachers are described. Many teachers used their past experiences in and out of school to construct a perception of technology education.

Secondary Teachers' Perceptions of Technology Education

Secondary teachers talked about technology in terms of the subjects that they taught. They interpreted technology education in terms of their subject area or in terms of the discipline that they were trained in. Included in these perceptions were teachers' views about what should be taught in technology, what students should learn, and the place of technology education in the school. When teachers were asked what they thought students should be learning in technology education the reply was often in terms of their existing subject areas.

All the *science* teachers who were interviewed saw technology education in terms of applications of science. In terms of teaching, technology was perceived to be a vehicle for teaching science and often something extra to the conceptual development in science. There was concern expressed about non-science teachers incorporating the scientific aspects of technology into their lessons. All five science teachers made similar comments:

> It [technology] would fit best in science . . . it depends what aspects of technology you are going to explore and what for . . . I try to [fit it in] as an application. If it is from a sociological point of view it is better to explore it in social studies . . . but from the scientific aspect it would be better through science rather than having social studies teachers trying to teach the science of technology. (Science teacher)

Social studies teachers emphasized the social aspects of technology particularly in terms of awareness and the human aspects of technology. They wanted students to develop skills to cope with life in the future and to become aware of technology so that they could cope with future changes:

> The purpose of education in technology is the skills which are necessary for students to take their place in a technological society. To give them the understanding necessary to use and not abuse technology and a technological approach to life. (Social Studies teacher)

English teachers associated technology education with media studies, techniques used in journalism and drama:

> . . . students learn a lot about organization, leadership, creativity, group skills, show originality and the satisfaction of seeing something completed, entrepreneurial skills . . . they tend to have a lot dished out to them, they expect handouts, they expect other people to do the work. Doing drama really teaches things about problem solving, the kids have got to find an audience, find a market, got to advertise . . . how much to charge them . . . designing and creating props. (English teacher)

The *accounting* teacher talked about students learning in technology education in terms of using computers and awareness of technology in our lives. While *economics* teachers emphasized concepts related to resources.

> In terms of my own subject it would be in terms of computer aided accounting. (Accounting teacher)

> Economics is concerned with resources and how technology might improve those resources. (Economics teacher)

Technical teachers at the secondary school had a broader view of technology which was influenced by their experience of the subject at the national level. The emphasis of the technical teachers at the secondary school were in terms of 'design and make' and using a variety of skills to realise practical outcomes.

> Students should learn how things work and operate, how materials behave some this way [some that way] and how you see tools to shape things to make things and eventually come out with some practical outcome. There is knowledge, there is designing and there is some practical outcome. (Technical teacher)

From the above quotes it can be seen that at the secondary school level the subjects that are taught by the teachers influence what they think technology education is about and what the students should be learning. These subject subcultures also influence the teacher in thinking about what the students might already be capable of in terms of technology. The teachers in the secondary school also lacked knowledge about what is taught in other subject areas that might contribute to technology education. In many of the discussions the teachers were concerned that the aspects of technology education that were already being taught in their subject areas might be removed when this new subject called technology was introduced. No one teacher had a broad view of technology education and their view was restricted to the subject within which they teach and within which they trained.

It became apparent that many of the secondary school teachers felt that, in terms of their current perceptions of technology education, they were already incorporating technology in their subjects. This was particularly true of the social studies and technical teachers. Science teachers, while not necessarily incorporating as much technology as they liked, nevertheless thought that technology was being covered in science:

> If technology education came in as a subject it would be interesting to see which departmental umbrella it came under — let's say technical departments, their teaching techniques tend to very different from other classroom teachers — we would probably just remove it from our course and let them teach it . . . we are already doing technology in a number of different subjects now . . . we already have design and make in schools now. (Social Studies teacher)

Primary Teachers' Perceptions of Technology Education

The primary teachers were not locked into their subject subcultures, although they were influenced by their past experiences, both in and out of teaching.

In both the primary and the intermediate[1] school, teachers were trying to integrate computers into their classroom. In the primary school there was one computer per class and at the intermediate school there were computers in a resource area. For many of the teachers at the primary and intermediate school they viewed technology in terms of computers. This meant using computers or other technology to solve problems. Although they might be aware of the range of technology, they tended to focus on computing. For example, as stated by one teacher, *not using pen or paper but using computers to solve problems*. Many intermediate teachers saw technology education as students using technology as part of their learning experiences and this was, in the main, using computers:

> We use technology across the curriculum for example some of the maths that we do can be done on the computer or on calculators. So technology is coming into the maths program. Word Processors are coming into language. (Primary teacher)

Another aspect of technology education mentioned by the teachers was for the students to find out how things work. Teachers also mentioned problem solving in relation to finding out how things work. 'Using examples of technology as a way of finding out how things work.' (Primary teacher). Technology is seen as a mechanism for solving a problem or as a vehicle for approaching a particular type of problem solving, that is, finding out how things work.

A group of teachers who did not emphasize computers in their perceptions of technology education emphasized the links between science and technology. Technology was seen to be closely linked to science and the teachers were trying to make the science courses more relevant by including technology. Some of these teachers had attended courses which emphasized this approach:

> Technology would be a more practical way of teaching science, more things to aid them, more equipment ... maybe children would work in a more individual way ... Technology is about science they go together. Technology is the practical awareness or help with science — make things to understand science things. Technology goes along with science. Children are interested in how things work ... it would involve using various apparatus or going into more depth in their own way. Children in this school have very enquiring minds and want to find out how things work. (Primary teacher)

Although teachers in the primary schools teach a range of subjects they appear to take a special interest in particular areas. This is apparent when one group of teachers place an emphasis on computers and technology education while others talk about the close relationship between science and technology. Many primary school teachers also placed importance on students being aware of technology and being confident with it. This was mainly in terms of new technology and computers.

> The closer we can relate school, home and the needs of society the better and we often do that through technology. It's keeping up with technology and making children familiar with them and not afraid of them. (Primary teacher)

Primary school teachers were generally positive about the introduction of technology, even though they had different perceptions of what it might be. They emphasized ownership, improved learning, student interest and flexibility as important factors in considering the uptake of technology education.

> A technology national curriculum subject would provide us with a challenge if we were allowed to integrate it into our program. We must be allowed to develop ownership of it. (Primary teacher)

> We are willing to try things . . . if it makes learning more exciting and children learn more then it has to be a good thing. (Primary teacher)

> I would look forward to technology because it would open up a new approach — for me that would be quite interesting. The children would be interested in that. It is always interesting to try something new — it would be refreshing for some of these children. The more able, creative students. (Primary teacher)

Some teachers may not be aware that they have already introduced aspects of technology into their existing teaching and learning programs. One teacher was asked about some children's work which was displayed on the wall, he comments:

> . . . so it [technology] might include something like we are trying to do to construct bridges and see what they come up with — I never thought of it as technology education just thought of it as problem-solving. We do that sort of thing all the time, I would never have thought of it as technology . . . I want them to learn to explore and try — I want them to experience failure so that they can experience success and have another go. I want them to use their imagination — will this thing work and then why. (Primary teacher)

Influence of Past Experiences on Teachers' Perceptions

Teachers' perceptions of technology education were closely linked with their life experiences. For example, music has moved towards the use of electronics and computing and this influenced two teachers. Both were music teachers in the primary school. As one of the teachers stated:

> I am involved in technology when doing my music. When I think of music I think of computers, drum machines . . . I mainly use the 'hi-tech' end in my teaching. Children doing programming on the drum machine, using recording equipment. (Primary teacher)

Another primary school teacher felt that there was a strong link between science and technology, finding out how things work and applications of science. The following extract illustrates why she links science and technology:

> I guess I see technology as using equipment and so forth in science . . . my partner is trained in science but he is often talked about as a technologist. My children are

doing physics and chemistry and there appears to be a lot of technology in those subjects . . . how things work. (Primary teacher)

Technology, for the teacher in charge of the library, was using computers to retrieve information and this tended to dominate her thinking about technology education in schools. As she says:

Everything is technology in terms of helping us . . . to help everybody . . . technology to help in learning . . . moving learning to, e.g. the library we hope to have all resources on the computer; e.g. searching for something on Vikings. (Primary teacher)

Teachers who had invested time into developing computer awareness and integrating computers into their classroom focused on information technology:

I think we are already doing a lot of technology education in schools like using computers and hypercard and I think we are using technology for problem-solving and for children to work cooperatively together. (Primary teacher)

The Influence of Preservice Teacher Education

Courses and activities undertaken during teacher training had an influence on perceptions of technology education. During training there was a course called educational technology which consisted of learning about technology used for teaching. This obviously influenced some to think about technology as being the use of technical equipment.

I did a course in educational technology such as videos and OHPs. (Secondary teacher)

For other teachers, the approach to the teaching and learning of science influenced how they viewed technology education and its close relationship to science.

One thing was the interactive science that I did at [Teachers'] college . . . we had to go to the school and do batteries and bulbs and it was electricity and I knew nothing about electricity and all I knew about science was that I loathed it at high school. Students had to find out solutions to real problems using batteries and bulbs . . . I guess that was technology . . . we went into the interactive science I realized it wasn't just science it was a whole way of thinking and doing. (Primary teacher)

The Influence of Inservice Education

In talking about how they developed their views of technology education, several teachers mentioned courses that they had attended which they perceived to have a technological focus:

> I've been on a course . . . That is technology — the use of science to solve prob-
> lems around you. The course also promoted technology in school, particularly
> electricity with the junior classes. You could only justify its use in terms of a
> teaching tool. (Science teacher)

Extended professional development programs also influenced teachers in their
perceptions of technology education. Some science teachers used technology as an
extension for more able students and had attended courses which emphasized this
approach. They were working with more able students and developing accelerated
courses with an emphasis on the applications of science. This then led to a view of
technology education as being for the more able science student and technology
being the applications of science.

Some teachers, particularly at the intermediate school, had attended courses
such as educational computing and they saw this as being technology education.
Some more senior teachers had taken courses in educational administration where
one of the emphases had been on using computers to solve administrative problems, such as using spread sheets for school accounting procedures.

The Influence of Being a Beginning Teacher

Beginning teachers were trying to come to terms with the subject areas they were
concerned with, and issues like technology education were seen as an extra.

> . . . basically in my first three years of teaching I have been trying to get everything
> together and tend to concentrate on the basics and then will start adding techno-
> logy into it. (Secondary teacher)

> I am just coping with the content areas of my subjects . . . I guess technology
> education is about awareness of computers — keeping up to date with computers
> and different apparatus. (Secondary teacher)

The Influence of National Association Involvement

Two teachers had been involved in their subject associations at the national
level, particularly at the policy decision-making level. These were both 'technical
teachers' and they appeared to have a broader view of technology education. They
had also had a chance to hear more about what the Ministry of Education was
thinking about technology education and they had both read widely about what was
happening in other countries.

> I am on the national executive . . . I have read a lot of information about what is
> happening in Britain. I don't think much of the British model — from what I can
> gather it is not as practically orientated as it is [here]. (Secondary teacher)

The Influence of Previous Work Experience

Not all teachers had taken the direct route to teaching. Some teachers had had careers outside of teaching. The use of technology in those careers influenced those teachers' perceptions of technology education. One teacher had been a secretary before returning to university and undertaking teacher training. In her view technology education was to use equipment such as word processors to make life easier:

> I guess I think of it as using computers and equipment to make the job easier. Like, for example, in offices now word processors are part of life and we should be making students aware of that. (Secondary teacher)

Another teacher associated technology with the 'hi-tech' that she had seen when she worked as an administrator in industry. When talking about technology she emphasized this and suggested that technology should be undertaken at polytechnics.

> The place for advanced technology studies is probably at the Polytech where there is money and resources — there is already an accepted relationship between education and the community. Schools struggle with the day-to-day running. We would have to have a major revolution in the school we run and management to really make it effective. (Secondary teacher)

A science teacher was influenced by his past career as an engineer and a career in sales. When he was a sales manager he was concerned with learning about the specifications and scientific theory behind the technology. His perceptions of technology education were dominated by applications of science to technology. He perceived technology as using difficult scientific concepts and hence these might not be accessible to the students. His views of technology education were also influenced by the constraints he saw himself working under in the classroom. Two teachers who had previously worked as research scientists were also concerned about the difficult scientific concepts involved in technology. They also linked technology with the applications of science.

> Some of the science concepts in the technology you are investigating can be quite complicated. Bringing it down to the level of the students can be a problem. (Secondary teacher)

A techni-craft teacher at the intermediate school was influenced by his career as a joiner and felt that it was important for students to be taught skills in woodwork. Throughout the interview he emphasized how important skills were in his past career.

> I want to stress the importance of manual skills — I see our job as being to teach the basic manual skills. I don't know what all the fuss is about. It has always been there and the skills I need I teach them. I now have had 40 years in the trade. Need to be 85 per cent skills how to use machines . . . no sitting down or writing — its all manual work. (Primary teacher)

Teachers have a range of perceptions of technology education and these have been influenced by their interests, experiences in both teaching and outside teaching, courses they have attended, their attitude to change and the stage they are at in their teaching career.

Discussion

Subject subcultures were found to be consistent and were a strong influence on secondary school teachers' perceptions of technology education. Science teachers emphasized applications, social studies teachers focused on societal aspects, English teachers on journalism, media studies and drama, accounting and economics teachers mentioned computing and resources, transition concentrated on computing, and technical teachers focused on skills, designing and making. While each of these subject areas contributes to technology, no one teacher had a broad view of technology education.

In the primary schools the subject subcultures did not appear to be as strong, although it did emerge in some of the teachers' comments. There was an emphasis in the school on problem-solving and many of the teachers talked about technology education as using technology, particularly computers, to solve these problems. Those teachers with a special interest in science emphasized science and technology. The science specialist saw technology as a vehicle to teach science or the applications and this view was written into the school schemes. The societal aspects of technology were mentioned by teachers in terms of making students comfortable with technology and awareness. In the intermediate school technical teachers felt threatened that other teachers in the school would become qualified in their area. They felt that what they were already doing was technology. It became apparent that because teachers had a narrow view of technology they may not be aware of the technology that was already in their teaching programs.

Teachers' perceptions of technology education were influenced by their past experiences both in and out of school. Interests in music, computing, and home have all contributed to teachers' views of what technology education might be. Teachers who were beginning their teaching career were concentrating on 'survival' and coming to terms with what they had to teach, and technology was seen as an extra. Those teachers who had worked outside of teaching were influenced by these past careers and tended to focus on 'hi-tech' as being the highly visible technology. Where the technology was in terms of construction the focus of the teacher was on manual skills. Those teachers who had been involved in some form of long-term teacher development program felt confident about the introduction of technology education, although this was often in terms of science and technology. Interactive teaching has had a big influence on teachers' confidence to tackle new subject areas such as technology.

Those teachers who have developed interactive teaching approaches in their classroom felt they had learnt science through an interactive approach and saw technology no differently. The teachers thought they would be learning with the children in this new area. The teachers who had adopted a more interactive approach in their classroom could also be seen as being innovative and therefore much more likely to try new areas if they felt it would enhance student learning. Although the teachers did not have a clear view of the knowledge base required for teaching technology they were confident enough in their pedagogical approaches to 'give it a go'.

In terms of teachers' views of the management of technology in schools, there are different issues depending on the level of schooling. For example, at the secondary school level there are problems in terms of developing a cross-curricular approach which teachers at the junior school level appeared to favour. At the intermediate school level, teachers teach a range of subjects, but problems arose in terms of trying to work in with the technical areas.

Some of the teachers interviewed could be termed as low-risk takers. They either had a narrow view of technology education, saw it as 'threatening', or 'felt they were already doing it'. Other teachers were challenged by what technology education might offer their subject area. Many of the less experienced teachers were just coming to terms with their subject area and either wanted to be told what to do or did not want anything to do with technology education. Particularly in the primary school — with all curriculum areas to teach as well as establishing classroom management approaches — a new subject area was seen as another burden. The teachers who might be classified as a high-risk takers were already doing innovative things in their classrooms, particularly at the primary school level. These teachers welcomed the challenge provided by technology education. They perceive technology education as an area worth developing and believed they had the skills to tackle a new area. Also their existing programs included aspects of technology education or used technology as a context for teaching other curriculum areas.

It is apparent from the interviews with teachers that there are a range of views about technology education and these views will influence the school development and implementation in the area of technology. A curriculum that is imposed that does not take account of the existing ideas of teachers and the realities of the school will become distorted in such a way as to threaten the improved learning that could take place. Already there is evidence, as the next section of this chapter will show, that teachers' different views of technology influence what occurs in the classroom even though they are working from a common curriculum document.

The Influence of Teachers' Subcultures on the Innovation

This next section of the chapter examines how subject subcultures and perceptions of technology and technology education influence the way in which the curriculum innovation is implemented in the classroom. Twenty-seven classrooms were observed in the Learning in Technology Education Project (Jones, Mather and Carr, 1995). Overall the research was both quantitative and qualitative. The methods included recording and analysing: individual and group interviews with teachers and students (approximately 60 teachers and 700 students); planning meetings, and; classroom observation, including fieldnotes (28 classes).

Also reported here are some of the research findings from two other projects which involved five primary teachers (Moreland, 1998) and seven science teachers (Northover, 1997). These teachers had had much more teacher professional development than the ones involved in the Learning in Technology Education Project. It could be argued with technology education becoming more established and with a national focus on technology teacher professional development that there would be some change in teacher perceptions and classroom implementation from 1993–94 to 1997.

In the Learning in Technology Education Research Project, it was found that the concepts of technology held by teachers had a significant affect on their planning of technological activities and their subsequent classroom strategies. For example, many secondary teachers, who considered that they were doing aspects of technology in their existing practice, often saw no need to change in any significant way — either their practice or their conceptualization. Change for these teachers was considered to require additions in order to meet the curriculum requirements. Some teachers commented in the interviews that reflecting on the technological activities and the discussions served to reinforce their initial concepts of technology. This conflicted with the researchers' perceptions that there appeared to be a change away from these initial concepts toward a concept more consistent with the curriculum.

> I don't think it's changed a whole lot, it's just probably strengthened a bit more, the ideas within it, I think I've set them a bit more firmly. Because my ideas really came from the courses that I've done up at varsity, mainly they were science courses. (Technology teacher)

Teachers also commented on the students' concepts of technology and expressed concern that they were often still quite far removed from their own, and those portrayed in the curriculum statement.

When students were carrying out technological activities, teachers often reverted to learning areas they were comfortable with as possible learning outcomes rather than technological outcomes. For example, they may emphasize discussion and debating skills rather than technological outcomes.

Teachers mentioned a certain level of 'expertise' as crucial to successful classroom practice in technology. What this referred to was difficult to ascertain, but it appeared that the suggestion was that teachers needed a combination of technological knowledge *and* a concept of technology education. The lack of such 'expertise' was reflected as problematic in the following comment:

> In the middle, I was lost, I did not know how to guide them, the start was good and the end was fine. (Technology teacher)

The tasks that were introduced in all of the classrooms were considered to be 'good' technological activities, in that lent themselves to technological outcomes for the students. When identifying what learning was important the teachers often emphasized learning in areas other than technology. Therefore, in looking for evidence the teachers focused on those aspects they were traditionally comfortable with, such as discussion and group skills:

> The initial ideas of what is technology and that stuff that we did with the brainstorming, I thought that went really well . . . at the end I felt as though it was a bit chopped off, like it sort of finished, luckily we had the debate. (Technology teacher)

Those teachers who were comfortable with their concept of technology but felt they lacked an understanding of technological knowledge and processes, often felt 'lost' in the middle of the activity. The beginning and end of the activity were primarily concerned with language and research-based skills that were undertaken in a technological context, and thus were seen as unproblematic as they fell within their area of 'expertise'. This situation was noticed in many of the classrooms involved in this research.

An alternative situation was evident in other classrooms where teachers had a sound technological knowledge base, but a narrow concept of technology education. This resulted in classroom activities emphasizing a design process without links to issues inherent in the technological knowledge, and technology and society, strands of the draft curriculum statement. This was also evident from the comments made by teachers when discussing their concepts of technology and technology education.

> I think at the same time we have to be careful we don't force the issue — stretching it to bring in society. (Technology teacher)

In other classes, particularly in secondary social studies classes, the focus moved from solving the technological problem to the presentation of the background ideas. For the primary teachers much of the focus was on language skills, for example;

> . . . language goes through everything . . . (Technology teacher)

Possible learning outcomes identified by teachers in technological activities were influenced by their views of assessment, their expectations of the students and their views of learning. When students were carrying out technological activities teachers often reverted to learning areas they were comfortable with as possible learning outcomes rather than technological outcomes. For example, they may emphasize discussion and debating skills over technological outcomes.

Some teachers had a view of learning which allowed them to take the role of co-learner with the students, and they were prepared to take risks in implementing technology. These teachers reflected that there were some important factors that enabled them to be more willing to attempt to implement technology in their classrooms. These factors might be referred to as teaching characteristics and were described by the teachers as: taking responsibility for their own professional development; risk-taking; learner-centred approaches, including taking into account the needs and experiences of the students; being flexible and open-minded to new approaches; and having a positive attitude to change.

Teacher and student conceptualization of technology is a complex issue and requires an understanding of the many factors which influence it. Some factors the researchers noted as having a large impact on how willing teachers were to change their own concepts of what technology and technology education include: perceived need for change, background experience, subject subculture, level of support given to teachers during any change process, and personal disposition towards dealing with implications of these changes.

The strategies developed by the teachers in their classrooms when implementing technological activities were often positioned within that particular teacher's teaching and subject subculture. The subcultures had a direct influence on the way teachers structured the lessons and developed classroom strategies. Teachers developed strategies to allow for learning outcomes which were often more closely related to their particular subject subculture than to technological outcomes. Teachers entering areas of uncertainty in their planned activities often reverted to their traditional teaching and subject subculture.

The teachers' technology and technology education concepts, which could not be reinforced through any type of technological experience, appeared to be somewhat fragile and transient in nature. This resulted in classroom practice often reverting toward a previous conceptualization, which was in turn reflected in subsequent classroom practice. The extent to which this occurred was largely determined by the level of comfort teachers felt with the concepts of technology developed during the intervention process, and the teachers were often unaware of a change/reversion. Other influences on the teachers' conceptualization and practice included: subject subculture: views of teaching and learning; other life experiences, and; aspects of their social positioning, e.g. school culture, background experience, constructions of gender, etc.

Teachers are positioned within a particular social environment which comes complete with community expectation of their practice. These can include views of learning environments, expectations of artefacts to be taken home, and value being placed on books full of notes. These, along with teachers' own expectations of their students' characteristics, ability, and prior experience, impact on the classroom strategies. For example, activities in the middle school were changed so that students could include project type reports, or were given science notes, to satisfy outside demands.

Students' concepts of technology and technological activities also appeared to influence teachers' classroom practice. For example, if a student's initial concepts of technology and technology education were inclusive of those underlying the technology unit, there appeared to be a significant level of reinforcement of the student's initial concepts due to participation in the unit. The student's technological practice in this case appeared to directly reflect their concept. If, however, the student's initial concepts of technology and technology education were significantly different to that on which the technology unit was based, there appeared to be little change in the student's initial concepts. Instead, initial concepts appeared to constrain the student's activity, or, alternatively, led the student to perceive their activity to be non-technological. The student's concepts would therefore appear to have more impact on the student's technological practice than the teaching strategies employed in the technological unit. Although the teachers had developed technology units more focused on concepts of technology as underlying the technology curriculum statement (Jones, Mather and Carr, 1995), student activity appeared no different from previous trials where this was not the case. This was further complicated by the teacher's own limitations in sustaining the planned technology unit, whereby the students' technological practice and narrower concepts of technology began to affect the teachers' own concepts of technology education. It was found that where a teacher's concepts of technology were somewhat fragile the students' concepts of technology appeared to dominate the learning outcomes e.g. including robotic arms or flashing eyes to make it more technological.

The outcomes from this research (Jones, Mather and Carr, 1995) led to a teacher development model which emphasized the importance of teachers developing an understanding of technology education and technological practice. In the previously discussed research, the teachers had had some professional development but not as intensive as that which was delivered in 1996 and 1997. The following discussion explores the results of two studies which examined teachers' classroom practice after involvement in a year-long program (Northover, 1997; Moreland, 1998).

Moreland (1998) reports that although the teachers stated that they needed to learn more about the teaching of technology, they felt they had enough skills and understanding to be teaching technology and could do it in the classroom. One teacher with a strength in science set the students applied science tasks (design a hot air balloon then study flight). Technological principles were not involved. The criteria were in terms of why things happened and a narrow focus of outcomes. For nearly all the other teachers they looked for language outcomes and social skills, not technological outcomes. These same concepts were reflected in the teachers' assessment practices where they concentrated on students' ability to be cooperative, to make decisions, to create a solution to problems, and to work from a design brief. The teachers' assessment procedures related more to their existing subcultures rather than assessment in technology.

Northover (1997) noted that all the teachers she worked with viewed technology as being applied science, skills and skill development. The teachers went for minimal change and added technology into existing programs rather than developing new ones. She found that these teachers generally expressed an interest in technology education and commented on the motivational aspects of technological activities. Teachers often saw changes in perceptions they held of technology and technology education as a means of better understanding the curriculum document, but did not see the importance of the development of a coherent technological knowledge base to their own learning and teaching practice. The dominant science subculture in schools proved to be a powerful conservative influence and teachers who evidenced a changed view of technology and biotechnology, by the end had often reverted to the perspective initially held. In fact, where teachers did make changes to their perceptions initially the cognitive dissonance set up by the disparity between their views and their practice was often resolved by reverting to a previously held view.

Conclusion

The strategies developed by the teachers in their classrooms when implementing technological activities were often positioned within that particular teacher's teaching and subject subculture. These subcultures are consistent and often strongly held. The subcultures had a direct influence on the way teachers structured the lessons and developed classroom strategies. Teachers developed strategies to allow for learning outcomes that were often more closely related to their particular subject subculture than to technological outcomes, e.g. science and language. Teachers entering areas of uncertainty in their planned activities often reverted to their traditional teaching and subject subculture. Possible learning outcomes identified by teachers in technological activities were influenced by their views of assessment, their expectations of the students and their views of learning. When students were carrying out technological activities, teachers often reverted to learning areas they were comfortable with for identifying possible learning outcomes rather than technological outcomes. For example, they may emphasize discussion and debating skills over technological outcomes. Even those teachers who were confident and competent in their pedagogical approaches in the classroom had difficulty in introducing a new curriculum area where they did not have a strong pedagogical content knowledge base.

This chapter has identified the difficult nature of teacher change, the powerful influence of teaching subcultures, and suggests that innovation takes time and ownership. The chapter suggests that teachers need to develop technological knowledge and an understanding of technological practice, as well as concepts of technology and technology education, if they are to become effective in the teaching of technology. This then illustrates the importance that teachers' professional knowledge must include a strong knowledge base in the relevant curriculum area. It is not enough to just have a strong pedagogical knowledge base. This has major implications for preservice and inservice courses. Teacher content knowledge is vital if appropriate classroom practice and student learning in particular knowledge areas is to occur. Jones and Compton (1998) and Compton and Jones (in press) show how these knowledge bases can be developed with teachers and how crucial they are for implementing a new curriculum area. However, although we have some insight to how these knowledge bases can be developed, the research evidence to date suggests that this will take a substantial period of time to become established in classroom practice.

Note

1   In the analysis they are classified as primary teachers.

References

BALL, S.J. and GOODSON, I.F. (1985) *Understanding Teachers: Concepts and Contexts*, in BALL, S.J. and GOODSON, I.F. (eds) *Teachers' Lives and Careers*, London: Falmer Press.

BELL, B., JONES, A. and CARR, M. (1995) 'The development of the recent national New Zealand science curriculum', *Studies in Science Education*, **26**, pp. 73–105.

COMPTON, A. and JONES, A. (in press) 'Reflecting on teacher development in technology education: Implications for future programs', *International Journal of Technology and Design Education*.

GOODSON, I.F. (1985) 'Subjects for study', in GOODSON, I.F. (ed.) *Social Histories of the Secondary Curriculum*, London: Falmer Press.

JONES, A. and CARR, M. (1992) 'Teachers' perceptions of technology education — implications for curriculum innovation', *Research in Science Education*, **22**, pp. 230–9.

JONES, A. and CARR, M. (1993) *Towards Technology Education*, p. 145, Centre for Science and Mathematics Education Research, University of Waikato.

JONES, A. and COMPTON, V. (1998) 'Towards a model of teacher development in technology education', *International Journal of Technology and Design Education*, **8**, 1, pp. 51–65.

JONES, A.T., MATHER, V. and CARR, M.D. (1995) *Issues in the Practice of Technology Education*, p. 125, Centre for Science and Mathematics Education Research, University of Waikato.

MINISTRY OF EDUCATION (1993) *New Zealand Curriculum Framework*, Wellington: Learning Media.

MINISTRY OF EDUCATION (1995) *Technology in the New Zealand Curriculum*, Wellington: Learning Media.

MORELAND, J.P. (1998) 'Technology education teacher development: The importance of experiences in technological practice', Unpublished MEd thesis, University of Waikato.

NORTHOVER, B.A. (1997) 'Teacher development in biotechnology: Teachers' perceptions and practice', Unpublished MEd thesis, University of Waikato.

PAECHTER, C. (1991) 'Subcultural retreat: Negotiating the Design and Technology Curriculum', Paper presented to the British Educational Research Association Annual Conference.

10   The Impact of Teaching Experiences on Student-teachers' and Beginning Teachers' Conceptions of Teaching and Learning Science

Helmut Fischler

Background

The recent growth in knowledge pertaining to the conditions associated with students' learning of scientific topics can really only influence teaching if teachers make this knowledge an explicit part of their thinking about, and actions in, teaching. This chapter examines some of the outcomes from researching learning about teaching science and acknowledges the inherent difficulties that student-teachers and beginning teachers face as the pressure to adjust to a full-time teaching allotment influences (and perhaps represses) the learning about teaching that was so crucial in their teacher education program.

Research findings about Learning Processes in Teacher Education

Understanding student-teachers' subject-related pedagogical competency is an important foundation stone in teacher education. This competency includes student-teachers' ability to plan teaching experiences that take into account their students' interests and ways of learning and should be followed up — after teaching the lesson(s) — by an evaluation of the resultant teaching and learning. Obviously, then, the preconditions and processes of learning, as well as the concepts and likely areas of interest related to the subject specific topics, is similarly important in the planning and teaching of lessons. Therefore, it is a central component of subject-related pedagogical education to convey the knowledge about subject-specific conditions of learning and to guide student-teachers in their lesson planning in ways that remind them of these preconditions of learning and teaching.

From research on learning processes in all branches of science education, an emerging dominant view is one that regards learning as a process of knowledge construction based on and extending existing knowledge. This comprises two aspects: first, the importance of the learner's own activities, and secondly, the significance of one's existing knowledge (Driver, 1988, 1989a). From early investigations of students' conceptions in physics (Jung, 1978), recognition of learning impediments has been important. Everyday conceptions of physics terms and phenomena are usually very different from scientific views and their effects on learners' thoughts and actions renders it more difficult for learners to take on the 'scientific' conceptions.

The existence of students' stable conceptions have been well noted (Duit, 1993) and according to Jung (1986), the following approaches to teaching are possible:

- initiating teaching with experiences of everyday understanding does not contrast with the scientific conceptions;
- contrasting everyday conceptions with scientific ideas; and,
- helping the students to rethink their conceptions towards a physics understanding.

While the method of confrontation aims to breach everyday conceptions, the strategies of 'linking up' and 'rethinking' are used in an attempt to find a continuous transition from everyday conceptions to the scientific. In early discussions about the likelihood of changing everyday conceptions (conceptual change, see Duit, 1995) the confrontational strategy in which a cognitive conflict is used to motivate students was regarded as being most effective (Posner, Strike, Hewson and Gertzog, 1982; Hewson and Hewson, 1988a). Concrete proposals for teaching units that consequently took into account students' conceptions, also drew on this instructional principle (Nussbaum and Novick, 1982; Champagne, Gunstone and Klopfer, 1985a, 1985b; Driver, 1988, 1989b). Meanwhile reflections on conceptual change have developed further in the direction of continuous transition (Stavy, 1991) and the use of analogies has also become important in this context (Duit, 1991).

Investigations of teaching and learning processes based on constructivist views, reveal claims of considerable impact while still raising some concerns about methodological problems (Wandersee, Mintzes and Novak, 1994). Positive findings exist in discontinuous teaching approaches as well as in conceptions approached via analogies. This is not surprising because teaching conceptions commonly contain similar instructional elements; teaching is not regarded as an arrangement of instructional strategies, but more a situation in which learning processes need to be recognized and supported. Clearly, then, this important knowledge base of teaching in science can create demands on the teachers as they need to:

- be sensitive to students' learning difficulties;
- be patient through the process of students' construction of new knowledge;
- take into account students' existing knowledge;
- create a classroom climate in which students are willing to express and discuss their ideas;
- create situations in which students can present their own opinions; and,
- accept a teaching role that is not so much that of communicator and examiner, but more as a person who advises and helps students to develop knowledge in science (Scott, Asoko and Driver, 1992).

In physics lessons, for example, the presentation of phenomena that are not immediately explained by the teacher offers opportunities for learning situations in which students can explore their own ideas using their existing knowledge (as well as that gained from their work in experimental investigations). In essence, these elements combine to make up that which I would describe as the subject-related pedagogical education that student-teachers should be exposed to in their learning about teaching and learning in physics. Obviously, researching teaching has been important in constructing this knowledge base and it needs to be acknowledged and called upon in teacher education programs.

Students' Conceptions and Teachers' Theories

Making the knowledge about science learning comprehensible and communicable in teacher education, though, creates problems similar to those described above in relation to science teaching. Student-teachers often begin their programs with fixed conceptions about teaching and learning, and, as a rule, are not usually willing to take on alternative conceptions unless they have experienced failure when using their own ideas. For example, Gunstone and Northfield (1986) see 'fundamental similarities in the requirements of achieving conceptual change in both groups'. Investigations of teachers' and student-teachers' conceptions about teaching and learning are embedded in a research paradigm, that, under the notion of 'Teachers' Thinking' aims at identifying teachers' cognitions in the context of teaching (Shavelson and Stern, 1981; Bromme and Brophy, 1986; Clark and Peterson, 1986; Borko and Shavelson, 1990). Using the construct 'Subjective Theories', German research literature demonstrates that cognitive aspects of teachers' behaviour are prevalent in this approach (Mandl and Huber, 1983; Groeben, Wahl, Schlee and Scheele, 1988). Nevertheless, the variety of different research activities comprises a wide spectrum of goals, methods and underlying theories. The restriction to teachers' thinking — for example, in the course of lesson planning (Bromme, 1981; Clark and Yinger, 1987) or in specific teaching situations (Crocker and Banfield, 1986) — is a part of this spectrum, as well as attempting to identify holistic views on the teaching process. The methods applied also reflect the breadth of positions held in psychological research — pre-structured questionnaires (Hewson and Hewson, 1987a) in contrast to more biographical and narrative methods (Elbaz, 1983; Butt, 1984).

Teachers' Conceptions and Their Behaviour:
Subject-related Findings

Compared to the mass of literature on 'Teachers' Thinking' the number of subject-related publications is relatively small. Unlike correspondent activities in mathematics (Heymann, 1982; Leinhardt and Greeno, 1986; Peterson, Fennema, Carpenter and Loef, 1989) investigations in natural science subjects only really began when attempts to integrate the growing knowledge about students' conceptions into programs of teacher education became problematic.

The few science-related investigations so far completed have focused on two groups of conceptions that are most likely to be relevant to aspects of teachers' cognitions in the teaching process:

- conceptions of the processes of scientific inquiry and of the status of the knowledge achieved (nature of science); and,
- conceptions of learning and teaching science.

Tests for identifying conceptions of the nature of science (Andersen, Harty and Samuel, 1986; Lederman, 1986; Koulaidis and Ogborn, 1989) exist, and investigations carried out using these tests demonstrate that some patterns do emerge. Findings that display attainments of an acceptable knowledge level are seldom (Carey and Stauss, 1970; Lederman, 1986); in fact most scores are such that researchers complain about students' and teachers' deficient knowledge about the nature of science. Conceptions prevail that describe the process of scientific inquiry as consisting mainly of experiments and inductive inferences. This view is close to that of naive empiricism and implicitly suggests that the task of natural science (and of science teaching) is to discover scientific laws as if they are independent of specific content.

Some findings concerning the influence of conceptions of the nature of science on teachers' ideas about teaching and learning suggest that teachers who assign a strict logic (determined by experiments) to the process of inquiry, hold specific conceptions of a systematic structure to be followed in the process of teaching and learning. 'It was not always the same students that held the view that the function of science is to "discover" the laws of nature, and the "knowledge intake" view of learning. . . . But many of these students showed an implicit connection between the two views' (Aguirre, Haggerty and Linder, 1990, p. 389).

The impact of teachers' conceptions of teaching and learning on their decision-making in teaching lessons has been identified with the help of questionnaires (Aguirre et al., 1990; Jonas, 1993; Huibregtse, Korthagen and Wubbels, 1994), and in other cases by a presentation of fictitious learning and teaching situations. The results of these investigations suggest that science learning in these cases relate to what the teacher presents, rather than that of a constructivist view. Aguirre et al. (1990) found that it was not uncommon for science teaching to be seen as planting appropriate topics into students' empty minds. In contrast to this, Huibregtse et al. (1994) found high scores for the category 'Physics teaching as facilitating knowledge construction' with physics teachers. It seems, then, that the common approach to teaching science is very teacher centred, such that in science lessons students are engaged in only a small part of all the activities which take place (Hage et al., 1985; Tobin and Gallagher, 1987).

Investigations into the relationship between teachers' intentions (stated by themselves) and their concrete actions show that it is problematic to imply that observed teaching practice reflects teachers' intentions. In many cases a significant discrepancy exists between teachers' stated intentions and decisions made during their lessons. This happens when teachers' student-oriented conceptions, under the perceived pressure of practice, are subdued by teacher-centred orientations in action. Rodriguez (1993) summarizes his observations as 'a disposition to act is not the same as acting on a disposition'. Beginning teachers also face enormous problems teaching according to their conceptions of teaching (Brickhouse and Bodner, 1992; Fischler, 1994). Experienced teachers are more successful in regard to this but, on the whole, also succumb to these pressures in classroom settings.

Modification of Teachers' Conceptions in Teacher Education

The majority of investigations noted in the previous section have identified conceptions of teaching and learning science which have very little in common with our knowledge of students' everyday conceptions and with the conclusions to be drawn from science teaching. The proposals for the modification of (student) teachers' conceptions towards a more 'constructivist' view suggests a need for instructional methods that are similar to the elements of constructivist-oriented science teaching (Fensham, 1987; Marion, Hewson, Tabachnick and Blomker, 1994; Parsons-Chatman, 1990). This means taking into consideration student-teachers' conceptions of teaching and learning and giving them the opportunity to construct new ideas in the light of their own experiences. Keiny (1994) points out that this conception of teacher education corresponds to the goals that Schön (1983, 1987, 1988) was striving for in the development of a teacher (or any professional) to be a 'reflective practitioner'. Therefore, many courses in teacher education seek a close connection to school practice situations (e.g. Baird, Fensham, Gunstone and White, 1991). Some authors regard this engagement as the most important way to evoke changes in student-teachers' conceptions as they reflect on concrete practical problems (Erickson and MacKinnon, 1991; MacKinnon and Erickson, 1988, 1992).

Investigations into the efficacy of courses that begin with student-teachers' existing conceptions report positive effects. Tobin and Fraser (1989) and Tobin (1990) focused on metaphors used for the description of teaching and learning science. By helping student-teachers to problematize these metaphors and to reflect on alternatives, they achieved a change. Tobin, Tippins and Gallard (1994) concluded that, 'The findings reviewed to this point suggest that significant changes in classroom practice are possible if teachers are assisted to understand their teaching roles in terms of new metaphors' (p. 59). Similarly, Hand and Treagust (1994) stated that teachers change their conceptions of teaching and learning when they begin to accept the value and the benefits of teaching that are oriented toward students' conceptions.

Stability and Change of Teachers' Conceptions in Teaching Practice

The teaching practicum is sometimes regarded as a didactical field for the construction of a theoretical awareness (Heimann, 1962); as a field for testing innovative teaching conceptions (Fichten, Jaeckel and Stinshoff, 1978); as a source of stimulation and as a motivation for further studies; as a place for the acquisition of practical knowledge, and; in general, as an appropriate place for 'professional growth' towards becoming a reflective teacher (Erickson and MacKinnon, 1991).

Subject-independent investigations into the influence of teaching experiences on teachers' conceptions have revealed some results on changes in teachers' attitudes in the course of their professional socialization (Koch, 1972). In general, investigations uncovered shifts to more student-centred attitudes during student-teachers' studies at university. This attitude then mostly changed again after the beginning of practical work/school placement (Koch, 1972).

Zeichner and Tabachnik (1981), after a detailed review of the literature, questioned the significance of the results of investigations done in the UK and the US which showed changes in student-teachers' attitudes and conceptions. They regarded students' statements as surface-effects and the observations as a confirmation of Lortie's (1975) argument that teachers' socialization happens through the thousands of lessons spent as students in schools themselves and therefore that they did not essentially change during their time in teacher education. Kagan (1992) also recently concluded, '. . . . preservice students enter programs of teacher education with personal beliefs about teaching images of good teachers, images of self as teacher, and memories of themselves as pupils in classrooms. These personal beliefs and images generally remain unchanged by a preservice program and follow candidates into classroom practica and student teaching' (p. 142). Bramald, Hardman and Lead (1994) used a questionnaire to identify the conceptions of teaching and learning held by 162 student-teachers during a postgraduate certificate in education course. The average scores on a seven-point scale with the poles 'pupil-centred' and 'teacher-centred' moved 'towards a more traditional approach'. This change was subject specific. Science was one of the subjects in which teachers' conceptions became more teacher centred.

Trends and Deficiencies

The investigation of student-teachers' and teachers' conceptions of teaching and learning in science are strongly influenced by the research knowledge of students' specific learning problems in science. Therefore, such investigations have the same subject-related features that are characteristic of research on students' conceptions. The connection between these research fields is established by the common interest in finding appropriate means of changing the identified conceptions. For students, aids to overcome the impediments of learning science are sought, for student-teachers research aims to give them knowledge of how they can achieve a conception of teaching in which students' learning problems in science play a significant role.

In Anglo-American countries a noticeable tradition of research on teachers' conceptions has been developed. Within this tradition, science as a subject is a considerable component because learning problems that result from the discrepancy between everyday and scientific knowledge barely plays a role in school subjects outside of science. The case-study is the prevailing research design therefore the results are very context related. But there are some themes that emerge in the findings:

- the majority of student-teachers hold conceptions of teaching and learning science that emphasize the methodically 'optimized' presentation of teaching topics to a greater extent than teachers' orientation toward students' learning problems;
- subject-related pedagogical courses in teacher education may lead to modifications of these conceptions if they take them as a starting point for corresponding efforts;
- student-teachers who hold conceptions of teaching and learning that are oriented toward students' learning processes are, in their teaching activities, guided by totally different orientations of action; and,
- there are no science specific results on the influence of field experiences on student-teachers' conceptions of teaching and learning. Investigations that comprise several subjects report on various outcomes.

The overview above demonstrates the importance of researching teaching in establishing a knowledge base of factors that influence learning about teaching in science. Obviously, although only briefly summarized in this chapter, such research into teaching is crucial in shaping our understanding of learning to teach (and teaching about teaching). With this in mind, I offer the following project into researching learning about teaching physics.

Researching Teaching and Learning in Physics

The main goal of this project was to investigate the impact of teaching experiences on conceptions of teaching and learning by student-teachers in physics. The focus of this research was on identifying these conceptions prior to, and after, the teaching phase of a teaching practicum. The following assertions influenced my approach to this research project:

- some student-teachers' orientation during teaching practicum changes toward teacher-centred principles based on the notion that a methodically well-arranged presentation of the topics is the main task of the teacher. For these student-teachers, their existing conceptions about teaching and learning are either suppressed during the time of the teaching practicum (and resurface after this phase) or are replaced by the conceptions developed in practice (and are not stated again after the practicum phase);
- some student-teachers, despite their subject-related pedagogical knowledge, have teacher-centred conceptions of teaching and learning which are reinforced during the practicum; and,
- the mentor and the coaching professor can influence these processes of suppression and modification in terms of their intensity but not their direction.

The examination of these assertions is important in helping to answer the following questions:

- Do learning-process related conceptions change during the practicum towards teacher-centred conceptions, or is it simply a temporary suspension of these conceptions? and, Which situations in lessons are responsible for processes of change or suppression?
- Do teacher-centred conceptions stabilize during the teaching practicum? and Which events are decisive in this confirmation?
- What influence do the mentor and the coaching professor have on these conceptions?

Program and Methods of the Investigation

Altogether 36 student-teachers and beginning teachers were interviewed and observed during the project. The design of this project differs from most comparable research approaches in which either only case-studies were carried out or, with a greater number of participants, only the identification of conceptions occurred without observations in practice. The general structure of the questioning and observation program comprised the following:

- Prior to the teaching practice: Identifying student-teachers' conceptions of teaching and learning.
- During the teaching phase: Video-recording of two lessons per student-teacher (with the presence of the mentor and the coaching professor).
- After the teaching phase: Questioning immediately on completion of the teaching practicum. Identifying the conceptions and addressing these in relation to the student-teacher's instructional behaviour.

For the beginning teachers, the research questions were modified because they did not start teaching without any practical background, but in principle, the three parts of the research program remained unchanged for the beginning teachers. However, the main questions referred to the relationship between their statements concerning their conceptions of teaching and learning on the one hand and their orientations for their actions in the classroom on the other.

Questioning and Data Gathering

The identification of conceptions about teaching and learning prior to the teaching phase was conducted about one week before each practicum. During the interviews, conceptions in the area of 'teaching and learning' were probed that, in preliminary investigations, proved to be relevant factors in physics teaching. These factors included: judgments about the role of students and teachers in the teaching process; ideas about the goals of physics teaching; views about what causes learning problems; reactions and opinions by teachers about philosophical foundations of physics; and their significance for physics teaching. The interview questions were constructed in a manner that would induce concrete answers because they referred to problematic statements on physics teaching and to teaching situations described or presented through the videotapes.

The collection of numerous data from the teaching phase was envisaged as helping to formulate a relationship between the modifications of conceptions which became visible in the student-teachers' statements after the teaching phase. Factors that could obviously influence the student-teachers during the practicum and needed to be considered and remembered during analysis included:

(a) In order to have at least a part of each student-teacher's practice available for the questioning after the practicum, two lessons by each student-teacher were video-recorded. Clearly, these experiences could influence student-teachers' understanding of these conceptions.

(b) The conversation between the student-teacher and the coaching professor that, as a rule, takes place directly after the lesson, uncovers both the student-teacher's main instructional principles as well as the coaching professor's conceptions about teaching and learning. This may also be the case if the mentor (school supervising teacher) is present. The audio-taping of these conversations therefore revealed important information about all participants' judgments concerning the teaching situation.

(c) The often intensive exchange of ideas between the student-teacher and the mentor was not open to observation for this project. The content and organizational framework for the lessons conducted by the student-teacher was set by the mentor. This is a legal requirement for the student-teacher placement. Obviously the identification of the mentors' conceptions would be important as it seems reasonable to assume that it would impact on teaching decisions made by the student-teachers.

Methods of Investigation

For identifying the complex conceptions about teaching and learning, structured interviews with mainly open questions and the presentation of problematic teaching sequences were used. The student-teachers are asked to react to these. The interview format was based on a combination of questions from various investigations (Hewson and Hewson, 1987b, 1988b, 1989; Aguirre et al., 1990; Statler, Stoddart and Niederhauser, 1994; Huibregtse et al., 1994). The selection of the questions was dependent on whether or not the expected responses were likely to reveal results about the following components of the field 'conceptions about teaching and learning':

(a) Tasks, contents and goals of physics teaching.
(b) Conceptions about the processes of students' physics learning.
(c) Ideas about suitable teaching methods in order to reach the goals striven for and the intended learning processes.
(d) Aspects of philosophy of science in the decisions concerning goals, topics and methods.

The subjects were confronted with problematic statements on teaching situations and asked to comment on, or propose solutions for, the situation. An example drawn from components (b) and (c) (above) is concretized in a way similar to that of Hewson and Hewson (1987b) such that, at the end of a lesson, the student-teacher is given a problematic situation in which the students responses to the teacher's questions demonstrate that the students did not learn anything about the essential terms which were introduced in the lesson. Therefore, the students' answers reflect that their everyday conceptions about the new terms are still effective. In the interview then, the student-teachers are asked how they would react to this situation in the next lesson, first with an open question and then with the presentation of several possibilities introduced in an order according to the student-teachers' preference.

In a procedure designed to summarize (a) to (d) in concrete teaching problems, participants were also asked to state the teaching principles that they regarded as essential to their teaching.

As has been noted by other researchers, Kelly's (1955) repertory grids are an appropriate tool for gaining information about the developmental process that leads to the identification of conceptions (Pope and Denicolo, 1993; Morine-Dershimer, 1993; Markham and Mintzes, 1994; Pope and Keen, 1981; Boei, Corporaal and van Hunen, 1989; Morine-Dershimer et al., 1992). Repertory grids support a constructivist view that is regarded as helpful not only for the investigation of students' conceptions (Whitelock, 1988), but also of teachers' conceptions, therefore it was used for this research project.

Kelly regards the perception and the understanding of reality as a construction process. In this context each person judges themselves, their environment, and the relationship between each. The repertory grid identifies the construct system that is a person's basis for perceiving a specific field of experience and for anticipating changes and developments within that field. 'Elements', as classes of similar events or things of special importance for the person, describe a section of reality. In the repertory grid technique, they are identified and linked with judgments concerning their similarity or difference. The criteria for this discrimination are called 'constructs'. Therefore, at the end of the procedure the researcher has a complete matrix of element–construct connections that can be evaluated by the application of different methods.

For the construction of the repertory grid as a research tool in this project, student-teachers' teaching principles served as elements for confrontation with the rated constructs which described the effects of these principles on students' characteristics, e.g. on their learning outcomes, their behaviour, and their attitudes toward physics. As a first step on the way to a complete repertory grid, the triadic method was applied: the teachers drew three of the element cards and were asked to describe two of the elements which had similar effects on students and how these were distinguished from the third element. The selection process is methodologically advantageous as it leads to characterization (namely the judgment about the similarity) as well as distinction (with judgment about the difference). The common property is regarded as the construct pole, whilst the contradictory property is the contrast pole. In the next step, the teachers are asked for a seven-step rating that is supposed to express how intensively each element contributes to the effect described by the construct.

The analysis of the repertory grid reveals structures and each interpretation requires the teacher's comments, confirmation, correction, or critical questioning. In this respect the individual phases of analysis are useful opportunities for further discussions in which the basic reflections during the construction process are intensified.

Results

A Gap Appears: Conceptions and Orientations of Acting

In both groups of teachers (student-teachers and beginning teachers) the observation and video-taping of lessons was an important part of research. For the student-teachers, information about classroom processes provided the researcher with details about possible reasons for modifications of their conceptions of teaching and learning, and for beginning teachers, the comparison between their stated conceptions and their actions revealed an insight into their ability to integrate theory and practice.

Independent of the teachers' stated conceptions of teaching and learning, some features in processes of instruction appeared that were common to both groups. These instructional features demonstrated that the lesson was conducted more as a progression of activities designed by the teacher rather than as a learning process in which students' ideas played a significant role.

Stimulated recall interviews with video-recorded lessons gave transcripts that highlighted participants' instructional orientations during teaching. Analysis revealed that, according to the teachers, the instructional principles for success in teaching was measured with certain criteria which referred to the external process of teaching and barely took into consideration the students' learning processes. The following instructional orientations were identifiable:

- *Activity-flow orientation*
The prevailing intention is to keep the lesson moving and to realize the planning of the teaching periods that are a part of the picture of the whole teaching process. In such an orientation, since the learning processes are of secondary importance, they are no longer included in the teacher's aims as he or she concentrates primarily on ensuring a continuous flow of activities.
- *Students' work as mere activity*
The planned experimental student activities are dominated by the activity-flow orientation, therefore these experimental activities lose their ability to induce learning.
- *Plan orientation*
It is understandable that the teaching plans become the deciding factors in the educational phase, routines to lighten the instructional load have still not been

developed. The consequence in this orientation are that a large amount of the teacher's attention is drawn away from the students. Students' statements are, in part, not noticed because a response to these statements would endanger the realization of the intended teaching plan.

• *Completion orientation*

From the middle of the lesson on, teachers formulate explanations that refer to the end that is staged as a completion of the teaching process instead of a learning process.

The orientations described above are supported by a view of physics learning that follows the schemata 'offer-reception'. Within this schemata, physics learning is regarded as a one time process which is started with a clever methodical presentation of the lesson's content.

For many student-teachers and beginning teachers who, prior to their teaching, have stated conceptions that are closely related to learning processes, this turning to decisions stressing students' actions means a gulf between their instructional intentions and their actual behaviour (Fischler, 1986, 1989, 1993a, 1993b, 1994). With these results the tendencies of the observations of other researchers could be confirmed and put in concrete terms for the field of physics teaching.

Teaching Principles

Analysis of the data produced a complex picture of the relationship between student-teachers' conceptions, their perception of the reality of the teaching processes, and their concrete reactions to specific events during their teaching. Some of the student-teachers stated similar conceptions of teaching and learning in physics education but drew different conclusions from their experiences. Others differed strongly in their conceptions and therefore interpreted similar situations in the classrooms quite differently.

For the construction of repertory grids, student-teachers in this project stated between 8 and 10 teaching principles and 5 to 7 constructs. The detailed analysis of the teaching principles showed that, beforehand, two groupings existed. One group of student-teachers who focused their planning activities on students' learning processes, and a second grouping who regarded teaching as a series of teacher activities which had to be planned precisely. However, for the description of the complex nature of the interaction between conceptions, perceptions and conclusions this grouping is too rough.

Promotion of students' learning processes is for many student-teachers one of their main instructional goals. However, there are significant differences about which decisions are most appropriate in promoting students' learning processes. Some of the teaching principles focus on more general requirements for instructional processes that promote learning, i.e. a positive classroom climate achieved by the teacher, while others refer to specific actions of the teacher which are supposed to increase students' willingness to learn. It is common to all student-teachers that they strive for a teaching process that they perceive as being successful. This goal includes student-related intentions of teachers' actions as well as intentions that emphasize a teacher role as a conveyor of knowledge.

The analysis of the teaching principles stated during the construction of the repertory grids reveals that each principle can be assigned to one of the following categories:

1   *Content related principles*
Student-teachers regard the selection of content, which is applicable in every-day life and therefore interesting to students, as a means of giving students insights into the various fields for the application of physics and to make them interested in understanding the physics basis of these applications.
Examples: Connecting physics topics with out-of-school topics
              Combining physics and life
              Selecting topics out of everyday life

2   *Principles related to the nature of presentation*
Student-teachers regard a clear and understandable presentation as a necessary prerequisite for successful learning, and if possible to support the presentation with a demonstration of an experiment.
Examples: Using correct physics terms during presentation
              Illustrating topics that are difficult to understand
              Writing down intermediate results

3   *Principles aimed to 'activate' students*
Student-teachers try to create situations in which students are stimulated to work actively.
Examples: Demonstrating exciting experiments to motivate students
              Amazing the students by using 'astonishing' phenomena
              Involving students in the processes of problem-solving

4   *Action oriented principles*
Student-teachers think that if students have a propensity to act on their own then they are motivated to learn.
Examples: Allowing students to carry out experiments they have planned
              themselves
              Giving students time to fully conduct their activities
              Giving students opportunities to handle physics devices

5   *Principles referring to classroom climate*
Student-teachers are convinced that a positive classroom climate contributes to successful processes of teaching and learning and that the teacher's behaviour is crucial in creating this climate.
Examples: Creating a friendly classroom climate
              Dealing with students in an informal way
              Being fair and just in dealing with students

For the 36 student-teachers and beginning teachers involved in this project, distribution of descriptors across these categories is outlined in Table 10.1.

Table 10.1   Distribution of participants' descriptors across categories (teaching principles)

1 Content-related principles	32
2 Principles related to the way of presentation	91
3 Principles aiming to activate students	127
4 Action-oriented principles	45
5 Principles referring to classroom climate	9

Student-teachers' statements in the interviews accounted for the majority of the principles in group 3: they remembered the physics lessons from their own school days that were either dominated by an active teacher or alternatively involved a great length of time as passive students. The 'bad image' of physics lessons, which is commonly reported in physics teaching and learning investigations, is as a result of these situations which the student-teachers would like to overcome.

Students' Characteristics

The construction of repertory grids requires constructs that in this research project are constituted by students' attributes as they were intended to be achieved through the instructional principles. The student related attributes stated by the student-teachers can be assigned to the following groups:

A   *Physics knowledge*
Students are knowledgable about the basic concepts of physics and they are able to solve physics problems.
Examples: Students acquire and retain physics knowledge
Students connect existing but isolated elements of physics knowledge
Students are able to think 'correctly' in physics
B   *Ability to connect physics and everyday life*
Students are willing and capable of applying physics knowledge to phenomena of everyday life.
Examples: Students understand devices of everyday life
Students connect physics and everyday life
C   *General intellectual abilities*
In physics lessons, students have developed understandings that are not context bound. They are able to think in abstract terms, they can work on their own and they master subject related discussion.
Examples: Students are able to discuss physics concepts
Students are able to concentrate on essential concepts and issues
D   *Interest, motivation, attention, active involvement*
Students are interested in physics topics and they behave accordingly in the classroom.
Examples: Students engage actively in classroom processes
Students are motivated to follow the instructional process

Helmut Fischler

Table 10.2   Frequency per category
(Students' characteristics)

A	Physics knowledge	61
D	Interest, motivation	53
F	Positive attitude	31
C	General abilities	25
B	Physics and everyday life	18
E	Experimental skills	15*
G	Social competence	8*

* The low numbers for the last two groups were
a little surprising because in method classes
experimental work is particularly emphasized.

E   *Experimental skills*
Students have learnt to carry out experiments.
Examples: Students are equipped with practical knowledge
Students are able to do measurements
F   *Positive attitudes toward physics and physics lessons*
Students value physics knowledge and think that physics lessons are an appropriate place to acquire this knowledge.
Examples: Students do not have any aversion to physics lessons
Students have experienced success in learning physics and
therefore have established a positive attitude
G   *Social competence, willingness and ability to work in groups*
Students have learnt to work cooperatively.
Example: Students demonstrate appropriate social behaviour

The frequency of each of the above groups is outlined in Table 10.2.

Resultant Tendencies

This section illustrates the data pertaining to the modifications of student-teachers' conceptions: The statements reported here are those elicited through the semi-structured interviews, repertory grids and video-tapes of the physics lessons.

First of all the student-teachers normally report on their general experiences with their teaching principles and the student-related goals (the intended attributes). They then express their opinions about whether or not their teaching principles have stood the test of teaching and which principles they wish to keep or reject. Their responses show a uniform picture, as demonstrated by:

- During their teaching practice student-teachers felt free to decide about principles in groups (2) to (5). They were convinced that they consciously made decisions within these categories. Content was the only aspect that they perceived as restrictive as a result of both their mentor's directions and the syllabus. Therefore, the goal of demonstrating to the students the connection between physics and everyday life was not achieved.

- For all of the student-teachers the previously described orientations of actions were distinctly effective. However, this was achieved without the student-teachers' being aware of it. Therefore, they perceived students' behaviour as reactions to their decisions that they themselves regarded as being much more student oriented than they were perceived to be by the observers, e.g. the mentor and the coaching professor.
- In the categories of students' intended attributes, the student-teachers only considered students' knowledge (A) and their motivation (D) as being 'controllable' in the period of practical experiences in a practicum setting. All the other aspects of these categories were considered to be long-term goals and therefore beyond their control in a practicum situation.
- Only one student-teacher actually deleted a teaching principle from his list and replaced it with another. In all other cases, the teaching principles and intended students' attributes were unchanged. However, there were some major changes in some parts of the rating scores in the repertory grids. These were most noticeable in those that described student-teachers' judgments about how strongly their teaching principles achieved the intended student attributes.

Principles to Activate Students

All of the student-teachers stated several teaching principles that could be categorized as intentions to activate students. Interest, motivation, and attention (group D) were the main consequences expected. Indirectly, there was also greater success in physics learning (group A) than expected. Student-teachers' prevailing experiences with the principles which aimed to activate students were disappointing because in the interviews about 75 per cent of all student-teachers spoke about their failed attempts to motivate students to engage in the processes of teaching and learning:

> Presenting a problem to the students was not successful because they are not willing to think about physics problems.

> It did not work to give the students the chance to discuss a problem. They are not used to talking with each other.

These statements reflect the subjective perception of the situation and at the same time describe the reasons the student-teachers attribute to this situation. However, both parts of these statements need to be considered against the background of the permanent effective orientations of actions which push away the teaching principles stated in the interviews and which they claim to be the guidelines for their actions. First, student-teachers call a teaching situation open and student oriented even though it is restricted by various planning elements which are supposed to ensure the free flow of activity. Secondly, the diagnosed students' unwillingness and inability to fulfill open situations is often as a consequence of students' experience that teachers normally draw narrow limits around the openness of a teaching situation.

The failure to achieve the intended students' attributes of interest, motivation, and attention is at the same time perceived as a failure of the efforts to establish a basic physics knowledge (group A) which, because of the missing feeling of success, entails negative consequences in terms of the development of a positive attitude towards physics and physics teaching (group F).

Only 25 per cent of the student-teachers were content with their efforts. The judgment of the student-teachers as well as the observers was that many of the successful cases were induced by student-teachers' integration of teaching principles which could be assigned to the group 'Principles referring to classroom climate' (group 5). For the student-teachers, before teaching practice, these goals had been a necessary prerequisite for achieving students' attention and engagement. After teaching practice, the student-teachers were convinced that a positive attitude towards physics lessons (group F) could only be achieved through the integration of such goals as physics learning (group A of students' attributes) and from successful learning experiences.

In some cases, students were motivated from the beginning so that any specific teacher effort was unnecessary in this regard. Consequently, the student-teachers did not see any reason to reflect on modifications of their teaching principles.

What consequences do student-teachers draw from their perceptions and experiences? The failure to engage students did necessarily lead to an abandonment of the teaching principle. Common reactions covered the following three components:

- An attitude of resignation that, despite the failure, does not see any alternative: 'Without any problem posing it did not work either.'
- Often this statement is connected with the expectation that under better conditions these efforts would be more effective (different students, better equipment).
- Student-teachers (and beginning teachers) to a large extent attribute failure to themselves. In their opinion, increased experience would improve the possibilities for the realization of their intentions.

A descriptive summary of expectations, perceptions and consequences that can be identified in the context of category (3) of the teaching principles comprises the following characteristics:

- Of the total teaching principles stated by student-teachers, a group in which teacher activities designed to have students stimulated, attentive and ready to solve problems independently is recognizable. These principles, according to their number, form the largest of all groups. Student-teachers hope that the realization of these intentions will create a classroom climate of interest and motivation that will entail positive attitudes. The majority of student-teachers perceived the reality of physics teaching as a failure. However, they maintained their teaching principles because they attributed their failure to the specific conditions of the teaching practicum.

The integration of teaching principles that aimed to create a positive classroom climate led to feelings of success for only a minority of student-teachers.

Content-related Teaching Principles

As mentioned above, most of the student-teachers felt restricted by their content-related decision-making that had to meet the scientific orientation of the syllabus and their mentor but was opposed to their own conception of good physics teaching. However, student-teachers themselves selected topics which were oriented towards the scientific body of knowledge because these topics gave them a certain self-confidence during teaching which they would not have had with everyday, and technical, topics which they did not encounter in teacher education. It was also clear that the dichotomy between teaching intentions and real decision making became more intensive following teaching experience. In the repertory grids, principle (1) (i.e. selection of content which is applicable in everyday life) received higher scores than students' attributes in group D (motivation) and group B (physics and everyday life).

Principles Related to Representation

Many student-teacher statements could be assigned to this category as they describe student-teachers' intentions to help students learn physics through concrete and illustrative experimental demonstrations. In the repertory grids, the student-related goals of interest, motivation and attention (group D) and physics knowledge (group A) were all highly scored prior to teaching. However, the teaching experiences gave the majority of student-teachers (about 80 per cent) grounds to change their judgment. Two reasons account for this:

- They recognized that it did not make much sense to optimize the presentation of topics which students cared little about. This situation intensified their dilemma because the problem of content selection created an internal contradiction. The topics in which they felt most competent were not generally those that the students thought were worth learning.
- The time-consuming and detailed planning necessary for experimental presentations and problem-solving tasks led to teaching situations in which student-teachers disliked deviating from the planned order of activities. Therefore, it is clearly difficult for students to bring in their conceptions and to influence the sequence of teaching within such tightly organized lessons. In such teacher-centred teaching, then, feedback to students is most likely missing.

Most of the student-teachers who prior to their teaching allocated great importance to an optimal presentation of physics topics reversed their judgment concerning the goals in group A and D and instead gave increased importance to content and interest related-teaching principles.

Action-oriented Teaching Principles

Two reasons account for the intention to give students the chance to do laboratory work. Firstly, student-teachers remembered doing experiments on their own as a most attractive part of science lessons from their school days. Secondly, the introduction of Piagetian theory (in method classes) and the influence of concrete–operational actions on learning fell on fertile ground. The student-teachers tended to connect their action-oriented teaching principles of group D (interest, motivation) and group A (physics knowledge) with students' expected characteristics but less with goals of group E (experimental skills) and even less with social goals which might only be achieved through cooperative group work.

After teaching practice, student-teachers' judgments about the influence of the action-oriented teaching principles on the student-related goals 'interest, motivation' and 'physics knowledge' noticeably decreased. In the interviews during the construction of repertory grids it became obvious that students' learning processes took longer to develop than the student-teachers expected and that this perception increased the 'pressure of time'. For many student-teachers, laboratory work independent of the teacher's direct guidance was not productive enough in terms of learning results, compared to the amount of time required for the work. Therefore, student conducted experiments created a conflict judgment for the student-teachers and the pressure of time and equipment problems were given as reasons for this. In repertory grids, the functions of supporting learning and promoting motivation are (after teaching) not so highly judged as they are before teaching. Nevertheless, in the interviews student-teachers on the whole maintained a positive judgment. Obviously they were in principle convinced of the significance of students' laboratory work, but they hesitated describing precisely the advantages of such work and chose to shy away from preparing and conducting it.

Consequences for teacher education

The main purpose of this research was to investigate the changes in teacher education that might help young teachers to realize their own conceptions of teaching and learning and at the same time meet the fundamental demands of practice. The findings deliver numerous suggestions that are discussed in the following section using the thematic structure of this section of the chapter.

Conclusion: Orientations of Acting

It was clear that the participants of this study needed to be made aware of their orientations of action uncovered through this study as it is important to one's own educational beliefs to be aware of effective unconscious orientations which (although not necessarily individually recognized) exist. For this process it turned out to be most valuable when the student-teacher and the coaching person (or in this case the researcher) observed the video-taped lesson and commented on situations which either found worthy of discussion. At no stage before this was there an opportunity for participants to view their own decisions and students' reactions without any pressure to act and being sufficiently detached from the situation in classroom.

The stimulated recall interviews gave some information about the roles of the coaching persons. Seldom did student-teachers refer directly to the university advisor. The mentor's influence though had two effects. When the mentor and the student-teacher had similar conceptions, student-teachers felt confirmation and approval, their conceptions having passed the first test of practice and therefore being reinforced. In the case of differences, the student-teachers tried to maintain their conceptions and adjust their decision-making sufficient to prevent conflict with the mentor.

It is still an open question as to how to help student-teachers overcome the identified orientations of acting. It would, however, seem reasonable to suggest that under 'good' teaching conditions (e.g. small groups) the likelihood of control over their decisions might well be more permanent.

Activating Students

It is reasonable that student-teachers, after their failure to activate students, maintain their teaching principles and wait for other opportunities to realize them. Teacher education is able to offer many opportunities and ideas for giving prospective teachers a variety of instruments to establish situations full of curiosity, astonishment, and surprise for their students. The small group of student-teachers who have successfully introduced affective and emotional components into their teaching and who have achieved a friendly classroom climate through their behaviour, points to elements of teaching that have been underestimated and neglected in teacher education for a long time. Psychologists continue to remind us about the importance of these aspects for the instructional process and that a teacher's friendly attitude towards students is essential, whether or not the students like to participate actively in the instructional process.

Content in Physics Teaching

Improving student-teachers' content-related demands for teaching does not seem too difficult. They should be set free from the dilemma described that they, on the one hand, are convinced of the significance of application-oriented topics for students' willingness to learn and, on the other, do not feel knowledgable about these topics and therefore avoid each risk to explore new ground. Although this is in principle a problem of science teaching, it cannot be solved within subject-related pedagogical education of teachers alone but requires support by the section of scientific studies. In view of the very systematically determined science courses, conflicts can be predicted. The age-old question about the extent to which science courses refer to the demands of teachers needs to be raised again. There are no simple answers, but scientists should clearly be concerned with attractiveness of science education.

Teachers' Planned Activities

Practice in the planning processes of subject-related pedagogical preparation for student-teachers' own teaching is most important. For beginning teachers, careful reflection on their intentions and precise analysis of the existing situation leads to the development of 'professional behaviour'. The large number of principles related to 'ways of presentation' and the visible assumption that these principles have an impact on students' engagement and on students' learning processes, show that student-teachers attribute an enormous significance to lesson planning before teaching practice. The video-taped lessons demonstrated that this lesson planning did not necessarily induce and promote learning processes but is crucial in helping the student-teacher to conduct lessons in accord with their ideas. Most of the student-teachers stayed near their notes during the teaching process and made use of them regularly during a lesson.

In teacher education, it is too easy to ignore the reverse of this intensive planning. After teaching practice, student-teachers often confirm the need for such detailed planning for their teaching, but they are also aware of the consequences for the teaching process. Students' contributions may not be taken on, or may even be ignored, because they do not fit the planned procedure for the lesson. Therefore a domination of teachers' planned activities may well have a negative effect on students' engagement and result in an outcome opposite to that which was intended. This situation should be considered in teacher education. It is possible, for instance, to prepare teachers more intensively for students' conceptions than can be foreseen according to the results of research in recent years.

Laboratory Work and Learning

Student-teachers' judgments about the influence of students' laboratory work changes during teaching practice. The impression that the learning outcomes are not sufficient with regard to the effort, results from student-teachers' focusing on an under-achievement in students' 'testable' knowledge. A widening of perspectives towards other functions for students' laboratory work would allow for cognitive achievements in a more realistic manner and would turn the student-teacher's attention to other teaching goals associated with laboratory work. Experimental skills, independent planning, conducting and evaluating experiments, and the ability to work cooperatively in groups are goals worthy of a teacher's energy and efforts. The preparation and design of laboratory work related to these aspects should therefore be increasingly a part of teacher education.

Stability and Change

This investigation has revealed that student-teachers' teaching experiences only meet their expectations to a small extent. The reactions to this discrepancy are subtly diversified. In regard to some of their teaching principles the situation for student-teachers is rightly described by the term 'dilemma'. They have experienced the narrow limits of their efforts (e.g. to activate students) but do not see an alternative and therefore hold on to their teaching principles with the hope of more favourable times. They realize that they have selected topics of little interest to students but do not see any solution because they do not want to move from their 'safe content-grounds'. They recognize the problems of detailed lesson plans which focus on teachers' activities, but know that as beginners they find this support indispensable. Finally, they maintain their opinion that students' laboratory work should play a major role in science teaching, although their decision-making illustrates a different view in terms of their conceptions of learning and teaching.

Overview

Attempting to maintain stable conceptions of teaching and learning whilst making modifications in terms of scepticism and reduced anticipation with regard to realistic student learning outcomes are key characteristics in student teaching experiences. The appearance of stability and change of this kind generates a tension that is difficult for student-teachers to stand. Easing this difficulty is the task of teacher education and I trust that this chapter has adequately demonstrated how one approach to researching teaching has offered genuine possibilities for the further development of our knowledge about teaching and the difficulties and complexities of learning in this most important profession.

References

AGUIRRE, J.M., HAGGERTY, S.M. and LINDER, C.J. (1990) 'Student-teachers' conceptions of science, teaching and learning: A case study in preservice science education', *International Journal of Science Education*, **12**, 4, pp. 381–90.
ANDERSEN, H.O., HARTY, H. and SAMUEL, K.V. (1986) 'Nature of science, 1969 and 1984: Perspectives of preservice secondary science teachers', *School Science and Mathematics*, **86**, 1, pp. 43–50.
BAIRD, J.R., FENSHAM, P.J., GUNSTONE, R.F. and WHITE, R.T. (1991) 'The importance of reflection in improving science teaching and learning', *Journal of Research in Science Teaching*, **28**, 2, pp. S.163–82.

BOEI, F., CORPORAAL, A.H. and VAN HUNEN, W.H. (1989) 'Describing teacher cognitions with the repgrid', in LOWYCK, J. and CLARK, C.M. (eds) *Teacher Thinking and Professional Action*, pp. 175–92, Leuven: University Press.

BORKO, H. and SHAVELSON, R.J. (1990) 'Teacher decision making', in JONES, B.F. and IDOL, L. (eds) *Dimensions of Thinking and Cognitive Instruction*, pp. 311–46, Hillsdale: Erlbaum.

BRAMALD, R., HARDMAN, F. and LEAD, D. (1994) 'Initial teacher trainees and their views of teaching and learning', *Teaching and Teacher Education*, **11**, 1, pp. S.23–31.

BRICKHOUSE, N. and BODNER, G.M. (1992) 'The beginning science teacher: Classroom narratives of convictions and constraints', *Journal of Research in Science Teaching*, **5**, pp. 471–85.

BROMME, R. (1981) 'Das denken von lehrern bei der unterrichsvorbereitung', *Eine empirische Untersuchung zu kognitiven Prozessen von Mathematiklehrern*, Weinheim: Beltz.

BROMME, R. and BROPHY, J. (1986) 'Teachers' cognitive activities', in CHRISTIANSEN, B., HOWSON, G. and OTTE, M. (eds) *Perspectives on Mathematics Education*, pp. 99–140, Dordrecht: Reidel.

BUTT, R.L. (1984) 'Arguments for using biography in understanding teacher thinking', in HALKES, R. and OLSON, J.K. (eds) *Teacher Thinking*, pp. 95–102, Lisse: Swets and Zeitlinger.

CAREY, R.L. and STAUSS, N.G. (1970) 'An analysis of experienced science teachers' understanding of the nature of science', *School Science and Mathematics*, **70**, pp. 366–8.

CHAMPAGNE, A.B., GUNSTONE, R.F. and KLOPFER, L.E. (1985a) 'Instructional consequences of students' knowledge about physics phenomena', in WEST, L.H.T. and PINES, A.L. (eds) *Cognitive Structure and Conceptual Change*, pp. 61–90, London: Academic Press.

CHAMPAGNE, A.B., GUNSTONE, R.F. and KLOPFER, L.E. (1985b) 'Effecting changes in cognitive structures among physics students', in WEST, L.H.T. and PINES, A.L. (eds) *Cognitive Structure and Conceptual Change*, pp. 163–88, London: Academic Press.

CLARK, C.M. and PETERSON, P.L. (1986) 'Teachers' thought processes', in WITTROCK, M.C. (ed.) *Handbook of Research on Teaching*, pp. 255–96, New York: Macmillan.

CLARK, C.M. and YINGER, R.J. (1987) 'Teacher planning', in CALDERHEAD, J. (ed.) *Exploring Teachers' Thinking*, pp. 84–103, London: Cassell.

CROCKER, R.K. and BANFIELD, H. (1986) 'Factors influencing teacher decisions on school, classroom, and curriculum', *Journal of Research in Science Teaching*, **23**, 9, pp. 805–16.

DRIVER, R. (1988) 'Theory into Practice II: A constructivist approach to curriculum development', in FENSHAM, P. (ed.) *Development and Dilemmas in Science Education*, pp. 133–49, London: Falmer Press.

DRIVER, R. (1989a) 'Students' conceptions and the learning of science', *International Journal of Science Education*, **11**, pp. 481–90.

DRIVER, R. (1989b) 'Changing conceptions', in ADEY, P. (ed.) *Adolescent Development and School Science*, pp. 79–103, London: Falmer Press.

DUIT, R. (1991) 'On the role of analogies, similes and metaphors in learning science', *Science Education*, **75**, 6, pp. 649–72.

DUIT, R. (1993) 'Schülervorstellungen — von Lerndefiziten zu neuen Unterrichtsansätzen', *Naturwissenschaften im Unterricht Physik*, **16**, 4, pp. 16–23.

DUIT, R. (1995) 'Conceptual change approaches in science education', Revised version of a paper presented at the 'Symposium on Conceptual Change', Friedrich-Schiller-University Jena, Germany, September 1–3.

ELBAZ, F. (1983) *Teacher Thinking: A Study of Practical Knowledge*, London: Croom Helm.

ERICKSON, G. and MacKINNON, A.M. (1991) 'Seeing classrooms in new ways: On becoming a science teacher', in SCHÖN, D. (ed.) *The Reflective Turn: Case Studies In and On Educational Practice*, pp. 15–36, New York: Teachers College Press.

FENSHAM, P.J. (1987) 'Theory in practice: How to assist science teachers to teach constructively', in ADEY, P. (ed.) *Adolescent Development and School Science*, pp. 61–77, London: Falmer Press.

FICHTEN, W., JAECKEL, K. and STINSHOFF, R. (eds) (1978) *Projektstudium und Praxisbezug — Reformmodelle der Lehrer- und Juristenausbildung*, Frankfurt/M.

FISCHLER, H. (1986) 'Schülervorstellungen und lehrertheorien: Zum programm einer rekonstruktion subjektiver theorien von physiklehrern', *physica didactica*, **13**, Sonderheft, pp. 67–79.

FISCHLER, H. (1989) 'Methodische konzeptionen, unterrichtsinhalte und lehrerentscheidungen', in WIEBEL, K.H. (ed.) *Zur Didaktik der Physik und Chemie*, Alsbach, pp. 58–75.

FISCHLER, H. (1993a) 'Von der Kluft zwischen Absicht und Handeln — Lehrervorstellungen und lehrerreaktionen', in BEHRENDT, H. (ed.) *Zur Didaktik der Physik und Chemie*, Alsbach, pp. 226–8.

FISCHLER, H. (1993b) 'Physiklehrer im unterricht — Was machen wir in der Ausbildung falsch?' *Didaktik der Physik, Vorträge der Frühjahrstagung der Deutschen Physikalischen*, Gesell-schaft, pp. 431–6.

FISCHLER, H. (1994) 'Concerning the difference between intention and action: Teachers' conceptions and actions in physics teaching', in CARLGREN, I., HANDAL, G. and VAAGE, S. (eds) *Teachers' Minds and Actions: Research on Teachers' Thinking and Practice*, pp. 165–80, London: Falmer Press.

GROEBEN, N., WAHL, D., SCHLEE, J. and SCHEELE, B. (1988) *Das Forschungsprogramm Subjektive Theorien: Einführung in die Psychologie des Reflexiven Subjekts*, Tübingen: Francke.

GUNSTONE, R.F. and NORTHFIELD, J.R. (1986) 'Learners-Teachers-Researchers: Consistency in Implementing Conceptual Change', Paper presented at the meeting of the American Educational Research Association, San Francisco.

HAND, B. and TREAGUST, D. (1994) 'Teachers' thoughts about changing to constructivist teaching/learning approaches within junior secondary science classrooms', *Journal of Education for Teaching*, **20**, 1, pp. 97–112.

HEIMANN, P. (1962) 'Didaktik als theorie und lehre', *Die Deutsche Schule*, **54**, pp. 407–27.

HEWSON, P.W. and HEWSON, M.G. A'B. (1987a) 'Science teachers' conceptions of teaching: Implications for teacher education', *International Journal of Science Education*, **9**, 4, pp. 425–40.

HEWSON, P.W. and HEWSON, M.G. A'B. (1987b) 'Identifying conceptions of teaching science', in *Proceedings of Second International Seminar on Misconceptions and Educational Strategies in Science and Mathematics*, Volume II, pp. 182–93.

HEWSON, P.W. and HEWSON, M.G. A'B. (1988a) 'An appropriate conception of teaching science: A view from studies of science learning', *Science Education*, **72**, 5, pp. 597–614.

HEWSON, P.W. and HEWSON, M.G. A'B. (1988b) 'Analysis and use of a task for identifying conceptions of teaching science', Paper presented at the Annual Meeting of the American Education Research Association, New Orleans.

HEWSON, P.W. and HEWSON, M.G. A'B. (1989) 'Analysis and use of a task for identifying conceptions of teaching science', *Journal of Education for Teaching*, **15**, 3, pp. 191–209.

HEYMANN, H.W. (1982) 'Zur erforschung subjektiver unterrichtstheorien von mathematiklehrern: Überlegungen zu einer empirischen studie', *Unterrichtswissenschaft* **2**, pp. 154–64.

HUIBREGTSE, I., KORTHAGEN, F. and WUBBELS, T. (1994) 'Physics teachers' conceptions of learning, teaching and professional development', *International Journal of Science Education*, **16**, 5, pp. 539–61.

JONAS, G. (1993) 'Subjektive theorien von physiklehrern zum experiment im physikunterricht', in GRAMM, A., LINDEMANN, H. and SUMFLETH, E. (eds) *Naturwissenschaftsdidaktik: Sommersymposium*, Essen, pp. 151–7.

JUNG, W. (1978) 'Zum problem der "schülervorstellungen"' (1. Teil). *physica didactica* **5**, 3, pp. 125–46.

JUNG, W. (1986) 'Alltagsvorstellungen und das Lernen von Physik und Chemie'. *Naturwissenschaften im Unterricht-Physik/Chemie*, **34**, 13, pp. 2–6.

KAGAN, D.M. (1992) 'Professional growth among preservice and beginning teachers', *Review of Educational Research*, **62**, 2, pp. 129–69.

KEINY, S. (1994) 'Constructivism and teachers' professional development', *Teaching and Teacher Education*, **10**, 2, pp. 157–67.

KELLY, G.A. (1955) *The Psychology of Personal Constructs*, New York: Norton.

KOCH, J.–J. (1972) *Lehrer-Studium und Beruf*, Ulm: Süddeutsche Verlags-Gesellschaft.

KOULAIDIS, V. and OGBORN, J. (1989) 'Philosophy of science: An empirical study of teachers' views', *International Journal of Science Education*, **11**, 2, pp. 173–84.

LEDERMAN, N.G. (1986) 'Students' and teachers' understanding of the nature of science: A reassessment', *School Science and Mathematics*, **86**, pp. 91–9.

LEINHARDT, G. and GREENO, J.G. (1986) 'The cognitive skill of teaching', *Journal of Educational Psychology*, **78**, pp. 75–95.

LORTIE, D.C. (1975) *Schoolteacher*, Chicago: University of Chicago Press.

MACKINNON, A.M. and ERICKSON, G.L. (1988) 'Taking Schön's ideas to a science teaching practicum', in GRIMMETT, P.P. and ERICKSON, G.L. (eds) *Reflection in Teacher Education*, pp. 113–37, New York: Teachers College Press.

MACKINNON, A. and ERICKSON, G. (1992) 'The roles of reflective practice and foundational disciplines in teacher education', in RUSSELL, T. and MUNBY, H. (eds) *Teachers and Teaching: From Classroom to Reflection*, pp. 192–210, London: Falmer Press.

MANDL, H. and HUBER, G.L. (1983) 'Subjektive theorien von lehrern', *Erziehung und Unterricht*, **30**, pp. 98–112.

MARION, R., HEWSON, P., TABACHNICK, B. and BLOMKER, K. (1994) 'Teaching for conceptual change in elementary and secondary science methods courses', Paper presented at the Annual Meeting of the National Association for Research in Science Teaching, New Orleans.

MARKHAM, K.M. and MINTZES, J.J. (1994) 'The concept map as a research and evaluation tool: Further evidence of validity', *Journal of Research in Science Teaching*, **31**, 1, pp. 91–101.

MORINE-DERSHIMER, G. (1993) 'Tracing conceptual change in preservice teachers', *Teaching and Teacher Education*, **9**, 1, pp. 15–26.

MORINE-DERSHIMER, G., SAUNDERS, S., ARTILES, A.J., MOSTERT, M.P., TANKERSLEY, M., TRENT, S.C. and NUTTYCOMBE, D.G. (1992) 'Choosing among alternatives for tracing conceptual change', *Teaching and Teacher Education*, **8**, 5/6, pp. 471–83.

NUSSBAUM, J. and NOVICK, S. (1982) 'Alternative frameworks, conceptual conflict and accommodation: Toward a principled teaching strategy', *Instructional Science*, **11**, pp. 183–200.

PARSONS-CHATMAN, S. (1990) 'Making sense of constructivism in preservice: A case study', Paper presented at the annual meeting of the National Association for Research in Science Teaching, Atlanta.

PETERSON, P.L., FENNEMA, E., CARPENTER, T.P. and LOEF, M. (1989) 'Teachers' pedagogical content beliefs in mathematics', *Cognition and Instruction*, **6**, pp. 1–40.

POPE, M.L. and KEEN, T.R. (1981) *Personal Construct Psychology and Education*, London: Academic Press.

POPE, M. and DENICOLO, P. (1993) 'The art and science of constructivist research in teacher thinking', *Teaching and Teacher Education*, **9**, 5/6, pp. 529–44.

POSNER, G.J., STRIKE, K.A., HEWSON, P.W. and GERTZOG, W.A. (1982) 'Accommodation of a scientific conception: Toward a theory of conceptual change', *Science Education*, **66**, 2, pp. 211–27.

RODRIGUEZ, A.J. (1993) 'A dose of reality: Understanding the origin of the theory/practice dichotomy in teacher education from the students' point of view', *Journal of Teacher Education*, **44**, 3, pp. 213–22.

SCHÖN, D.A. (1983) *The Reflective Practitioner. How Professionals Think in Action*, New York: Basic Books.

SCHÖN, D.A. (1987) *Educating the Reflective Practitioner*, San Francisco: Jossey-Bass.

SCHÖN, D.A. (1988) 'Coaching reflective teaching', in GRIMMETT, P.P. and ERICKSON, G.L. (eds) *Reflection in Teacher Education*, pp. 19–29, New York: Teachers College Press.

SCOTT, P.H., ASOKO, H.M. and DRIVER, R.H. (1992) 'Teaching for conceptual change: A review of strategies', in DUIT, R., GOLDBERG, F. and NIEDDERER, H. (eds) *Research in Physics Learning: Theoretical Issues and Empirical Studies*, pp. 310–29, Kiel: IPN/Institute for Science Education.

SHAVELSON, R.J. and STERN, P. (1981) 'Research on teachers' pedagogical thoughts, judgements, decisions, and behavior', *Review of Educational Research*, **51**, 4, pp. 455–98.

STATLER, R., STODDART, T. and NIEDERHAUSER, D. (1994) '*Beginning teachers perspectives on didactic and conceptual approaches to science teaching*', Paper Presented at the Annual Meeting of the National Association for Research in Science Teaching, Anaheim.

STAVY, R. (1991) 'Using analogy to overcome misconceptions about conservation of matter', *Journal of Research in Science Education*, **28**, pp. 305–13.

TOBIN, K. (1990) 'Changing metaphors and beliefs: A master switch for teaching?' *Theory into Practice*, **29**, 2, pp. 122–7.

TOBIN, K. and FRASER, B.J. (1989) 'Barriers to higher-level cognitive learning in high school science', *Science Education*, **73**, 6, pp. 659–83.

TOBIN, K. and GALLAGHER, J.J. (1987) 'What happens in high school science classrooms?' *Journal of Curriculum Studies*, **19**, 6, pp. 549–60.

TOBIN, K., TIPPINS, D.J. and GALLARD, A.J. (1994) 'Research on instructional strategies for teaching science', in GABEL, D.L. (ed.) *Handbook of Research on Science Teaching and Learning*, pp. 45–93, New York: Macmillan.

WANDERSEE, J.H., MINTZES, J.J. and NOVAK, J.D. (1994) 'Research on alternative conceptions in science', in GABEL, D. (ed.) *Handbook of Research on Science Teaching and Learning*, pp. 177–210, New York: Macmillan.

WHITELOCK, D. (1988) 'Repertory grid elicitation: A potential tool for studying secondary school pupils' ideas of dynamics?' in SCHMIDT, H.-J. (ed.) *Proceedings of the International Seminar "Empirical Research in Science and Mathematics Education"*, pp. 233–44, Dortmund: Universität Dortmund.

ZEICHNER, K. and TABACHNICK, B.R. (1981) 'Are the effects of university teacher education "Washed Out" by School Experience?' *Journal of Teacher Education*, **32**, 3, pp. 7–11.

11   Researching Formative Assessment

Beverley Bell and Bronwen Cowie

Formative Assessment

Teaching includes a range of skills and draws on the professional knowledge of the teachers. One aspect of teaching is that of formative assessment. Within the research reported here, formative assessment, as classroom-based assessment for better learning, was defined as:

> . . . the process used by teachers and students to recognize and respond to student learning in order to enhance that learning, during the learning. (Cowie and Bell, 1996)

Formative assessment can be viewed as the process by which teachers gather assessment information about the students' learning and then respond to promote further learning. It is the component of teaching in which teachers find out about the effectiveness of the learning activities they are providing. Learning activities provide common ground for the teacher–student interactions (Newman, Griffin and Cole, 1989) and through these teacher–student interaction, students receive feedback on what they know, understand and can do and they are able to generate opportunities for furthering their understanding. Feedback or dialogue is an essential component of formative assessment interaction where the intention is to support learning (Clarke, 1995; Sadler, 1989).

   The process of formative assessment always includes students. It is a process through which they find out about their learning. The process involves them in recognizing, evaluating and reacting to their own and / or others' evaluations of their learning. Students can reflect on their own learning or they may receive feedback from their peers or the teacher. Formative assessment is viewed as occurring within the interaction between the teacher and student(s) and so is at the intersection of teaching and learning:

> Assessment is in dynamic interaction with teaching and learning. (Gipps, 1994, p. 16)

In recent years, the importance of formative assessment in the teaching and learning processes has become more widely acknowledged and, in New Zealand, government educational policy documents recognize and emphasize the importance and value of assessment in informing learning. For example:

> The primary purpose of school-based assessment is to improve students' learning and the quality of learning programs. (Ministry of Education, 1993a, p. 24)

The *New Zealand Curriculum Framework* (Ministry of Education, 1993a, p. 24) and, for example, the science curriculum (Ministry of Education, 1993b, p. 18) include specific reference to assessment for better learning; diagnostic, formative and summative assessment; self-assessment by students; and assessment examples. Formative assessment has been given importance as it is seen as giving students and teachers feedback so as to improve learning outcomes. But despite formative assessment being included in government policy documents, there has been little classroom-based research to document what teachers do when they undertake formative assessment. The nature of the teaching activity called formative assessment is under-researched, under-theorized and hence largely lacking in the professional practice studies of preservice and inservice teachers. The research described in this chapter investigated classroom-based formative assessment in science education, in an attempt to clarify what it is that teachers do and think during formative assessment activities, and the purposes for which they do formative assessment. Full details of the research are documented in Bell and Cowie (1997a, 1997b) and Cowie (in progress). The research was funded by the New Zealand Ministry of Education in 1995–96 and its main aim was to investigate assessment and, in particular, formative assessment, in Years 7–10 classrooms where the teacher of science was taking into account students' thinking (Bell, 1993).

Research Design

There were four main considerations in planning the research: ethics, combining research and development, multiple perspectives, and multiple data collection methods.

Ethics

The ethical concerns were principally those of the ongoing maintenance of confidentiality with respect to the data; obtaining informed consent from all participants; monitoring for potential harm throughout the project; and the methods for dealing with any concerns of the (volunteer) participants with respect to being involved in a research project. These concerns were addressed throughout the project as well as at the beginning. The researchers felt it necessary to address these concerns due to the relatively small size of the city in which the research was undertaken. Hamilton, New Zealand, has a population of approximately 120,000, and is New Zealand's fourth largest city. But it is still, by international standards, a small city, with most people in the education community knowing each other. Therefore, the research had to be undertaken in a context where ethics and care regarding the people involved were of utmost importance. If the researchers alienated a group of teachers through their research design and methods, they would find a diminishing pool of teachers to work with in future years.

It was the policy of the researchers to be open about the purpose and methods of the research with all participants. The teachers selected to take part in the project were invited to a briefing meeting early in March 1995. At this meeting, the aims and questions which formed the basis of the research were discussed; the opportunities for professional development provided by the project were elaborated; and the requirements of the project in terms of data collection; and the teachers developing and trialing new material explained. The ethics governing the conduct of the project were then outlined. These included procedures the researcher would follow in setting up interviews and observations; ownership of the data (by the teachers and students) and data analysis (by the researchers); in obtaining informed consent from all participants; in maintaining the confidentiality and accuracy of transcripts; in monitoring for potential harm; the methods for dealing with concerns; and the method for withdrawing from the project. The proposed use of the data and procedures for the teachers to review the data analysis were outlined. The teachers' written informed consent for the procedures was obtained at the meeting. School principals and, through them, Boards of Trustees, were contacted and informed of the ethical procedures which would govern the project. Their informed consent for the involvement of their teachers and students was obtained. The students and their caregivers were also asked to sign an informed consent form.

Combining Research and Development

The second main consideration in the research design was that of deliberately combining research and development. This was done for four reasons. Firstly, the researchers held a view that the research process should have reciprocal purposes and gains for both the teachers and researchers. However, the gains for the researchers and teachers may not necessarily be the same. Whereas the main aim for the researchers was the creation of new knowledge about classroom-based assessment, teachers in previous research projects had indicated that they often got involved in major research projects for the opportunities for professional development. The teachers valued these opportunities for sharing ideas with other teachers, time for reflection, the input of new theoretical ideas and classroom activities, the support for trialing new classroom activities and for the information about wider educational developments (Bell and Gilbert, 1996). These activities could best be fostered in teacher development days although it is also acknowledged that these activities also occurred in the data collection activities of interviews, surveys and classroom observations.

Secondly, teachers' knowledge is often tacit knowledge. It was felt that some professional development activities would enable the teachers to raise their awareness of what they were doing in the classroom by way of formative assessment; develop a shared understanding and language in the group to make explicit their knowledge and skills about formative assessment; have shared experiences of formative assessment in the classroom by doing set tasks (for example, the coke and mystery box activities as recorded in Bell and Cowie, 1997a) in between meetings; and discuss and contribute to the developing model of formative assessment.

Thirdly, the teacher development days were included so that the teachers and researchers could meet to discuss the emerging and ongoing data analysis and negotiate a shared meaning of formative assessment. The teachers tended to talk about their teaching in the form of situated case studies by way of anecdoting (Bell and Gilbert, 1996). This discussion provided a forum for the teachers' voices to be heard with respect to their theorizing about formative assessment. This theorizing was considered valuable by the researchers as it was theorizing arising from practice rather than just theoretical perspectives arising from the disciplines of psychology, sociology, etc. This theorizing was in a form that could be seen as useful by other teachers in any subsequent teacher development days for teachers not involved in the research. The discussion also provided an ongoing secondary data generation and collection opportunity for the researchers and further reflective opportunities for the professional, personal and social development (Bell and Gilbert, 1996) of the teachers. The discussions of the teachers were sequential in nature. They initially focused on concerns about assessment (and in particular summative assessment); then the nature of formative assessment; how summative and formative assessment relate to each other (and especially in policy documents); the exchange and trialing of classroom formative assessment activities; discussion of the similarities and differences between the two types of formative assessment; and discussion of the model to describe and explain formative assessment.

Lastly, data to inform future teacher development courses on classroom-based assessment was sought.

As part of the research project, eleven teacher development days were held over the two years of the project. These teacher development days were included in the research design so that the ten teachers and two researchers could meet:

- to reflect on past and future assessment practices in science classrooms;
- for the input of new ideas for assessment in science classrooms from each other or from guest speakers;
- to discuss the trialing of new assessment activities in their classroom in between meetings;
- to discuss the data analyses and emerging model of formative assessment.

These four activities have been shown to promote teacher development (Bell and Gilbert, 1996) and the format of the eleven meetings was based on these research findings. The teacher development days were held from 9.00am to 3.00pm in one of two venues, with lunch being provided. The main activities on each of the days were:

- an input of new ideas for classroom assessment activities;
- sharing with each other how an assessment activity had worked in the classroom through the use of anecdoting (Bell and Gilbert, 1996);
- presentations by guest speakers who clarified educational policy on assessment and how formative assessment interfaced with other assessment procedures in the school;

- planning for tasks to be done by the teachers in between meeting times;
- discussions on the emerging data analysis;
- discussions of the developing model of formative assessment and the development of the model diagrams;
- the distribution and sometimes discussion of articles, books and Ministry of Education/Education Review Office documents.

Multiple Perspectives

The third main consideration in the research design was that of multiple perspectives. Formative assessment involves both teachers and students. Therefore, the research needed to explore formative assessment from the perspectives of both teachers and students. The researchers wished to research the teacher's and students' thinking about formative assessment and what they did in the classroom by way of formative assessment. Hence, three perspectives on formative assessment in the classrooms were obtained: those of the teachers, students, and the researchers. The researchers also thought that the teachers' involvement in the development of the model and the theorizing would be necessary as they were interested in how the teachers constructed the reality of their work and classrooms. Therefore, the research was designed with the following three strands.

Ideas about assessment

In this strand of the research, the views of assessment of the teachers and some of their students were elicited at the beginning of the project and monitored throughout the project. Data for this strand was collected through interviews and surveys.

Classroom-based studies

In this strand of the research, the classroom assessment activities of the teachers and their students were studied and documented in the form of eight case studies. In particular, formative assessment was researched. Data for this strand was collected by participant observation, involving fieldnotes, headnotes, and documentary data such as the writing on the board, student books, the wall displays, the teachers' 'plan' for the unit and the teachers' record books. The data included reflections by teachers and students on their experiences of classroom assessment in interviews.

Teacher development studies

In this strand of the research, teacher development activities were undertaken by the teachers to develop the formative assessment activities they used in their classrooms and to reflect on the data collected and analysed. This occurred on eleven days over 1995–96. Data for this strand was collected by audio-taped discussions, surveys and fieldnotes.

Three different groups of people were involved in generating data — the teachers, students and researchers. Each of these is discussed in turn.

The teachers involved

The teachers involved were volunteers as the researchers did not have the authority to compel teachers and students to work with them. All Hamilton urban schools with Year 7–10 (students aged 10–14 years) classes were sent a letter in February 1995 inviting them to register interest in being involved in the research, along with information on the purpose of the project, the professional benefits, and their obligations if they joined the project. All schools responded positively as they had teachers who wished to be involved. Ten teachers were then selected so that initially two teachers came from each of five schools; there was a mix of intermediate (Years 7, 8) and junior secondary school teachers (Years 9, 10); and there was a mix of teachers with and without experience of being involved in previous Learning in Science Projects and recent curriculum implementation inservice work. There was a mix of beginning and experienced teachers and some of the teachers had management responsibilities in their schools. Details of the teachers are given in Bell and Cowie (1997a).

Students

Each of the ten teachers chose a class to work with them on the project (and hence a different class in 1995 and 1996). All students, in the class chosen by the teacher to work with them on the project, were asked by the researcher or by their teacher if they would be prepared to be interviewed individually. The response varied from most wishing to be involved in the more junior classes, to only three or four responses in the Year 10 classes. The criteria for selection of the three from the sample of volunteers were that the students be thoughtful and able to communicate — a high level of performance in science was not a criteria.

The researchers

In qualitative research, the background of the researcher is of importance when considering the research design, data collection and data analysis. It is felt that it is important to record the background of the researchers so that readers of the research can be fully informed.

Beverley is a qualified and trained secondary teacher of science and biology, teaching for five years before undertaking postgraduate studies in science education. She has been involved in five major research projects on classroom-based teaching and learning, this assessment research being her sixth. She has also worked for four years as a national curriculum developer for the government Department of Education in the late 1980s, having responsibility for the revision of a national science curriculum. She is currently at the University of Waikato teaching masters and doctoral students in science education and researching into science education in the areas of teaching, learning and assessment and teacher development.

Bronwen is a qualified and trained teacher of secondary mathematics and physics. She taught for 15 years, before accepting the position of full-time researcher on this research project. She is currently writing up her doctoral thesis, exploring students' views of formative assessment, at the University of Waikato, where she also teaches primary and secondary preservice teachers.

Multiple Data Collection

Multiple kinds of data and multiple ways of collecting data were used to increase the validity of the data collected and the data analysis. The data were collected by interviews, surveys, participant observation and the audiotaping of discussions on the teacher development days. Aspects of these are now discussed:

The interviews and surveys

There were three sets of interviews with the teachers and the selected students. The nature of the interviews changed as the research progressed in response to the data being collected. In the first set of interviews (Phase 1, January–June 1995; reported in Cowie and Bell, 1995), the teachers and three of their students were interviewed, using a semi-structured approach, about aspects of assessment.

The second set of interviews was the end-of-lesson and end-of-unit interviews conducted following the 1995 and 1996 classroom observations, with the teachers and students. These enabled the researcher to obtain the teacher's and some students' impressions and interpretations of the learning, teaching and assessment which had taken place during the unit. The teacher end-of-lesson interviews in 1995 and 1996 ranged from informal discussions to semi-structured interviews depending on the teacher's work commitments immediately following the lesson.

The third set of interviews (the end of year interviews) was conducted at the end of 1995 and 1996 with each teacher. At these times, the teachers were interviewed using semi-structured interviews, as a part of monitoring the teachers' views on assessment over the two years of the research and to ask them to reflect on the emerging model of formative assessment.

Three surveys were given to the teachers to complete as part of the teacher development strand — one in June 1995, May 1996 and November 1996 — on their views of teacher development and formative assessment.

Participant observation

Data from classrooms were collected by participant observation. It was decided that in order to construct a rich, coherent and useful interpretation of assessment within a classroom, it was important for the researcher (Bronwen) to 'see' the whole story of a teaching unit. This would allow her to become familiar with the context of the learning within the particular classroom for the particular unit. She would be present through the complete teacher planned and delivered unit of work and she would observe the students' interactions and meaning making throughout the unit. Such continuity is important for naturalistic research where the researcher wishes to develop a valid interpretation of a complex process (Guba and Lincoln, 1985; Maykut and Morehouse, 1994). For this purpose, the five intermediate and five secondary teachers were observed throughout their units of work in 1995 or 1996 and data collected and recorded through a variety of techniques.

At one stage in the research, a visiting researcher (Carol Boulter, University of Reading) was working with the project team. The opportunity for two researchers to be involved in the classroom observations provided different opportunities for data collection and interpretation. In particular, the reliability and validity of the participant observation and fieldnotes could be explored.

The observation of classrooms-in-action requires an empathetic approach on the part of a researcher, who needs to balance the demands of collecting rich data with the degree to which she or he will alter what is happening. The purpose of the sequence of observations was to collect data on assessment as it was occurring within the classroom. The researcher was interested in the assessment activities of both the teacher and their students. The role of the researcher was agreed as that of participant observer — she would become part of the classroom in the role of researcher in a manner which would minimally influence the learning, while keeping her integrity as a person deeply interested in what was happening (Ball, 1985). The actions appropriate to this role varied depending on how the teacher had structured the learning activities. During whole class discussion, the researcher observed the teacher and 'the class', she did the work which was assigned to the students, sometimes discussing it with the student beside her as the other students did. During group work, she participated in a group with the group leader's permission. In this case, she observed what was happening within the group or within the class from the perspective of the group. Blending in with different groups within the classroom required a variety of strategies, ways of behaving. At times, the researcher was specifically invited to join a group. For example, one group invited her to join them, re-established their view of the researcher's purpose for being in the classroom, and continued to work independently but within the group structure as they had before her arrival. She was included in smelling, looking at or commenting on any apparatus or the experiment in the same way as any other member of the group. She spent several days working within this group and always felt welcome and accepted.

The different data collection techniques used in support of the participant observation were fieldnotes, headnotes (the record of the observation which the researcher retained in her head — what she remembered of the lesson, see Sanjek, 1990) and documentary data (the board, student books, the walls, the teacher's plan for the unit, the teacher's record book). The multi-faceted data collection and data analysis were managed within a framework provided by triangulation. Triangulation through the use of two or more methods of data collection is a technique used to increase the validity and reliability of the data collection and interpretation. In this research, different forms of triangulation (data triangulation, investigator triangulation, respondent triangulation, time and space triangulation) were achieved through a variety of methods (Cohen and Manion, 1994; Maykut and Morehouse, 1994).

The Findings

The findings of the research are fully documented in Bell and Cowie (1997a, 1997b); Cowie (in progress); Cowie and Bell (in press).

What was Assessed in Science Classrooms?

The findings indicated that the teachers assessed a wide range of learning outcomes in their lessons — wider than it was originally thought by the teachers and researchers at the beginning of the project. What was being assessed was related to the purposes of formative assessment and linked to the students' learning within the classroom — their personal, social and science development (Cowie, Boulter and Bell, 1996, p. 30). Students' personal development related to their learning about themselves as learners of science, asking questions, self-assessment, behaviour, time management, motivation and attitude. Their social development related to their interacting with others (students and teachers), peer assessment, leadership skills, group work, discussion and listening skills. Their science development related to the development in the knowledge and understanding of science and their ability to do science — for this was their unique purpose for being in a science classroom. These three aspects were assessed by the teachers of science (Bell and Cowie, 1997a). The three aspects were not independent of each other; the complexity and richness of their interactions was a contributor to the diversity and complexity of the classroom.

The aspects of science which were assessed in the science lesson were the science content (the body of scientific knowledge — the concepts and ideas of science), science context (the contexts in which the science is learnt and used) and science processes (those skills and processes used by scientists to investigate phenomena).

Two Kinds of Formative Assessment

At the start of the research, the teachers stated that they did formative assessment but had difficulty describing what it was exactly that they did. A strong trend in the survey data was for the teachers to acknowledge that they were more aware of what they did, by way of formative assessment, by the end of the research. What they did was a complex process involving many professional skills and knowledges.

The findings suggested to the researchers and teachers that two forms of formative assessment were being used by the teachers and students in the classrooms observed:

Figure 11.1   Planned formative assessment

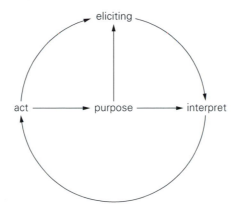

- planned formative assessment;
- interactive formative assessment.

Planned formative assessment

The process of planned formative assessment was characterized by the teachers eliciting, interpreting and acting on assessment information. The purpose for which the information was being collected and what was being assessed determined how the information was collected. Hence, these four aspects are interrelated and mutually determining. These aspects are represented diagrammatically in Figure 11.1. An example of planned formative assessment in the data was a teacher asking the students to brainstorm their understanding of aspects of electricity at the beginning of a lesson. The assessment was planned by the teacher before the lesson began and was formative in that it gave feedback to both teachers and students about the learning outcomes of the students in the previous lesson. The teacher used the information obtained to determine the exact content of the day's lesson.

Interactive formative assessment

The second form of formative assessment was interactive formative assessment. Interactive formative assessment was that which took place during student–teacher interactions. It differed from planned formative assessment in that the details were not planned and could not be anticipated. Although the teachers often planned or prepared to do interactive formative assessment, they could not plan for or predict what exactly they and the students would be doing.

Interactive formative assessment occurred during student–teacher interaction and so had the potential to occur any time students and teachers interacted. The teachers and students within the project interacted in whole class, small group and one-to-one situations. The teachers' interaction with selected students in a whole

Figure 11.2   Interactive formative assessment

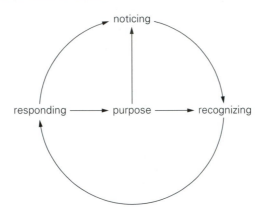

class was public as all of the students were able to observe and listen to what happened. The teachers interacted more privately with students in small group and one-to-one situations.

The process of interactive formative assessment involved the teachers noticing, recognizing and responding to student thinking during these interactions. Interactive formative assessment is represented diagrammatically in Figure 11.2. An example of interactive formative assessment in the data was when a teacher noticed in a lesson that some of the students held a scientifically unacceptable view of cooling and contraction. She recognized that some teaching was required, and she responded by moving the class discussion to whether matter contracted or expanded on cooling.

The teachers indicated that they were prepared to do interactive formative assessment in a lesson. They prepared for it by planning to increase the number of interactions between them and their students. They prepared by providing opportunities for students to approach them. They prepared for interactive formative assessment by rehearsing their responses to possible student alternative conceptions. They also planned to increase their opportunities for observing students interacting with each other.

Interactive formative assessment depended on the teachers' skills of interaction with the students and the nature of the relationships they had established with the students. The teachers viewed interactive formative assessment as an integral part of teaching and learning, not separate from it. The responding as an action could be viewed as a part of formative assessment or a part of teaching from this perspective.

Interactive formative assessment is more complex and more difficult to execute in the busyness of the classroom than planned formative assessment. Hence, the teachers indicated that interactive formative assessment tended to be done more by experienced teachers and when they knew the students better; for example, in the middle and end of the school year.

Figure 11.3   A model of formative assessment

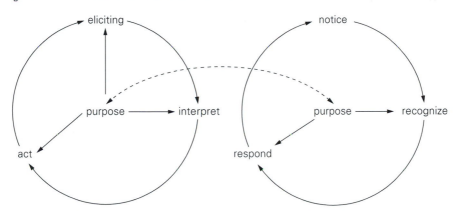

planned formative assessment   interactive formative assessment

The main distinctions between interactive and planned formative assessment were the degree and type of planning done by the teachers and the purposes for which they did formative assessment. Planning for planned formative assessment involved preparing in advance of the lesson, specific assessment activities. Planning for interactive formative assessment involved being prepared to notice and recognize students' ideas and planning to respond to them.

The purpose of planned formative assessment was perceived as obtaining information from the whole class about progress in learning the science as specified in the curriculum to inform the teaching. The purpose of interactive formative assessment was perceived as mediating in the learning of individual students with respect to science, personal and social learning.

Using Both Forms of Formative Assessment

The teachers indicated that a developing professional skill was the ability to move 'to-and-fro' from planned to interactive and back again. In the discussions held on the last two teacher development days in November 1996, the teachers and researchers considered the two forms of formative assessment and how they interacted with each other. The two kinds of formative assessment and the links between them, had been represented diagrammatically on the whiteboard, as shown in Figure 11.3. The teachers discussed the interaction of the two kinds of formative assessment. They commented: that the two kinds of formative assessment were linked through the *purposes* for formative assessment (the dotted lines); that the planned formative assessment was typically more explicit to the teachers and students; that some teachers used interactive formative assessment more than other teachers; and that a teacher could move from planned to unplanned and back. As one teacher commented:

Beverley Bell and Bronwen Cowie

> I quite like the idea that now we've got sort of two (parts to the) model. Because I know that when I plan assessment tasks, that they would certainly obviously fit in to that planned formative assessment section. And yet a lot of interactive things are happening during the lessons, either directed by me or even directed by students. There'll be students who will make a self-assessment and they'll reset goals and they'll work towards something else, so I think that interactive one is not just for us, but it's for students as well. (TD10/96/28.4)

(This and the other quotations are from the transcripts of the teacher development day — (TD). This quote is from the 10th teacher development day, in 1996, tape 28).

For another teacher, the righthand side part of the model acknowledged the role of professional knowledge and 'gut-feelings' in the process as had been discussed in previous teacher development meetings:

> But that second circle [on the righthand side], there, is quite exciting because that puts a definite professional skill onto teaching. You know . . . [some people say] . . . anyone could teach, therefore you don't have to train, . . . you can have non-registered teachers . . . anybody can teach. But it's not everybody that can do that . . . second circle. (TD10/96/28.13)

The righthand side of the model was noted to involve the teacher's disposition and motivation to assess (and teach) in this way:

> *Teacher*: I'm still really interested in this idea that, in particular, the righthand side diagram requires the teacher to have a particular disposition . . . And the example that's given . . . is playing a piano. A disposition consists of the ability to play the piano, which is one aspect of the disposition. The inclination to play the piano, like you want to play, and sensitivity to times when it's appropriate to play the piano.
> *Researcher*: Is that part of what the motivation means?
> *Teacher*: Well I think it is care . . . that's got something to do with motivation.
> *Researcher*: And by care, you would mean?
> *Teacher*: Well, that you think it's worthwhile to try and pass on that knowledge or skill to other people. I mean, if it's, if you feel in yourself that it's a waste of time, what you're doing, then you don't come across as a motivated teacher. (TD10/96/28.39; TD10/96/28.40)

The role of the teacher's knowledge of science was noted:

> Yes, well you see that's the whole notion about whether you need to have some science yourself to teach it. . . . I would say you do. I mean, you don't have to have heaps of it, but you have to have some to be able to interact with the students. To be able recognize and respond, you have to have some scientific knowledge in order to respond to it. Otherwise, you're just talking around on ill-formed ideas and we have a responsibility in teaching . . . [to teach] . . . the scientific ideas. That's not saying that all students are going to learn it and that's the only goal of the lesson, but the government and parents charge you with responsibility of teaching science. (TD10/96/28.6)

210

The teachers made many comparisons between the two parts of the model, for example:

> Yeah, well the one on the lefthand side is definitely more formal, you can plan it. How you're going to gather information, how you're going to do it . . . Whereas on the right is more intuition. (TD10/96/28.14)

> Because that one [on the lefthand side], there's almost like it's . . . you start your lesson, you've got your purpose set. Whereas this one over here [on the righthand side] is you're halfway through your lesson, you notice something that your purpose can change or your lesson plan changes to fit it. (TD10/96/28.8)

The link between the two parts of the model was seen to be centred around the purposes for doing formative assessment:

> . . . You start out with your planned purpose, and you're teaching along and you notice something happens which changes what happens during the lesson which gives you a new purpose, which will lead to your next planned purpose. (TD10/96/28.31)

The distinction was made between an initial purpose (arising out of some planning) and a purpose that evolved or emerged from what was happening in the lesson:

> Well, for me, you have your purpose and you'll be going through that gather, interpret, act cycle, and that's when you notice. Your purpose is not when you notice, your purpose is what you set out to do. So you're not going to notice anything when you're setting out to do it. You only notice it when you've got into interpreting, acting or gathering. (TD10/96/28.31)

The teachers confirmed that they changed from planned to interactive formative assessment (see the dotted lines in Figure 11.3) by noticing something in the course of planned formative assessment. The purpose for the interactive formative assessment took them back to planned formative assessment.

The discussions up to this point in the teacher development days are evident of the teachers collaboratively reflecting on their practice to develop the model with the researchers. Further discussions indicated that the teachers were going beyond the model to the use of metaphors. One of the researchers commented that the diagram looked like a bike:

> . . . it sort of looks like a bike model. (TD10/96/28.33)

This analogy of the diagrammatic representation of the formative assessment process with a bike was built on by the teachers. The pedals were equated with what drove the process of formative assessment:

> . . . the pedals to me are the skill of the teacher, the level of expertise of the teacher in facilitating learning. Because that one [cycle] on the right, you said that's a

higher order thing that teachers do. And you could be stuck with your back pedal forever if you're not a really good teacher. That pedal is not just motivation, it's also having that expertise to be able to make the thing go. I mean, it's like you haven't learned to ride your bike yet and you have not got the pedals under control. (TD10/96/28.43)

The bell was equated with reporting and the brakes were equated with the perceived restraints on assessment and teaching:

Your brakes could be the parents or the outside community . . . [the brakes] controls how fast and slow you go . . . the brake could be the limitation of resources. (TD10/96/28.48)

The relative size of the two bike wheels was equated with the relative importance and use of each kind of formative assessment (planned formative assessment on the lefthand side of the model and interactive formative assessment on the righthand side of the diagram). The purpose for doing each type of formative assessment was also acknowledged to be different:

I think one of the key things would be making sure that people understand that the one [the circle in the model diagram] on the left you might use say three or four times during a period of three weeks, whereas the one on the right you're using every day. So that's a really key issue, that they've got to hone in on the fact that yes, there are planned ones, and you might do three of them. The interactive one is one that you really need to enlighten yourself with. . . . It's the crucial one.

And if that one [the righthand side cycle], if . . . the expertise and those sorts of things, are not very highly developed. So that wheel becomes a smaller one or not used very much. You're not going to go anywhere near as far as you could do if you had that one the righthand side cycle as a bigger wheel.

A penny farthing is not as advanced as the two wheels.

Well also, some people [have an idea] . . . that you put people under more stress and are more insecurity and therefore they're going to perform better. I think, here, if you are more secure and have less stress, then that [righthand side] wheel gets bigger because you have time to notice and recognize and respond and do things properly. And the more stress and the more tunnel visioned you become, the smaller that wheel gets.

Because I found that this year, since I've been sick, you tend to narrow your purpose because you're trying to get the most important things done, and that one on the righthand side gets smaller. And it's only when you sort of learn to relax a bit and take the bigger picture that [right] wheel starts getting big again.

So your focus is on covering the syllabus or doing a particular task rather than looking at the students' learning.

So that's an interesting comment in terms of the two purposes of those two wheels. The hub is different, isn't it?

Yes, the left is curriculum and the right is student.

So the righthand one is more about focusing on the student, that student-referenced one we talked about. Whereas the lefthand side, what is driving your planning in that is the curriculum plan that you might do that translates to the teaching . . . (TD10/96/28.53; TD10/96/28.54)

In this last transcript segment, the teachers explored the possibilities of the metaphor of bike, emphasizing the important role of purpose in assessment. These discussions were possible because of the shared, negotiated meanings of formative assessment and trust that had been generated during the eleven teacher development days. The process of combining research and development enabled the teachers and researchers to arrive at a place where this kind of talk was possible.

Summary and Conclusion

Formative assessment as described by this research is a complex, skilled task. The formative assessment done by the teachers in the research reported here (when considering both forms of formative assessment) was either planned for or prepared for, contextualized, responsive, ongoing, done during the learning to improve the learning, and relied on the teacher's pedagogical knowledge (Shulman, 1987).

Knowing about the details of the formative assessment process raised the awareness of the ten teachers about what they do by way of formative assessment in their classrooms (Bell and Cowie, 1997a). That is, the teachers were doing formative assessment but they were not always aware of exactly what they were doing that could be called 'formative assessment'. The increased awareness enabled the teachers to reflect in new ways on their practice. The increased awareness was perceived by the teachers to be the main aspect of their teacher development during the two years of the research project (Bell and Cowie, 1997a). The teachers also indicated that eliciting and noticing were easier to do in the classroom than acting and responding. The feedback obtained to date suggests that other teachers and researchers are also interested in this clarification of the formative assessment process. The research findings lend themselves to the development of workshop materials for use in teacher education programs to develop teachers' skills of formative assessment, both with respect to knowing about formative assessment and to being able to carry it out in the classroom.

It is our view that combining the research and developmental processes enabled both the researchers and teachers to gain from this collaborative project. In particular, the teacher development strand and the data collection techniques enabled the teachers to reflect on their trialing of new classroom activities, the data generated, the data analysis, the model and the implications of the bike metaphor. The teachers valued these reflections to increase their awareness of their practice, to extend their theoretical frameworks and to contribute to the development of the model. These reflections also supported them to change their classroom practice.

We, as researchers, valued both the research and development strands to enable us to document teachers' tacit knowledge and practice. Although we have both secondary and tertiary teaching experiences ourselves, we enjoyed being surprised and amazed at the unanticipated data and the complexity of the formative assessment process as it emerged in the data analysis. Hence, both the teachers and the researchers gained from having one aspect of teachers' knowledge and professional practice articulated, described and theorized.

Beverley Bell and Bronwen Cowie

References

BALL, S. (1985) 'Participant observation with pupils', in BURGESS, R.G. (ed.) *Strategies of Educational Research*, London: Falmer Press.

BELL, B. (1993) *Taking Into Account Students' Thinking: A Teacher Development Guide*, Hamilton: University of Waikato.

BELL, B. and COWIE, B. (1997a) *Formative Assessment and Science Education. Research Report of the Learning in Science Project (Assessment)*, p. 340, Hamilton: University of Waikato.

BELL, B. and COWIE, B. (1997b) *Formative Assessment and Science Education. Summary Report of the Learning in Science Project (Assessment)*, p. 80, Hamilton: University of Waikato.

BELL, B. and GILBERT, J. (1996) *Teacher Development: A model from Science Education*, London: Falmer Press.

CLARKE, D. (1995) 'Constructive assessment: Mathematics and the student', in RICHARDSON, A. (ed.) *Flair: AAMT Proceedings*, Adelaide: AAMT.

COHEN, L. and MANION, L. (1994) *Research Methods in Education*, London: Routledge.

COWIE, B. (in progress) 'Assessment in science classrooms', Unpublished DPhil thesis, University of Waikato.

COWIE, B. and BELL, B. (1995) *Learning in Science Project (Assessment) Research Report 1: Views of Assessment*, SMTER Centre: University of Waikato.

COWIE, B. and BELL, B. (1996) 'Validity and formative assessment in the science classroom', Invited Keynote Paper to *Symposium on Validity in Educational Assessment*, 28–30 June, Dunedin, New Zealand.

COWIE, B. and BELL, B. (in press) 'A model of formative assessment in science education', Invited paper to a special issue of *Assessment in Education*.

COWIE, B., BOULTER, C. and BELL, B. (1996) 'Developing a framework for assessment of science in the classroom', Working paper, CSMTER: University of Waikato.

GIPPS, C.V. (1994) *Beyond Testing: Towards a Theory of Educational Assessment*, London: Falmer Press.

GUBA, B. and LINCOLN, S. (1985) *Naturalistic Inquiry*, Newberry Park, CA: Sage Publications.

MAYKUT, P. and MOREHOUSE, R. (1994) *Beginning Qualitative Research: A Philosophical and Practical Guide*, London: Falmer Press.

MINISTRY OF EDUCATION (1993a) *The New Zealand Curriculum Framework*, Wellington: Learning Media.

MINISTRY OF EDUCATION (1993b) *Science in the New Zealand Curriculum*, Wellington: Learning Media.

NEWMAN, D., GRIFFIN, P. and COLE, M. (1989) *The Construction Zone: Working for Cognitive Change in School*, Cambridge: Cambridge University Press.

SADLER, D.R. (1989) 'Formative assessment and the design of instructional systems', *Instructional Science*, **18**, 2, pp. 119–44.

SANJEK, R. (ed.) (1990) *Fieldnotes: The Makings of Anthropology*, Ithaca: Cornell University.

SHULMAN, L. (1987) 'Knowledge and teaching: Foundations of the new reforms', *Harvard Educational Review*, **57**, 1, pp. 1–22.

12 Researching Teaching Through Reflective Practice

Christopher Day

Introduction

This chapter examines the nature of reflective practice, its purposes and contexts, and the kinds of investment which are needed by the individual and the organization in order to build, sustain and develop quality of teaching over the course of a career. It discusses the purposes of reflective practice, different modes of reflection, and the need to address emotion as well as cognition in the context of maintaining teachers' substantive selves and preventing burnout. It charts the cultural, organizational and practical time constraints and the need to take account of teachers' own development phases as part of the conditions for reflective practice; and it highlights the difficulties in promoting reflective practice as a part of systemic development efforts. Finally, it suggests a model of reflective professionalism through partnership.

> ... to cope with a changing world, any entity must develop the capability of shifting and changing, of developing new skills and attitudes: in short the capability of learning ... the essence of learning is the ability to manage change by changing yourself — as much for people when they grow up as for companies when they live through turmoil. (de Gues, 1997, p. 20)

The credibility of teachers as professionals in all countries is now being judged more than ever against ability to deliver government results-driven reform agendas which emphasize success in terms of implicit cause-and-effect relationships between the quality of teaching and pupil achievement across a relatively narrow band of knowledge and skills at key stages in their school lives. The effects of home, peer and school environments upon students' dispositions (motivations) to learn and their achievement levels have been well documented over the years; and although governments have attempted to address these in a variety of ways, they remain important variables not only in curriculum achievement but also in school attendance, citizenship and employment potential. Yet in the years since it was argued that at least half the differences in pupils' performances in their late teens were due to differences in their social backgrounds and prior attainments (Jencks et al., 1972), considerable research has also taken place on factors in school which make a difference to the learning lives of pupils. Such 'value added' formulae appear to enable school effectiveness to be judged in relation to these and other factors. Surprisingly, less attention has been given to the impact on learning of the values of the school (Goodlad, Soder and Sirotnik, 1990), the relationships between teachers and students (Rudduck, Day and Wallace, 1997) and the quality of teachers' long-term motivation and intellectual and emotional commitments. A necessary condition of effectiveness as a teacher is regular reflection upon the three elements that make up teaching practice: the emotional and intellectual selves of the teacher and students; the conditions that affect classrooms, schools and students' learning and achievements; the experience of teaching and learning.

Reflective Practice: Contexts and Purposes

It is reasonable to predict that classroom teaching roles and the intellectual and emotional demands placed upon teachers will become more rather than less complex as the expectations of society and the needs of learners change. Engaging routinely in reflection upon thinking and practice is, therefore, a necessity in order to sustain professional health and competence. Yet research over the years has established that most teachers become locked into 'single loop' learning (Argyris and Schön, 1974) as they develop 'routines' (Clark and Yinger, 1979) in school cultures which often discourage the sharing and critiquing of practice (Rosenholtz, 1989). Furthermore, many teachers become either disenchanted as the toll of teaching and conditions of service erode early aspirations, or remain on the plateau of competence, which indicates underperformance. In doing so, they lose their extended view of their responsibility — of teaching as a moral enterprise. Yet it has been argued that teachers must be seen, and see, themselves as more than technicians:

> . . . teachers must be seen as occupying key roles in classrooms — not simply as technicians who know how to run good discussions or teach encoding skills to beginning readers but as persons whose view of life, which includes all that goes on in classrooms, promises to be as influential in the long run as any of their technical skills. It is this extended view of a teacher's responsibility that makes it appropriate to speak of teaching as a moral enterprise. (Jackson et al., 1993, p. 277)

To practice effectively, then, means engaging routinely in conscious, systematic collection and evaluation of information about these areas and the relationships between them which affect and result from practice. In this respect, teaching is similar to, though more complex than, other caring professions. For example, it is similar to social work in that teachers have a responsibility to assess (need), plan (to meet need) and evaluate (through feedback) whether the needs of both the individual and society have been met. It is different because teachers must work almost exclusively in crowded social settings which militate against extended interaction with individual students and because they have a core responsibility to 'educate' through the transmission of agreed curricula. A relationship may be drawn, however, between achieving the instrumental goals of education and achieving the social work goals of:

- understanding better some client population;
- understanding better some particular situations or circumstances affecting clients;
- understanding better the process of some service delivery system or helping network;
- evaluating the impact and outcomes of some practice procedure or care system;
- comparing the outcomes of different practice procedures;
- evaluating the impact of local or national policy or legislation on a case load or how we work with clients. (Whitaker and Archer, 1990)

Teaching also has similarities with nursing. Like nursing, the ability to exercise discretionary or professional judgment is essential to practice and this is based upon interaction between personal, experiential and scientific knowledge. Growth and expertise will be limited if practitioners reply only one kind of knowledge. In much the same way that van Manen (1995) presents the case for pedagogical tact so, in the context of nursing, Rolfe (1998) argues that the expert practitioner's judgments represent the appropriate integration and application of personal, experiential and scientific knowledge. In short, teachers must engage in reflective practice. Further parallels between these three professions are the conditions of increasing performance expectations, work loads and accountability pressures which affect their abilities to engage in reflection. Reflective practice in all three demands a considerable investment over the course of a career both by individuals and their employers.

There is a body of literature (Elbaz, 1992; Hargreaves, 1997; Guskey and Huberman, 1995; Jackson et al., 1993; Fried, 1995; Barth, 1990; Tedesco, 1997) which recognizes the need to recruit and retain teachers who will not only be rich in their knowledge of content and pedagogy, but also remain caring, enthusiastic about, and committed to making a difference in the lives of their students over the 40-year span of their careers — no mean feat in the face of declining morale, increased stress, and punitive working conditions. However this tends to be written about by academic researchers and practitioners, and seems to have had little impact upon government policy. It is difficult for teachers to remain hopeful in the face of a perceived lack of understanding of the complexity of the business of teaching and learning by governments. This statement, by an Australian teacher, might well have been made by teachers in any of a dozen countries:

> They don't really care. It's purely a numbers and monetary game. I wouldn't mind so much if there was a purpose or master plan. Pressure and stress are up, and I'm not convinced that the government has the best interests of the kids at heart. (Bishop and Mulford, 1996, p. 232, cited in Hargreaves, 1997)

Yet, if teachers are to strive to fulfil the expectations placed upon them, they must retain the capacity and willingness to intervene effectively in the classroom in order to promote knowledge, skills and achievement outcomes and, perhaps more important in the longer term, a love of learning itself among their students. Effective intervention suggests more than a knowledge of students' needs and the possession and application of a repertoire of teaching skills, it is more in line with what van Manen (1995) has called, pedagogical tact:

> ... improvisational pedagogical–didactical skill of instantly knowing, from moment to moment, how to deal with students in interactive teaching–learning situations. (van Manen, 1995, p. 41)

It implies a continuing motivation and ability on the part of teachers to interrogate their own practice and its results in order to continue to connect with students' changing needs — and the changing expectations of government and others — and meet both. To be a professional, then, is to be an inquirer (Yinger and Hendricks-Lee, 1995).

Modes of Reflection

A reflective teacher is one who, given particular circumstances, is able to distance herself from the world in which she is an everyday participant and open herself to influence by others, believing that this distancing is an essential first step towards improvement (Mezirow, 1981, p. 105). Donald Schön (1983) popularized the notion of reflection 'in' and 'on' action, the former taking place during the action and often being tacit, and the latter outside the action, thus enabling more conscious, systematic evaluation of performance. Both seek to identify areas for change by seeking consistencies and inconsistencies within and between intentions and practices and then planning for action which will improve these. The notion of reflection-in-action has been criticized because there is simply no time to reflect in the busyness of classroom action (Eraut, 1994). Additionally, in order to survive in and manage the complexity of life in crowded classrooms, teachers naturally develop routines so that much of what they do and many of the decisions they take will become 'intuitive' and thus unexamined (Clark and Yinger, 1979). 'Intuition' can enhance the quality of teaching but it can also detract from it. It can enhance because it can represent teaching and teachers at their intellectual and emotional best; it can detract because it may also represent a routine, unconscious response to a new situation which is formulated on the basis of experience of other situations which have superficial similarities but which also have significant differences which are either unrecognized or unacknowledged.

Reflection-on-action may appear to be the ideal solution to the need for teachers to review their teaching. However, it has been criticized as: i) being managerially driven and focusing principally on increasing teaching efficiency only in terms of instrumental purposes defined through measurable gains in a narrow range of subject content areas; and, ii) failing to address the emotional intra- and interpersonal and professional dimensions of teaching which are key drivers of teacher care, commitment and quality.

Different modes of reflection on action have been identified (and categorized) according to purpose. Figure 12.1 provides a summary of these and illustrates the

Figure 12.1   Types of reflection related to concerns and contexts (adapted from Hatton and Smith, 1995, p. 59)

REFLECTION TYPE	NATURE OF REFLECTION	POSSIBLE CONTEXT
Reflection-in-action (Schön, 1983, 1987)	**5. Contextualization of multiple viewpoints** drawing on any of the possibilities 1–5 below applied to situations as they are actually taking place.	Dealing with on-the-spot professional problems as they arise (thinking can be recalled and then shared with others later).
Reflection-on-action (Schön, 1983; Smith and Lovat, 1990; Smith and Hatton, 1992, 1993)	**5. Intrapersonal**, recognizing the self as contributing to social action, examining one's own behaviour in the context of personal values and emotions.	Thinking about the effects of one's own biography and feelings upon the management of classroom relationships.
	4. Critical (social reconstructionist), seeing as problematic, according to ethical criteria, the goals and practices of one's profession.	Thinking about the effects upon others of one's actions, taking account of social, political and/or cultural forces.
	3. Dialogue (deliberative, cognitive, narrative), weighing competing claims and viewpoints, and then exploring alternative solutions.	Hearing one's own voice (alone or with another), exploring alternative ways to solve problems in the broader school context.
	2. Descriptive (social efficiency, developmental, personalistic), seeking what is seen as 'best possible' practice.	Analysing one's performance in the professional role (probably alone), exploring reasons for actions taken.
Technical rationality (Schön, 1983; Shulman, 1988; van Manen, 1977)	**1. Technical** (decision-making about immediate behaviours or skills), drawn from a given research/theory base, but always interpreted in light of personal worries, previous experience and employer expectations.	Examining one's use of essential teaching knowledge and pedagogical skills in the classroom in relation to results-driven demands.

need for reflective practice to be connected to purpose. Many management-led reflective practice initiatives have been criticized by academic researchers as being limited to 'technical' reflection aimed at increasing efficiency — for example, in the delivery of curriculum — without consideration of the social, political or economic conditions and contexts which influence both the quality of teaching and the efficacy of the curriculum itself. Thus efficacy cannot be equated with effectiveness. Such researchers suggest the need for 'critical reflection' which promotes examination of the values which are implicit in the curriculum and social fabric of schooling itself; and many have particular ethical value stances concerning the need for social justice, equality and emanacipatory discourse in schools which are themselves open to debate (Zeichner, 1993; Carr and Kemmis, 1986).

Even these lofty purposes and the moral stance of their advocates fail to take into account the emotional needs of teachers which are linked, so closely, with their commitment and enthusiasm over careers in which their functions, roles and 'clients' will be subject to considerable change.

Emotional Intelligence

Emotions are usually acknowledged and discussed, according to Hargreaves (1998), 'only insofar as they help administrators and reformers "manage" and offset teachers' resistance to change, or help them set the climate or mood in which the "really important" business of cognitive learning or strategic planning can take place'. Yet they are at the heart of teaching and learning relationships.

In order to teach successfully, teachers need to have the capacity to notice and make distinctions between the moods, motivations and temperaments of their students, to exercise what Howard Gardner calls 'interpersonal intelligence' (Gardner, 1993). The ability to handle relationships, to recognize and manage emotions in others is a basic competence in teaching and it is strange that so little attention is given in preservice and inservice education to developing this capacity.

Closely linked to skills of empathy in the management of others is the capacity to access one's own emotional life, so-called 'intrapersonal intelligence' (Gardner, 1993). In crowded and emotionally charged classrooms, peopled as they are at any given time with enthusiastic, disadvantaged and disenchanted students, teachers need to be able to draw upon self-awareness as a means of understanding their own behaviour and thus manage their own feelings appropriately.

Emotional intelligence has been defined as:

> . . . persistence in the face of frustrations; the ability to control impulse and delay gratification, to regulate moods and keep distress from swamping the ability to think, to empathise and to hope. (Goleman, 1995, p. 34)

It follows that reflection on self — one's motivations, values, and inner life — is a necessary part of teachers' career-long development.

Teachers' Lives

> Teachers teach in the way they do not just because of the skills they have or have not learned. The ways they teach are also grounded in their backgrounds, their biographies, in the kinds of teachers they have become. (Hargreaves, in Smyth, 1995, p. vii)

There is a plethora of research on beginning teachers which highlights problems of need, transition, survival and development in relation to preservice education, personal histories and, more recently, the effects of school cultures. Much of the research confirms the importance of appropriate induction for beginning teachers and underlines the need for a wide variety of learning opportunities for teachers throughout their careers. Recent empirical research over the first seven years of teaching, for example, has illustrated how, 'even for an experienced teacher, the development of teaching expertise is remarkably uneven, and a product of a complex interaction of person and place' (Bullough and Baughman, 1995). Teachers develop in different ways according to disposition and circumstance. Combining the findings of Oja and colleagues (1989) on the development of expertise, and Michael Huberman (1989) on career-cycle development, Ken Leithwood charted three interrelated dimensions of teacher development (see Figure 12.2). This conceptualization provides a useful reference point for researching teaching through reflective practice, for it may be used as a diagnostic as well as developmental tool. To be effective, however, two further dimensions need to be considered: life-cycle factors and the development of emotional intelligence.

> Evidence from studies of teachers' professional life cycles illustrates important changes in teachers' concerns, relationships with pupils, and relationships with colleagues that suggested differentiated learning interests and processes throughout their careers. (Butt, McCue and Yamagashi, 1992, p. 54)

One key phase identified by Huberman is when teachers reach a 'plateau'. Such a phase signals a security that comes with the development of proficiency and expertise (Stage 4 in Career-cycle Development and Professional Expertise in Figure 12.2) but, ironically, may lead to stagnation or decline if new challenges are not provided. The application of these may be complicated, however, by a number of related factors, e.g. lack of opportunity for career advancement and, in terms of mid-life phase, declining energy, and a shift of focus to family matters outside the school. Such key events or critical phases in teachers' lives indicate a time to re-examine purposes, values and direction.

Sustaining Purpose, Preventing Burnout

Fundamental to the notion of reflective practice is that good teachers need to maintain not only their intellectual but also their emotional health over the span of their careers if they are to serve the interests of society and provide high-quality learning opportunities for the many thousands of students whose dispositions towards learning and achievements they will influence — positively or negatively — over four or five decades of teaching. Fundamental to this is that teachers need to be both technically competent and 'passionate' in teaching — a recognition that teaching requires not only an appropriate range of knowledge and skills but also immense emotional investment.

Figure 12.2   Interrelated dimensions of teacher development (Leithwood, 1990)

Psychological Development (ego, moral, conceptual)		Development of Professional Expertise		Career-cycle Development
		6 participating in broad range of educational decisions at all levels		
	—	5 contributing to the growth of colleagues' instructional expertise	—	5 preparing for retirement: focusing
4 autonomous/inter-dependent, principled, integrated		4 acquiring instructional expertise		4 reaching a professional plateau
3 conscientious, moral, conditional dependence	—	3 expanding one's instructional flexibility	—	3 new challenges and concerns
2 conformist/moral, negative, independence		2 becoming competent in the basic skills of instruction		2 stabilizing: developing mature commitment
1 self-protective, pre-moral, unilateral dependence	—	1 developing survival skills	—	1 launching the career
Psychological Development (ego, moral, conceptual)	—	**Development of Professional Expertise**	—	**Career-cycle Development**

> Teachers' emotional commitments and connections to students, both positive and negative, energise and articulate everything they do. Teaching involves immense amounts of emotional labour . . . This kind of labour calls for a co-ordination of mind and feeling, and it sometimes draws on a source of self that we honour as deep and integral to our personality. (Hochschild, p. 7, cited in Hargreaves, 1997)

Unfortunately, considerable research evidence shows that the immense amount of emotional investment which teachers make during the early years of their careers declines. Many become disillusioned and demoralized in worlds which appear to undervalue their efforts or fail to appreciate the often adverse circumstances in which they work — whether caused by crowded classrooms, low resource levels, excessive bureaucratic demands or unrealistic performance expectations. Early aspirations and vision fades for many teachers and commitment dulls as they fail to live up to their own, and others', expectations. By mid-career they may have become disenchanted, feel undervalued, perhaps no longer hold the good of their students as a high priority, take responsibility of a minimalist kind for what goes on in the classroom and school, become 'defensive focusers' (Hargreaves, 1993). Such negative consequences of being a teacher are demonstrated directly in falling levels of recruitment and retention, evidence of increased stress-related illness in some countries (Cooper and Kelly, 1993) and an ageing teaching population. For example, in England and Wales in 1996, two thirds of teachers were aged 40+, one quarter aged 50+; and premature retirements accounted for the majority of all retirements (School Teachers Review Body, 1996).

Little is to be found in school development guidelines and models for the improvement of teaching which relates directly to the need for teachers to maintain their identities, what Woods (1994) has termed their 'substantive selves':

> Teaching is very much part of . . . teachers' substantive self. They have a strong sense of professionalism. They know how they want to teach and are not going to be dictated to. They consequently strongly resist the notion that they are being deprofessionalized. (Woods, 1994, p. 402)

Research in which teachers in England traced their professional learning and career lives during a 10-year period of imposed government reform (Day, 1999) revealed the different ways in which their attitudes to teaching, their practices and their confidence in their professionalism were challenged. It was those who found 'room to manoeuvre' in their personal and professional lives who maintained their optimism, passion and commitment to their vocation. From being potential 'victims', they reasserted their autonomy in new cultures of accountabilities and restructured their work within imposed guidelines in accordance with their own professional judgments (Helsby and McCullogh, 1997).

Cultural Influences

> When a school or school system deliberately sets out to foster new skills by committing everyone to required workshops, little happens except that everyone feels relieved, if not virtuous, that they have gone through the motions of doing their job. So, by and large, the district staff development activities we employ insult the capable and leave the competent untouched. (Barth, 1990, p. 50)

This former elementary school principal highlights the importance of attending to the culture of the school, recognizing that teacher development is closely related to the relationships within the school. Where the learning of teachers as well as students is not seen as integral to school development — is not part of teachers' everyday expectations — then it is unlikely to flourish. Traditional cultures of class-room teaching and existing cultures of many schools do not promote reflection of different kinds on a regular basis. Even when reflection is encouraged by govern-ment reform efforts, teachers' 'practicality' ethic (Doyle and Ponder, 1977) often militates against the kinds of critical discourse promoted by academics as being essential to the developing professional. In Norway, for example, the provision of time for collaborative planning and evaluation of teaching in secondary schools resulted in reflection at the technical level only (Handal and Lauvas, 1987). Restructuring does not always mean reculturing. Indeed, there are few recorded examples of processes of reculturing aimed at promoting schools as learning com-munities which are — for students and teachers — built around reflective processes which are planned alongside structural reform.

It might be argued that systematic reflection of different kinds is not a natural process in the busy worlds of classrooms (Johnston, 1994), and that it is not for teachers to question the policies of their employers, but to implement them. Indeed there is some evidence that even when teachers are provided with time to reflect in different ways, they tend to focus upon the planning and evaluation of everyday practice and not the ethical–moral issues espoused by some academics. However, this may be explained by the traditional cultures of teaching, in which teachers are educated to be self-reliant (at least publicly) in organizational and social cultures which are critical of weakness. External inspection systems which are punitive rather than developmental, results-driven curricula and the burgeoning list of behavioural competencies by which teachers are judged together with widespread media coverage, do not encourage disclosure. Conditions of service which do not allow teachers time to engage in systematic examination of practice and the think-ing behind their practice serve to reinforce the notion of action research as a luxury, principally carried out by those attending university courses. Paradoxically, one consequence of these cultures is that they work against the improvement aims of policy-makers in all but the most basic skill areas.

In recent years there has been much writing on school cultures. Hargreaves (1994) identified four kinds: 'individualism', in which the autonomy of the indi-vidual teacher is prized so much that the needs of the school are unlikely to be realized; 'contrived collegiality', in which teachers are brought to work together by management for administrative purposes — this may be a transition stage towards more collaborative cultures; 'balkanized', in which groups of teachers compete for resources and the values and purposes of departments in schools may be different and contradictory; and 'collaborative'. Others have characterized schools as 'stuck' or 'moving' (Rosenholtz, 1989), finding that, in the latter, improvements in teach-ing were seen as a collective endeavour and joint responsibility.

It is worth noting that cultures are not static and that if they are to continue to develop they will, like teachers, need time and investment. Like teachers they have life cycles. For example, Schön identified the 'dynamic conservatism' which is often present in organizations and serves to resist change (Schön, 1972); and Hall (1992) writes of five periods in the organizational life cycle. These are illustrated in Figure 12.3.

Figure 12.3   The organization life cycle (from Hall, 1992)

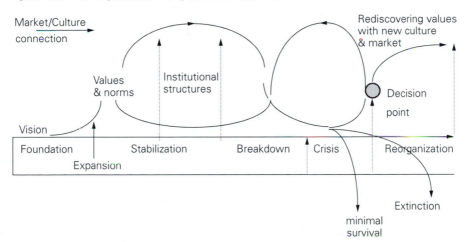

The *foundation* period is characterized by the strong and clear vision of the leader which 'connects with the needs of the times' and has the support of the teachers. The *expansion* period is a time when the vision is being implemented. It is characterized by a heightened sense of commitment by staff. Syllabi are written, plans draw up. The *stabilization* period marks an emphasis on unity and loyalty of staff who are secure in the knowledge that the school is successful and have a sense of professional achievement. The *breakdown* period marks a period of crisis when existing (often long held) values and practices are questioned as a result of 'a natural alteration in society and cultural values and needs that change with time and history'. One consequence may be a loss of self-esteem, and professional institutional loyalty. It is quickly followed by the *critical* period. Should the school adopt only a survival strategy (for example, a minimalist approach to the implementation of externally imposed change) or try to 'renew' itself? The critical factor here is the ability, skill and vision of leadership, and their tolerance of the uncertainties and ambiguities which characterize this period. Finally, there is the *reorganization* period. For this to occur, the leadership has to 're-examine its founding values, articulate them, and redefine them so that they . . . are in line with the present values and needs of society' (Hall, 1992, p. 22).

By being aware of such periods, and by locating the school in these, it is possible to focus investment upon particular needs; for example, to ensure that 'stabilization' does not lead to complacency, and that a 'breakdown' period provides opportunities to re-examine values.

Appraisal and Action Research: Differences and Similarities

We have observed that those schools which recognize that enquiry and reflection are important processes in school improvement find it easier to gain clarity and

> establish shared meanings around identified development priorities, and are better
> placed to monitor the extent to which policies actually deliver the intended out-
> comes for pupils. (Hopkins and West, 1994, pp. 192–3)

Whilst there can now be no doubt of the importance of inquiry and reflection as
endeavours which should be a part of systemic improvement efforts, their purposes,
processes and quality will be affected by the cultures in which they occur. For
example, reflection and inquiry as part of an appraisal system in a school which
does not promote collaboration as a part of its daily interactions is likely to be
perceived by teachers as being limited to fulfilling bureaucratic or management
determined demands. Action research, on the other hand, may be seen as an activity
which does not contribute to system needs. So whilst the broad intentions of
appraisal and action research may be similar, the specific purposes will inevitably
relate to context. For example, action research is voluntary, the agenda is set by the
teacher and, if collaborative, likely to be supported by self-selected critical friends.
Its purposes, like those of appraisal, are to improve practice, but definitions of
improved practice may differ. Underpinning action research is a view of teaching
as a complex task, requiring teachers to be skilled and wise in their use of discretionary judgment about students and events in their classrooms; and a view of
teachers themselves as having broad moral purposes which require intellectual and
emotional commitment to their students in order to perform at their best in conditions which essentially provide few opportunities for their own learning. Action
research also implicitly recognizes the need for teachers to review and renew their
commitment, motivation, knowledge and skills in order to sustain quality throughout their careers. The assumption is that schools will benefit directly through the
increased capacity of teachers to engage in critical evaluation of self, students and
the local and broad cultural and socio-economic cultures of their work.

   Appraisal, on the other hand, is employer initiated, management driven, and
bureaucratic. Whilst it may focus upon both development and contractual accountability, it is the latter which will be perceived to be its prime purpose. Because it is
management driven and bureaucratic, it will always be likely to be underpinned by
a view of teaching as being primarily concerned with achieving the instrumental
ends determined by government, district or school level policy or the school development plan. Whilst it is perfectly legitimate that this should be the case, such ends
will have the effect of narrowing the learning agenda and even — in day-to-day
school cultures of individuality, balkanization, comfortable or contrived collegiality
— alienating the teacher-learner.

Time

> Like us, teachers in many schools . . . find themselves too busy bailing out the
> water to plug the leak in the boat. (Hargreaves, 1997, p. 99)

Much has, and will continue to be, written about teacher research and its relationship to the development of teachers' and organizations' effectiveness. Research is,

of course, necessary for learning. However, in the busy lives of teachers who are in different phases of expertise, life, psychological and emotional maturity, with different responsibilities, learning dispositions and personal and professional concerns, there is not always the time or energy needed to undertake in depth inquiry either alone or collaboratively. The availability of time itself may be governed by any one or a combination of four dimensions: the **micropolitical** which relates to the distribution of time in relation to status; the **phenomenological**, which relates to the way in which the use of time is constructed in schools; the **socio-political**, which relates to claims made on teachers' time by administrators (Hargreaves, 1994); and the **personal**, which relates to the ways in which individuals themselves construct their priorities. These constraints upon the use of time ensure that most teachers will not be able to undertake long-term, systematic research regularly. Given the 'right' organizational culture, leadership support and personal commitment, there will be regular opportunities to reflect on practice and the conditions which affect it alongside colleagues from within and outside the school. However, opportunities for the systematic collection and analysis of data from self, classroom and school without support from colleagues are likely to be less frequent. Traditionally, it is those in school development and improvement networks and those in partnerships with higher education who are able to engage in this kind of research. All the more important, then, that opportunities for all teachers are provided at the most appropriate phases of their learning lives. This requires leaders who are themselves committed to learning. It also requires a recognition that healthy organizations, like healthy families, need to be places not only of challenge, but also of support and trust:

> The healthy families will be clear about their emotional needs so they won't have any hesitation about stopping to take a rest if they need to, or asking for help or advice when they want that. But it's the last of these factors, the degree of emotional support that they can draw on, which mainly accounts for the ease with which they deal with change. (Skynner and Cleese, 1993, p. 32)

Personal Change

Reflection is a necessary but insufficient condition for change. Some modes of reflection described in this chapter may pose challenges to the efficacy of closely held beliefs, values and practices, and teachers may not always wish to confront these or lack the practical and appropriate moral support to begin the process of change with its accompanying uncertainties:

> We may . . . be at our most vulnerable when studying closely our own persona as a teacher — the images others hold of us and those we hold of ourselves. In this, we may be entering into processes by which we deconstruct some basic, historically rooted views of ourselves. In such processes our existing images of the professional self will be challenged, questioned, re-thought and re-shaped in some degree. These processes are necessary if change and development are to occur and

if self study is to lead to new learning. We cannot escape them, nor the discomfort they may bring if we value our commitment to professional development. (Dadds, 1993, p. 288)

It is vital, then, that critical friendship support is available.

Constructing a Model of Reflective Professionalism

Successful confrontation by self or others requires a particular set of organizational conditions. In Australia, Judyth Sachs identified five core values which, she claims, are essential to a proactive, responsible approach to professional development:

1 Learning in which teachers are seen to practise learning individually with their colleagues and students;
2 Participation in which teachers see themselves as active agents in their own professional worlds;
3 Collaboration in which collegiality is exercised within and between internal and external communities;
4 Co-operation through which teachers develop a common language and technology for documenting and discussing practice and the outcomes;
5 Activism in which teachers engage publicly with issues that relate directly or indirectly to education and schooling, as part of their moral purposes. (Sachs, 1997)

Engaging in reflective practice enables such core values to be played out. Yet work of this kind requires huge personal and professional commitment to the practice of lifelong learning. To be most effective there needs to be principled and practical support in relation to school (and, where applicable, departmental) leadership and colleagues, in cultures which encourage disclosure and feedback, in environments which are focused upon improvement rather then punitive assessment.

Building communities of reflective practice is not easy, for it requires that expectations and traditional practices of teaching and its management is changed. To achieve this means that teaching purposes and values need to be revisited. It requires also acknowledgment that teachers are schools' greatest intellectual and emotional assets and that their health must be monitored over the whole of their careers. Opportunities to reflect on teaching represent one crucial contribution to efforts to maintain and nurture these assets in challenging, changing circumstances. Yet such opportunities require that time — the most precious commodity in teaching — be given, and that the complexity of teachers' work be recognized. Recognition by policy-makers, whether in or outside schools, of the need for reflection which goes beyond the valuable but limited and limiting 'learning from experience' in which most teachers engage, and the provision of appropriate support to enable this to occur, are to key factors in raising teacher morale for so long battered by reforms which seek to simplify the nature of their work by judging it through narrowly conceived measures of student achievement. Such measures, moreover, are essential if their capacities to develop and sustain the cognitive and emotional intelligences so necessary to the exercise of judgment in the classroom are to be built.

The core values identified by Sachs imply that schools, for long characterized as psychologically lonely places for adults to work (Cole, 1997), need to engage in 'sustained interactivity' in which learning partnerships within the school and between teachers and others from outside the school can be formed and developed over time.

There are many examples of partnerships between schools and universities through inservice work and other task-related consultancies; and between individual teachers attending award-bearing programs in which much of the inquiry work undertaken is school and classroom centred. School 'improvement' networks and consortia have also grown over the last 10 years. All these have the effect of reducing isolation and increasing participants' opportunities to reflect in different ways on their teaching, students' learning, and the contexts in which these occur. In such partnerships and networks, the relationships between university tutors and schools are based upon a common belief in the value of collaborative research and development. Systematic collection, analysis and reflection upon data about practice are the principal means of problem-identification, problem-solving and improvement. A key factor in their success is that all participants are committed to work together in equitable relationships. The role of the university is to provide appropriate, negotiated critical friendship, whether through didactic input, coordination, collection of data, or collaborative action research. Work of this kind demands that university tutors possess a range of human-relating skills and are themselves able to engage in reflection, particularly in areas related to their intra- and interpersonal intelligences.

Endnote

Making the professional knowledge base of teaching explicit and valuable for school teachers and higher education tutors is fundamental to pursuing their common goals of increasing understanding of the ways in which children and adults learn most effectively and the personal and social contexts which inform their (and our) thinking and actions; and improving the ways in which they teach. In this sense, research is fundamental to good teaching if we are to translate the rhetoric of continuous, lifelong learning into practice. The perceptions we have of ourselves and the societies in which we live, the ways we interact with others, our views of the past and the present, our visions for the future and the ways we initiate and respond to change are of immense importance to the ways we construct and carry out teaching. Without routinely engaging in reflective practice it is unlikely that we will be able to understand the effects of our motivations, prejudices and aspirations upon the ways in which we create, manage, receive, sift and evaluate knowledge; and, as importantly, the ways in which we are influencing the lives, directions and achievements of those whom we nurture and teach.

References

ARGYRIS, C. and SCHÖN, D.A. (1974) *Theory in Practice: Increasing Professional Effectiveness*, New York: Jossey-Bass.

BARTH, R.S. (1990) *Improving Schools from Within: Teachers, Parents and Principals Can Make a Difference*, San Francisco: Jossey-Bass.

BULLOUGH, R.V. and BAUGHMAN, K. (1995) 'Changing contexts and expertise in teaching: First year teacher after seven years', *Teaching and Teacher Education*, **11**, 5, pp. 461–77.

BUTT, R.D., McCUE, G. and YAMAGASHI, L. (1992) 'Collaborative autobiography and the teacher's voice', in GOODSON, I.F. (ed.) *Studying Teachers' Lives*, London: Falmer Press, pp. 51–98.

CARR, W. and KEMMIS, S. (1986) *Becoming Critical: Education, Knowledge and Action Research*, London: Falmer Press.

CLARK, C.M. and YINGER, R.J. (1979) *Three studies of teacher planning*, (Research Series No. 55) East Lansing: Michigan State University, Institute for Research on Teaching.

COLE, A.L. (1997) 'Impediments to reflective practice', *Teachers and Teaching: Theory and Practice*, **3**, 1, pp. 7–27.

COOPER, C.L. and KELLY, M. (1993) 'Occupational stress in headteachers: A national UK study', *British Journal of Educational Psychology*, **63**, pp. 130–43.

DADDS, M. (1993) 'The feeling of thinking in professional self study', *Educational Action Research Journal*, **1**, 2, pp. 287–303.

DAY, C. (1999) *Developing Teacher: The Challenge of Lifelong Learning*, London: Falmer Press.

DE GUES, A. (1997) *The Living Company*, Cambridge, M.A.: Harvard Business School Press.

DOYLE, W. and PONDER, G. (1977) 'The practicality ethic and teacher decision making', *Interchange*, **8**, pp. 1–12.

ELBAZ, F. (1992) 'Hope, attentiveness and caring for difference: The moral voice', *Teaching and Teacher Education*, **8**, 5/6, pp. 421–32.

ERAUT, M.E. (1994) *Developing Professional Knowledge and Competence*, London: Falmer Press.

FRIED, R.L. (1995) *The Passionate Teacher*, Boston: Beacon Press.

GARDNER, H. (1993) *Multiple Intelligences: The Theory in Practice*, New York: Basic Books.

GOLEMAN, D. (1995) *Emotional Intelligence*, New York: Bantam Books.

GOODLAD, J.I., SODER, R. and SIROTNIK, K.A. (eds) (1990) *The Moral Dimensions of Teaching*, San Francisco: Jossey-Bass.

GUSKEY, T.R. and HUBERMAN, M. (eds) (1995) *Professional Development in Education: New Paradigms and Practices*, New York: Teachers College Press.

HALL, B.P. (1992) 'The holographic organisation: Transforming corporate culture through values', Paper presented to Second World Congress on Action Learning, University of Queensland, Australia.

HANDAL, G. and LAUVAS, P. (1987) *Promoting Reflective Teaching*, Milton Keynes: Open University Press.

HARGREAVES, A. (1993) 'Dissonant voices, dissipated lives: Teachers and the multiple realities of restructuring', Paper presented to the Fifth Conference of the International Study Association on Teacher Thinking, Gothenburg, Sweden, August.

HARGREAVES, A. (1994) *Changing Teachers, Changing Times: Teachers' Work and Culture in the Postmodern Age*, New York: Teachers College Press.

HARGREAVES, A. (ed.) (1997) *Rethinking Educational Change with Heart and Mind*, Alexandria, V.A.: Association for Supervision and Curriculum Development.

HARGREAVES, A. (1998) 'Feeling like a teacher: The emotions of teaching and educational change', Paper provided in private correspondence.

HATTON, N. and SMITH, D. (1995) 'Facilitating reflection: Issues and research', *Forum of Education*, **50**, 1, pp. 49–65.

HELSBY, G. and McCULLOGH, G. (eds) (1997) *Teachers and the National Curriculum*, London: Cassell.

HOCHSCHILD, A.R. (1993) *The Managed Heart: Commercialisation of Human Feeling*, Berkeley: University of California Press.

HOPKINS, D. and WEST, M. (1994) *Creating the Conditions for School Improvement: Some Propositions*. London: Cassell.

HUBERMAN, M. (1989) 'The professional life cycle of teachers', *Teachers' College Record*, **91**, 1, pp. 31–57.

JACKSON, P.W. et al., (1993) *The Moral Life of Schools*, San Francisco: Jossey-Bass.

JENCKS, C., SMITH, M., ACLAND, H., BANE, M.J., COHEN, D., GUIFIS, H., HEYNS, B. and MICHELSON, S. et al., (1972) *Inequality: A Reassessment of the Effects of Family and Schooling in America*, New York: Basic Books.

JOHNSTON, S. (1994) 'Is action research a "Natural" Process for Teachers?', *Educational Action Research Journal*, **2**, 1, pp. 39–48.

LEITHWOOD, K. (1990) 'The principal's role in teacher development', in JOYCE, B. (ed.) *Changing School through Staff Development*, Alexandria, V.A., Association for Supervision and Curriculum Development.

MEZIROW, J. (1981) 'A critical theory of adult learning and education', *Adult Education*, **32**, 1, pp. 3–24.

OJA, S.N. (1989) 'Teachers: Ages and stages of adult development', in HOLLY, M.L. and McLAUGHLIN, C.S. (eds) *Perspectives on Teacher Professional Development*, London: Falmer Press.

ROLFE, G. (1998) *Expanding Nursing Knowledge*, Oxford: Butterworth Heineman.

ROSENHOLTZ (1989) *Teachers' Workplace: The Social Organisation of Schools*, New York: Longman.

RUDDUCK, J., DAY, J. and WALLACE, G. (1997) 'Students' perspectives on school improvement', in HARGREAVES, A. (ed.) *Rethinking Educational Change with Heart and Mind*, ASCD Yearbook, Alexandria, VA, Association for Supervision and Curriculum Development.

SACHS, J. (1997) 'Reclaiming teacher professionalism: An Australian perspective', Paper presented to the 5th Norwegian Educational Research Conference, Oslo, May.

SCHÖN, D.A. (1972) *Beyond the Stable State*, London: Penguin.

SCHÖN, D.A. (1983) *The Reflective Practitioner: How Professionals Think in Action*, New York: Basic Books.

SCHÖN, D.A. (1987) *Educating the Reflective Practitioner*, SanFrancisco, CA: Jossey-Bass.

SCHOOL TEACHERS REVIEW BODY (1996) London: HMSO.

SKYNNER, R. and CLEESE, J. (1993) *Life and How to Survive It*, London: Methuen.

SMYTH, J. (1995) *Critical Discourses in Teacher Development*, London: Cassell.

TEDESCO, J.C. (1997) 'Enhancing the role of teachers', in DAY, C., VAN VEEN, D. and WONG-KOOI, S. (eds) *Teachers and Teaching: International Perspectives on School Reform and Teacher Education*, Leuven/Apeldoorn: Garant.

VAN MANEN, M. (1995) 'On the epistemology of reflective practice', *Teachers and Teaching: Theory and Practice*, **1**, 1, PP. 33–50.

Christopher Day

VAN MANEN, M. (1977) Linking ways of knowing with ways of being practical, *Curriculum Inquiry*, **6**, 3, pp. 205–228.

WHITAKER, D.S. and ARCHER, J.L. (1990) 'Using practice research for change, social work and *Social Science Review*, **2**, 1, pp. 9–21.

WOODS, P. (1994) 'Adaptation and self-determination in English primary schools', *Oxford Review of Education*, **20**, 4, pp. 387–410.

YINGER, R. and HENDRICKS-LEE, M. (1995) 'Sustaining reform through teacher learning', *Language Arts*, **72**, 4, pp. 288–92.

ZEICHNER, K.M. (1993) 'Action research: Personal renewal and social reconstruction', *Educational Action Research*, **1**, 2, pp. 199–219.

Section Four

Conclusion

13   Changes in Research Since 1969

Richard White

It is a truism that books are products of their times. Each is written in accord with the purposes and beliefs of the day, and as those change so does the nature of the books. That applies to this book as to any other. It could not, for instance, have been written in 1969, the year I turned to formal research on learning after a decade of school teaching.

The research outlined in this book differs markedly from that of 30 years ago. Although varied, the present studies share qualities that cannot be found in the earlier work. Variation is, indeed, one of the qualities that has changed. In the 1960s, research design followed clear principles that were taught in most graduate schools, and it encouraged a uniformity that is absent today. These principles were enunciated by Campbell and Stanley (1963) in a brilliant analysis of experimental methods that still merits attention. Change does not equate to even progress and, though present research has many advances on that of the 1960s, it may be that some things of value have been lost. Future developments in research might follow from a synthesis of the principles of Campbell and Stanley with those of the present.

The main theme of Campbell and Stanley was that research must be designed in such a way that its conclusions are valid. They must be true for the learners who took part in the experiment, which is internal validity, and true for any broader group to which the results might be generalized, which is external validity. Campbell and Stanley described 16 types of experimental design, and evaluated each for how well it overcame certain threats to internal and external validity. One of the weakest designs, according to their analysis, was the one-shot case-study in which an innovation was tried and the participants' performance on some outcome was measured. In the face of the devastating criticism that Campbell and Stanley made of this design, it is remarkable that not only did it survive but it is well represented in the research described in the present book.

Hardly any examples of one-shot case-study were published in the 1970s. Guided by Campbell and Stanley, reviewers and editors rejected the few that might have been attempted. Instead, investigators employed stronger designs such as the pretest-posttest control group or the posttest-only control group, in which they allocated students randomly to one method of teaching or another. I liked these myself, and used a version of the latter in the study I have chosen to illustrate the early style of research. I chose a study of my own because I need to make sharp criticisms of the research of the time, and I can do that to my own work with fewer

Figure 13.1   Schematized learning hierarchy

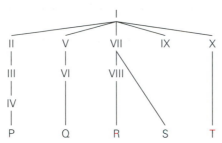

(Basic skills possessed by all learners at commencement of program)

inhibitions. The study, White (1976), exemplifies reasonable quality work of the period. I executed it early in 1970, though it did not appear in print until six years later — some things, such as the delay between doing the research and seeing its report in print, have not changed.

There is one further point to make before I describe my early study. Among the many ways of categorizing research is the distinction between experimental and descriptive forms. The basic notion in experiments is direct causal effect, in which a change that the researcher makes in one thing, such as method of teaching, which is termed the independent variable, is expected to produce a change in another, such as the amount learned, the dependent variable. A descriptive study has no intervention by the researcher, who merely records aspects of an existing situation. In the 1960s this commonly involved measuring two variables and seeing whether their values were related, for instance whether age is correlated with liking for mathematics, or whether the sexes differ in reasoning ability. Although both forms can be perceived in present research, they are much altered in style and have moved closer together, so it is less easy to classify a study as one or the other type. A study such as PEEL (Mitchell, this volume) is experimental, but involves much description.

There were plenty of correlational studies in the 1960s and 1970s, but the dominant form of research was the experiment. My early study (White, 1976) is typical of experiments of the time. Like many others, it involved more than one independent variable. This made it a factorial experiment. The chief factor that interested me was the amount of guidance given to learners as they attempted mathematical tasks that formed a learning hierarchy (Gagne, 1965; White, 1974). Figure 13.1 shows a schematized learning hierarchy. The principle of a learning hierarchy is that each element or skill in it stands upon certain prerequisite skills that may be identified by asking 'What *must* a learner be able to do in order to learn this new skill?' Thus in Figure 13.1, Skill II can only be learned by those who have first learned Skill III.

There was much interest at this time in discovery learning. Bruner (1961) had argued for superiority of discovery methods over transmissive teaching or drill. This superiority might evince itself in initial learning of a skill, but should show out even more in the ease with which the learner could use that learning in the next step (called vertical transfer), and in retention of the skill. Many studies of Bruner's assertion followed, with inconclusive results (Hermann, 1969). One reason for the unclear results was confusion of terms: one researcher's discovery method was similar to another's transmissive one. So I made my chief independent variable the amount of guidance students would receive, and took much care in defining before the experiment four levels of it. For the greatest amount of guidance, learners were to be given a mathematical task plus a reminder of its subordinate skills that the learner had acquired already, instructions of the steps to follow, and a worked example. The next level lacked the worked example, the next both the example and the instructions, and the least guidance level had only the task itself. Under all four levels learners were to attempt examples of the mathematical skill, would be told if they were correct and the answer if they were not, and were to attempt further examples until they got three correct in succession. They would then move on to another skill in the hierarchy. The dependent variable was the number of attempts. This now seems ridiculous. Of course those who got most guidance took fewer attempts. I can only say that it seemed less silly at the time, and certainly I had no difficulty in getting my report of the experiment published in a refereed journal. Perhaps current research will look silly in 2030.

A little less silly was the point that although greater guidance could help students to learn faster, they might not retain the knowledge as well nor be as able to use the knowledge in further learning. For a second dependent variable I tested their retention of the skills eight weeks later. To check on transfer of the knowledge, for the next skill in the hierarchy, I divided the four groups of students into four again, so that of those who got level 4 guidance for Skill IV, say, one quarter got level 4 again for Skill III, one quarter level 3, and so on. If Bruner's assertion about transfer were correct, those who got less guidance for Skill IV would acquire Skill III faster. This, too, might seem ridiculous to modern readers.

Another variable that researchers were studying then was the sequence in which information was given to learners. There was a theory that a random sequence would promote better learning and retention than a logical one, because in making sense of it learners would have to process it more thoroughly. I was interested in this, too, although even at the time I thought it silly. If I were a subject in an experiment and had randomly sequenced material given to me, would I bother to process it at all? In any event, I could not see school teachers, one of whom I had recently been, deliberately presenting information in a mixed-up order, no matter how incoherent they might be inadvertently. There were, however, two obvious alternatives of sequence for presenting the elements in my learning hierarchy: up each leg in turn, or zig-zagging across the legs taking the lowest element in each before moving to the next leg. I called these the ladder and snake sequences. It is relevant to note that there was no theory about this; one of the differences between research then and research now is the more sophisticated theoretical base of present research.

I now had a complicated experiment in which there were three factors: Amount of guidance (4 levels), Amount of guidance given with subordinate skill (4 levels), and Sequence (2 levels). Factorial experiments like this were common. I would need a certain number of students in each of the 32 combinations. There was a mathematical way of working out how many this should be, which took into account the chance the experimenter was prepared to take of incorrectly concluding that a factor had a real effect (known as Type I error) and the chance of incorrectly concluding that it had not (Type II error). I did the calculation, and found that I should need a greater number of students than I thought I could obtain, so I compromised on 4 per cell, 128 students in all. This sort of calculation and compromise was common at the time. Its intricacies tended to distract one from reflecting on the sense of doing the experiment at all. The idea behind it, however, had a lot of force that remains relevant today; it was to warn scholars against generalizing too confidently from limited data.

In 1970, bureaucracy had not made it too difficult to get access to schools. Teachers provided me with my 128 students, who good-humouredly cooperated and worked their ways through my materials, which were pencil-and-paper learning programs. It was a break from other activities that they might have found equally pointless. Perhaps in 1970 students were less ready to question the sense of what they were told (not asked) to do. I did not ask them for their reactions to the task, nor how they went about it. The only data I collected were their written attempts at the examples. We spent less than an hour together, then I collected their sheets and went away to count the numbers of tries each took to get three correct in a row for each element of the hierarchy.

After I had done the counting, I compared the mean number of tries for each cell, slice, row and column of the experiment. Of course there would be differences, but these could have arisen through accidents of allocation of more or fewer able students to the various cells. Inferential statistics existed to check on this. Experimenters at the time made much use of a classic work, Winer's (1962) *Statistical Principles in Experimental Design*, which gave formulae for arrangements such as mine. I did the calculations, although the results were already obvious: the greater the amount of guidance the fewer trials needed to get three correct in succession, but amount of guidance for the subordinate element and sequence made no difference. None of the factors had any influence on retention.

There was something else that made no difference: the experiment itself (other than any advantage it gave to my academic career). No teachers would change their methods because of my result. They would not have changed, whatever the outcome. The experiment had taken place in an educational vacuum. In reflecting on this in the years and further experiments that followed, I came to appreciate why teachers were right to ignore studies such as this early one of mine. It was too artificial. Some years after my study, the notion of ecological validity began to appear in research journals: an experiment should not be too different from the venue in which its results are to be applied. In our attempt to eliminate alternative sources of differences between experimental groups, as Campbell and Stanley advised us to do, we researchers created a laboratory and left it to teachers to work out how to apply our findings in their much more complex settings. Teachers, however, saw that the laboratory left out many factors that they could not ignore. Consequently the laboratory results were of no help to them.

I had something else to reflect upon. In experiments such as mine, one compared the mean scores of groups of learners. Within each group the scores of individuals differed. The larger the variation within a group, the less likely it was that a difference in means of groups would turn out to be statistically significant — that is, to be large enough to be unlikely to have occurred by chance. The researchers did the experiment because they were interested in the innovative method of teaching, and generally hoped to show that it was superior to some traditional method that was being used as a comparison. Variation within a group was therefore a nuisance which researchers tried to reduce, by further blocking of the learners into high, medium and low ability groups or by a statistical adjustment such as analysis of covariance. My reflections on my experiment led me, however, to think about these variations. Why did some learners take fewer attempts than others? Labelling them as 'more able' explained nothing. What was this ability? Were they consistently better across the skills? Why was the variation greater in the cells where low guidance was given? When learners were given the minimum of guidance, how did they get to the right answer at all? Why didn't I think to ask any of them about these matters? Although the experiment had had no impact on teachers, its generation of such questions meant that it was not completely sterile after all.

A comparison of studies of the 1960s and 1970s, such as mine, with recent ones like those described in other chapters of this book, reveals marked differences. Then, there was a cleavage between researchers and teachers, with none of the teacher research groups that Grimmett and Dockendorf, Austin, and Mitchell describe here, or partnerships such as the one Bell and Cowie describe. In set terminology, the intersection of teachers and researchers was an empty set, while now it has many members. Then, the research questions were fixed before the experiment began and remained unaltered. Now, they are outlined beforehand but remain open to amendment and supplementation during the course of the investigation. In the earlier research, the tenor is one of checking on predetermined propositions; in the latter, of exploring. In consequence, unexpected events tended to be put aside in the early research as distractions, irrelevancies or nuisances, while in the later work they are more likely to be noted and followed up as interesting phenomena.

Initial specification of research questions was coupled with meticulous planning of the design. No change in procedure was envisaged to occur once the investigation began. In much present research, however, the design and methods evolves in the course of the study. The research is reactive, shaped by events. Rigidity has been replaced by fluidity. This can be carried too far. Reactivity is sometimes used to justify sloppy work.

The great length of many present investigations makes evolution of procedure possible, and even unavoidable. Most studies in the earlier period were brief. Mine lasted less than an hour; others took only a minute or two. Nothing of the scale of PEEL (Mitchell, this volume) was attempted. Length of studies is connected with the appearance of teacher-researchers. When researchers and teachers did not overlap, researchers had to impose on schools and teachers to get access to the learners. Teachers have syllabi to complete, so they could release only limited time for researchers' use. Once the teacher became a true partner or principal in the research, the study could be fitted to the syllabus and greater time could be found for it. Greater length is also associated with concern for ecological validity. A short experiment will often be artificial, even if it is run in a classroom, as students take time to accept that an innovation is a proper, normal part of their schooling.

Longer studies made the subject matter that is to be learned an important item. Researchers, whether teachers or not, cannot justify taking much of students' time on learning something that is unimportant in the terms of the curriculum that is authorized for them. In the early, and brief, experiments, subject matter was merely a vehicle: in a study of learning, the participants had to learn something, but it did not matter much what it was. So in the 1960s there were studies in which the subject matter was characteristics of fictional planets, artificial vocabularies, and passages on glaciers and problems in Rhodesia, which had negligible educational interest or value for the students who were supposed to learn them. The research that Treagust and Harrison review in this book illustrates how crucial subject matter has become in current research. Content has become a variable of interest, and as Jones' chapter in this book shows, so has teachers' perceptions of content.

A major difference between the 1960s and now is the regard given to perceptions of the learners. These were ignored in the early research. There was negligible use of interviews (White, in press). It is as if we were doing research on mute animals rather than on communicable human beings. Following this change, reports of research include anecdotes and transcripts of interviews and lesson sequences, as is evident throughout this book as well as in many journals. Interest in the perceptions of individual learners goes with interest in variations between their performances, which formerly were regarded as nuisances rather than matters for study.

In the earlier research the dependent variable was usually restricted to scores on pre-designed tests. Test scores are still an important part of research outcomes, but only a part and not the whole as they once were. Along with this change is a reduction in the prominence of inferential statistics. There was hardly a research report in the 1960s and 1970s that did not refer to an inferential statistical procedure such as analysis of variance, t test, chi square, or the like. This is no longer the case. Reports now often contain only descriptive statistics such as counts of certain occurrences, or no statistics at all (White, in press). The function of inferential statistics is to legitimize the generalizing of the results from the sample of learners who took part in the experiment to a broader population (which in practice is rarely clearly defined). In recent research, generalization is seen as a different issue, one better approached by replication in diverse situations or by full description of the context in which the study took place.

Generalization across contexts is associated with implementation of results. In the earlier studies, researchers saw their responsibility to be to show whether some method of instruction could, in the circumstances of their experiment, produce a difference in the learning of the students in their sample. They did not consider, nor include in the design of their experiments, the effect of a particularly powerful variable, that of context. Of course the experiment took place in one context, while the implementation would be in another. The difference in context was not their concern, but that of the teachers, curriculum designers, and administrators who might choose to apply the experimental result. In present research, implementation is of direct concern to researchers. This follows from the blurring of the distinction between researcher and teacher.

People do whatever they think is most appropriate at the time, so those who read this book close to when it was written are bound to see the changes that have occurred in research as progress. The present form of research will not, however, be the last word, forever accepted as the way to do things. There will be further developments. It is not easy to see what they will be. If it were easy, we would already have introduced them. We might, however, get a hint of what is needed by going back to the days of Campbell and Stanley and imagining what criticisms they might level at present-day research.

A critic from the period of Campbell and Stanley might say that several of the projects described in this book have the simple structure of the one-shot case-study, which fails to overcome any of the threats to validity of conclusions. One such threat is termed Selection: the participants in PEEL, for instance, teachers or students, might have been more able than average, so the claimed success of PEEL could really have been due to their superior nature. Or, if it were argued that they had not been more successful than average before, then it could have been the combination of their latent abilities with the new procedures that worked, so one cannot be sure that the project would work with average people. Another threat is History: it might not have been the project that worked, but something else, some other change such as a new curriculum or a general change in class size, that happened to occur around that time. Or perhaps testing was responsible: the students got more used to the tests used to evaluate the program, or became alerted to the behaviour that was expected and changed to fit the tests. Instrumentation might be the cause: there was no real change but the tests or observations gradually became degraded as observers became more attuned to what to look for. Then there is the Hawthorne effect: novelty, the sense of being a pioneer, could have produced the positive results no matter what the form of the instructional program.

Researchers in PEEL and the other innovations described in this book no doubt can counter these criticisms. They might say that their research is not the simple one-shot case-study that Campbell and Stanley had experienced in the 1950s. Their projects run for so long and often in so many sites the outcomes cannot credibly be due to some other event, nor could the Hawthorne effect operate for years. The replications of PEEL in many schools and in several countries on different continents reduce the likelihood of Selection being responsible.

Although criticisms may be rebutted, there could be value in a synthesis of present research methods with the notions of Campbell and Stanley. I mean by this more than the reintroduction of inferential statistics and a return to rigour of design. We might, for instance, think about Instrumentation. Campbell and Stanley pointed out that measures, especially subjective ones, can change during a study as observers get better or worse or more blinkered. This suggests that in a long study there should be a succession of observers, with fresh ones overlapping with stale. Campbell and Stanley also refer to misplaced precision of observations. This brings to mind procedures where observers are practised in seeing and classifying events until there is high agreement between them. Often this is sensible, but there is a case to be made for diversity. Max van Manen (this volume) makes the point that different observers *can* see different things, so often it would be better or more complete research if there were not just multiple observers but observers with different interests and viewpoints.

Other hints for improvements in research can be gained from its trajectory from 1969 to 1999. Comparison of my early example with the approaches described in the chapters of this book shows how superficial observations and measurements have been replaced by detailed and penetrating ones. As teachers have become partners and principals in research it has become possible to study in depth their individual motives and actions. This could be taken further, to detailed studies of single learners. But just as the movement of the teacher from a subject or passive element in research to an active one opened up new possibilities, so would studies of learners be enhanced by the learner becoming a true partner. This has not yet happened to any marked extent. We interview learners more than we did, but rarely involve them in planning and in interpreting our research. The intersection of researcher and learner might cease to be an empty set.

The shift in research style has introduced new measures, such as the Good Learning Behaviours that teachers in PEEL defined (Mitchell, 1992). This could go much further. Admission of teachers and students into partnership in research enables measurement of intentions, which can then be compared with behaviour. Discrepancies between intention and action could then be probed for the factors that produce them. Baird (1986) provides an early example of this, which may come to be seen as a primitive prototype of an advanced form of research.

Other improvements must be possible. They could follow from deep consideration of the outcomes of research. Given that a key function of research is to improve practice, how should the outcomes be framed? In the 1960s, research reports contained conclusions which were judgments that this method or that had been shown to be superior. This format was taken over from physical science. It is not, however, the only or even the most productive way in which scientists nor another important group of scholars, the historians, present their findings. History is more than the telling of a tale, an account of what happened. It includes analysis of why, and so provides insights into human affairs that help us not only to understand new events but also to some extent to control them to our benefit. Between the 1960s and 1990s, educational research moved some way from the stereotype of the physical sciences to that of history. We might like to consider whether there are other ways of working in yet other disciplines that could be useful. I do not advocate a simple shift from one approach to another. Just as a synthesis of present methods with the principles of Campbell and Stanley would be useful, so would a synthesis from several disciplines of the ways of conceiving and presenting research produce a powerful advance in our understanding of pedagogy and in the capacity of research to influence the quality of teaching and learning.

References

BAIRD, J.R. (1986) 'Improving learning through enhanced metacognition: A classroom study', *European Journal of Science Education*, **8**, pp. 263–82.

BRUNER, J.S. (1961) 'The act of discovery', *Harvard Educational Review*, **31**, pp. 21–32.

CAMPBELL, D.T. and STANLEY, J.C. (1963) 'Experimental and quasi-experimental designs for research', in GAGE, N.L. (ed.) *Handbook of Research on Teaching*, Chicago: Rand McNally.

GAGNE, R.M. (1965) *The Conditions of Learning*, New York: Rinehart & Winston.

HERMANN, G. (1969) 'Learning by discovery: A critical review of studies', *Journal of Experimental Education*, **38**, pp. 58–72.

MITCHELL, I.J. (1992) 'The class level', in BAIRD, J.R. and NORTHFIELD, J.R. (eds) *Learning From the PEEL Experience*, Melbourne: Monash University Faculty of Education.

WHITE, R.T. (1974) 'The validation of a learning hierarchy', *American Educational Research Journal*, **11**, pp. 121–36.

WHITE, R.T. (1976) 'Effects of guidance, sequence, and attribute-treatment interactions on learning, retention, and transfer of hierarchically ordered skills', *Instructional Science*, **5**, pp. 133–52.

WHITE, R.T. (in press) 'The revolution in research on science education', in RICHARDSON, V. (ed.) *Handbook of Research on Teaching*, 4th edition, New York: Macmillan.

WINER, B.J. (1962) *Statistical Principles in Experimental Design*, New York: McGraw Hill.

Notes on Contributors

Terri Austin is a co-founder and teacher at a public charter school in Fairbanks, Alaska, and she is also a teacher educator at the University of Alaska, Fairbanks. She is an ongoing teacher-researcher with a continuing interest in examining all aspects of community. She is also the Chair of the Self Study in Teacher Education Practices Special Interest Group in the American Educational Research Association.

Beverley Bell taught in several secondary schools before coming to the University of Waikato in 1979 to do a masters and doctoral degree in science education. While a graduate student, she worked on the first Learning in Science Project team. She then worked as the project co-ordinator for the Children's Learning in Science Project, University of Leeds. On her return to New Zealand, she joined the Curriculum Development Division in the Department of Education and had responsibility for the revision of the F1-5 Science Syllabus. In 1989, she joined the Centre, where she was Director from 1994–1998. Her research interests include teaching, learning and assessment in science education, curriculum development and teacher development.

Shawn Bullock is enrolled in the Waterloo-Queen's Science Teaching Option at the University of Waterloo. After completing his BEd course requirements at Queen's University in 1997–98, he extended his teaching experience with a second 16-week practicum in Fall 1998 before returning to Waterloo to complete his BSc (Honours Physics) degree in 2000. Outside the classroom, Shawn shares his love of the Martial Arts by teaching karate to people of all ages.

Bronwen Cowie has taught science and mathematics in secondary schools for fifteen years and was the research officer for the Learning in Science Assessment Project from 1995–1996. She is now in the School of Education, at the University of Waikato, lecturing in mathematics education. Her research interests include mathematical thinking, reflection, open ended questions, cooperative work and assessment.

Christopher Day is Professor of Education, Head of Humanities Division of the Graduate School, and Co-director of the Centre for Teacher and School Development. He has worked as a schoolteacher, teacher educator, and local authority adviser. He has extensive research and consultancy experience in England, Europe, Australia, South East Asia, and North America in the field of teachers' continuing professional development, action research, leadership and change. Recent publications include *Developing Leadership in Primary Schools* (co-authored with C. Hall and P. Whitaker, 1998, Paul Chapman Ltd) and *Research on Teacher Thinking: Understanding Professional Development* (co-edited with J. Calderhead and P. Denicolo, 1993, Falmer Press). He is editor of *Teachers and Teaching: Theory and Practice* and co-editor of *Educational Action Research* and *Journal of In-service Education*. His abiding interest is in the interplay of teachers' thinking and action, and in this context, how schools and universities may provide effective management and support for their long-term professional development through research and teaching. In recognition of his work internationally in the field of continuing professional development for teachers he was awarded an Honorary Doctorate from the University of Linköping, Sweden, in 1993.

Maureen E.J. Dockendorf is currently Principal of Mountain View Elementary School in Coquitlam, British Columbia, and an author of a new English Language Arts Program. She has worked extensively throughout the province of British Columbia as a facilitator of teacher classroom action research and as an educational consultant. She also worked as a Faculty Associate (seconded teacher as clinical faculty) at Simon Fraser University and has served as a writer for various BC Ministry of Education resources, including the assessment components of the most recently mandated curriculum.

Dr. Helmut Fischler is Professor of Physics Education, Free University of Berlin and has been a teacher in Studies in Physics, Mathematics, Education from 1958–1965, then a teacher at German Gymnasium (Physics, Mathematics) 1965–1972 before completing a PhD in Physics Education in 1973. He has been actively engaged in physics teaching education and research since 1975. His research interests include: students' understanding of the particulate nature of matter, student-teachers' conceptions of teaching and learning physics and modern physics and students' conception.

Peter P. Grimmett is Professor of Education in the Faculty of Education and Co-Director of the Institute for Studies in Teacher Education at Simon Fraser University. His research interests focus at the pre-service and in-service levels on the relationship between teachers' development of their craft and the processes of reflection, collegial consultation and classroom-based action research. He has consistently collaborated with the numerous teacher research groups around the province of British Columbia. His recent publications include *Reflection in Teacher Education* (Teachers College Press, 1988, with Gaalen Erickson); *Craft Knowledge and the Education of Teachers* (American Educational Research Association, 1992 with Allan MacKinnon); *The Transformation of Supervision* (Association for Supervision and Curriculum Development, 1992, with Olaf Rostad and Blake Ford); *Teacher Development and the Struggle for Authenticity: Professional growth and restructuring in the context of change* (Teachers College Press, 1994, with Jon Neufeld); and *Changing Times in Teacher Education: Restructuring or Reconceptualizing?* (Falmer Press, 1995, with Marv Wideen). He is currently completing a three year study of pre-service teachers funded by the Social Sciences and Humanities Research Council of Canada.

Notes on Contributors

Allan G Harrison is a Lecturer in Science Education at Central Queensland University, Rockhampton, Queensland, Australia. Allan taught secondary science — biology, chemistry and physics — for 23 years in Western Australian public and private secondary schools before earning his MSc and PhD degrees at Curtin University. For the past seven years, he has researched the influence of analogies, metaphors and models on students' understanding of foundation concepts in chemistry and physics. This led to an interest in the ways expert teachers teach and explain science ideas — especially conceptual change teaching and learning strategies. His current research interests include student modelling abilities, effective practical work and the development of a model of expert teaching for beginning teachers.

Alister Jones is currently Director of the Centre for Science, Mathematics and Technology Education Research at the University of Waikato. He has taught science and physics in secondary schools before and after completing a doctoral degree in science education. He then worked in the OPENS project, researching into open-ended problem solving at King's College London for three years. Part of this research examined ways of developing teachers' knowledge in open investigations in science. In 1991, he joined the Centre and focused more on technology education where he has been involved in research on teacher development, particularly subcultural influences and subject knowledge, and student learning. He has also been involved in national curriculum development in science and technology.

John Loughran is the Director of Pre-service Education and Professional Development in the Faculty of Education at Monash University. He has been actively involved in teacher education for the past decade through his teaching in Science and Teaching and Learning in Pre-service Teacher Education. His research interests include teacher-as-researcher, reflective practice, science education and teaching and learning. Recent publications include *Developing Reflective Practice, Opening the Classroom Door* (Loughran and Northfield), and *Teaching about Teaching* (Loughran and Russell, Falmer Press).

Max van Manen is a professor in the Faculty of Education, University of Alberta, Edmonton, Canada. He received his teacher preparation in the Netherlands and he has taught at OISE and the University of Victoria. His research interests include epistemology of professional practice, the pedagogical significance of experiences of recognition, pedagogy of teacher education, the phenomenology of the body in illness and health, and human science methodology. Professor van Manen teaches courses in curriculum studies, pedagogy, and qualitative research. He is the author of many articles, translations, and several books including *The Tone of Teaching* (1986), *Researching Lived Experience: Human Science for an Action Sensitive Pedagogy* (1990), *The Tact of Teaching: The Meaning of Pedagogical Thoughtfulness* (1991) and *Childhood's Secrets: Intimacy, Privacy and the Self Reconsidered* (with Bas Levering, 1996). His books and articles have been translated into various languages.

Ian Mitchell is one of the co-founders of the Project for the Enhancement of Effective Learning (PEEL). Ian spent 23 years as a secondary school teacher of chemistry and mathematics from 1975 to 1997. For the past 14 of those years he lectured past-time in the Faculty of Education at Monash University. This long-term, dual role provided opportunities for extended classroom research that linked theory and practice. Ian has a wide experience in stimulating, advising, supporting and leading change in many educational settings. In 1998 Ian accepted a full-time lectureship at Monash and has continued his work through his research interest in teacher knowledge and teacher-as-researcher. Ian is currently involved as chief investigator (with Loughran) in a Large Australian Research Council grant exploring the development of Principles for Quality Learning through the PAVOT (Perspective and Voice of the Teacher) Project.

Tom Russell is a Professor in the Faculty of Education at Queen's University in Kingston, Ontario. He teaches pre-service courses in physics methods and in professional practice, as well as an MEd course in action research. His research focuses on the process of learning to teach, and he is also interested in innovative pedagogy, action research, and self-study of teacher education practices. Recent publications include *Teachers who Teach Teachers* (Munby and Russell), *Teaching about Teaching* (Loughran and Russell) and *Finding a Voice While Learning to Teach* (Featherstone, Munby and Russell) (all Falmer Press).

John Smyth is Foundation Professor of Teacher Education at the Flinders University of South Australia, and Associate Dean (Research). He is Director of the Flinders Institute for the Study of Teaching. He was a Senior Fulbright Research Scholar at University of Pittsburgh in 1990, Distinguished Scholar at University of British Columbia in 1991, and received the Palmer O. Johnson Award from AERA in 1993. In 1994 he was one of the judges of the ASCD Outstanding Dissertations Awards. John Smyth has authored/edited 12 books, among the most recent of which are *Critical Discourses on Teacher Development* (Cassell), *Being Reflexive in Critical Social and Educational Research* (Falmer), *Remaking Teaching: Ideology, Policy and Practice* (with Shacklock, Routledge), *Schooling for a Fair Go* (The Federation Press) and (with Hunt) *The Ethos of the University: West and Beyond*.

David Treagust is Professor of Science Education in the Science and Mathematics Education Centre at Curtin University in Perth, Western Australia. He holds graduate degrees in science education from the Science Education Centre at the University of Iowa, and undergraduate degrees in psychology and mathematics from the University of Western Australia, and in physics and chemistry teaching from Worcester College, England. He moved to Curtin after completing a Post-doctoral Fellowship at Michigan State University. Prior to working in universities in the USA and Australia for 20 years, he taught secondary school science for 10 years in England and Australia. His research interests are related to understanding students' ideas about science concepts, and how these ideas contribute to conceptual change and can be used to enhance the design of curricula and teachers' classroom practice. He is the author or co-author of over 100 science education articles in refereed journals and has presented over 200 papers at international, and at Australian national and state conferences.

Richard White is the Dean of Education at Monash University. He taught general science, physics and chemistry for ten years in high schools before joining Monash University in 1971. He has been Professor of Educational Psychology since 1981. His professional interest in the quality of learning has led him into research on learning hierarchies, episodic memory, cognitive structure and metacognition. Active participation in sailing and painting and more passive pursuits of reading, listening to music, computer games and admiring Australian plants supplement his professional life. Recent publications include *The Content of Science* (Fensham, Gunstone and White), *Probing Understanding* (White and Gunstone) and *Thinking Books* (Swan and White) (all Falmer Press).

Author Index

Subject Index